Fredericksburg City, Virginia

Deed Book

1794–1804

Ruth and Sam Sparacio

HERITAGE BOOKS

2020

HERITAGE BOOKS
AN IMPRINT OF HERITAGE BOOKS, INC.

Books, CDs, and more—Worldwide

For our listing of thousands of titles see our website
at
www.HeritageBooks.com

Published 2020 by
HERITAGE BOOKS, INC.
Publishing Division
5810 Ruatan Street
Berwyn Heights, Md. 20740

International Standard Book Number
Paperbound: 978-1-68034-488-2

pp.
1-
5

THIS INDENTURE made this 23 day of July in year of our Lord Christ one thousand seven hundred and Ninety four Between ZACHARIAH LUCAS and POLLY HARRISON, his Wife, of the Town of Fredericksburg of one part and FIELDING LUCAS of the Town aforesaid of other part; Witnesseth that ZACHARIAH LUCAS and POLLY HARRISON, his Wife, for sum of Sixty seven pounds to them in hand paid by these presents do bargain and sell unto FIELDING LUCAS his heirs part of a Lott of ground lying in the Town aforesaid known by Lott number 74, Beginning at the upper corner of said lott on CAROLINE STREET, thence running down said Street sixty eight feet, from thence running back one hundred and thirty two feet paralel to FAUQUIER STREET, from thence runing up said Lott sixty eight feet paralel to CAROLINE STREET and from thence runing one hundred & thirty two feet on FAUQUIER STREET to the beginning, together with all houses and appurtenaces belonging; To have and to hold the premises unto FIELDING LUCAS his heirs free and clear from all other gifts sales and incumbrances whatsoever; In Witness whereof ZACHARIAH LUCAS and POLLY HARRISON his Wife have hereunto interchangeably set their hands and affixed their seals the day month and year first afore written
Signed sealed acknowledged and Delivered in presence of

GUST. B. WALLACE,	JOHN MUNFORD,	ZACHARIAH LUCAS
JAMES BAGGOTT,	THOS: LONG	POLLY HARRISON LUCAS

The Commonweath of Virginia to GEORGE FRENCH & FONTAINE MAURY Gentlemen of the Corporation of Fredericksburg Greeting; (the Commission for the privy Examination of POLLY HARRISON, the Wife of ZACHARIAH LUCAS); Witness JOHN CHEW, Clerk of our said Court the 24th day of July 1794 in the 19th year of the Commonwealth
Corporation of Fredericksburg Sct. Agreeable to the within Commission to us directed (the return of the execution of the examination of POLLY HARRISON LUCAS); Given under our hands this 25 day of July 1794   GEO: FRENCH
                                                                          FONTAINE MAURY
At a Court of Hustings held for the Town & Corporation of Fredericksburg the 25th day of July 1794   This Indenture from ZACAHARIAH LUCAS & POLLY HARRISON, his Wife, to FIELDING LUCAS was proved by the oaths of three witnesses thereto & together with the Commission annexed & Certificate of Execution thereof indorsed, were ordered to be recorded
Examd. & delivd. to FIELDING LUCAS   Teste JNO: CHEW, C.C.H.

pp.
5-
7

THIS INDENTURE made this 13th day of June in year of our Lord one thousand seven hundred and Ninety four Between JAMES ABBOTT of County of Spotsylvania and ANN his Wife of one part and WILLIAM SMITH of Town of Fredericksburg of other part; Witnesseth that JAMES ABBOTT in consideration of the rents and covenants on part of WILLIAM SMITH to be paid and performed, said JAMES ABBOTT hath demised and to farm let unto WILLIAM SMITH his heirs one Lott of Land number 168 in Town of Fredericksburg running sixty six feet on the Cross Street and the length of the Lott on the Corse of the other Street which JAMES ABBOTT leased of PHILIP EVANS as per Lease bearing date the fourth day of September one thousand seven hundred and eighty nine, Together with all profits commodities and appurtenances belonging; To have and to hold the Lott of Land with all appurtenances unto WILLIAM SMITH his heirs from the first day of June one thousand seven hundred and eighty nine forever,

paying unto JAMES ABBOTT his heirs during the time the sum of Five pounds current
money of Virginia (at its present value); In Witness whereof the parties have hereunto
set their hands & seals the day and year above written
Sealed & Delivered in presence of (as to JAMES ABBOTT)
    CHS. MORTIMER,   JAMES ABBETT
    THOMAS GOODWIN, JOHN ASTON,   ANN ABBETT
    WILLIAM LOVELL
  At a Court of Hustings held for the Town & Corporation of Fredericksburg July 25th
1794   This Indenture from JAMES ABBOTT & ANN his Wife to WILLIAM SMITH was acknowledged by the sd. JAMES & ANN, she being first privately examined as the Law
directs, and ordered to be recorded
Examd. & Delivered WM. SMITH   Teste JNO: CHEW, C. C. H.

pp.   KNOW ALL MEN by these presents that I CHARLES YATES of the Corporation of
7-   of Fredericksburg by these presents appoint Major BENJAMIN DAY of said Cor-
9   poration my true and lawfull Attorney for me and to my use to ask demand sue
       for recover and receive of all persons whom it may concern all sums of money
debts and dues which now are due owing or belonging unto me and in default of payment to take all lawfull ways and means for the recovery thereof hereby confirming
all my said Attorney shall in my name lawfully do or cause to be done about the premises by virtue of these presents; In Witness whereof I the said CHARLES YATES have
hereunto set my hand and affixed my seal the fourth day of June in year of our Lord
one thousand seven hundred and Ninety four
Signed sealed & Delivered in presence of
    JNO: ANDERSON,   CHS. YATES
    JAMES BLAIR, ANTHONY BUCK
  At a Court of Hustings held for the Town & Corporation of Fredericksburg July 25th
1794   This Power of Attorney from CHARLES YATES to BENJAMIN DAY was proved by
the oaths of three witnesses thereto and ordered to be recorded
Examd. & Deld. Major B. DAY   Teste JNO: CHEW, C. C. H.

p.   TO ALL TO WHOM these presents shall come, Know ye that I FRANCIS THORNTON
9   (for and in consideration of the many good qualities and fidelity of CHARLES
      BUTLER, late the property of Mrs. FRANCES THORNTON deceased) have emanci-
pated and set free the sd. CHARLES BUTLER from me & my heirs forever. In Witness
whereof I hve hereunto set my hand and seal this 25th day of July 1794
                            FRAS. THORNTON
CHARLES BUTLER is about 40 years of age, 5 feet 3 inches.
  At a Court of Hustings held for Town & Corporation of Fredericksburg July 25th 1794
This Writing of Emancipation from FRANCIS THORNTON to CHAS. BUTLER was acknowledged by sd. FRANCIS THORNTON and ordered to be recorded

pp.   TO ALL WHOM it may concern, be it known that I JOSEPH CHRISTY of the Cor-
9-   poration of Fredericksburg being persuaded that Liberty is the just and natural
10   right of men, do for myself my heirs set free and Emancipate in the manner
      following; A Negroe man named Jack aged about thirty two years to be entitled
to his Liberty from the date of the presents; he paying me the sum of Thirty pounds in
three equal annual payments; Als a Negro Woman named Nanny aged about thirty four
years to be free from the date hereof with whatever progeny she may hereafter have;
Likewise her Son named George eight years to be free and entitled to his Liberty when
he arrive at the age of Twenty seven years; All which slaves I do for myself my heirs

discharge and liberate in the manner above expressed. As Witness my hand and seal this 26th day of September Seventeen hundred and Ninety four
                                        JOSEPH CHRISTY
   At a Court of Hustings held for Town & Corporation of Fredericksburg September 26th 1794   This Writing of Emancipation from JOSEPH CHRISTY to Jack, Nanny and George, was acknowledged by the said JOSEPH CHRISTY and ordered to be recorded

pp.   KNOW ALL MEN by these presents that I GEORGE W. B. SPOONER of Corporation
11-   of Fredericksburg in consideration of the love and affection I have for my
12   Father, GEORGE WILSON SPOONER & for the sum of One Dollar to me in hand paid
           by said GEORGE WILSON SPOONER, by these presents do bargain and sell unto
GEORGE WILSON SPOONER the following slaves; to wit, Charles, Diana, Lucy, Anna, Grace, Alcie and her two Children, Andrew & Silvey, and their increase; To have and to hold the said slaves and their increase to said GEORGE WILSON SPOONER his heirs for ever; and GEORGE W. B. SPOONER for himself his heirs warrent and forever defend the said slaves against the claims of all persons; In Testimony whereof I have hereunto set my hand and seal this twenty second day of August in year of our Lord one thousand seven hundred and ninety four
Signed sealed and delivered in the presence of
        SIDNEY WISHART,   GEO: W. B. SPOONER
        SAMUEL SMITH
   At a Court of Hustings held for Town of Fredericksburg on Friday the 24th of October 1794   This Deed for slaves from GEORGE W. B. SPOONER to GEORGE W. SPOONER was acknowledged by said GEORGE W. B. SPOONER and ordered to be recorded
Examd. & deld. Mr. VASS, G. W. B. SPOONER's Store Keeper

pp.   THIS INDENTURE witnesseth that GEORGE HUGHES (Son of SUSANNA HUGHES) of
12-   Corporation of Fredericksburg hath put himself with the consent of his Mother
14   of his own free will and accord Apprentice to GEORGE NORWOOD of the Corpora-
           tion aforesaid to learn his art trade and mystery and after the manner of an Ap-
prentice to serve said GEORGE NORWOOD from the day of the date hereof during the term of Five years & two months next ensuing; during which time in all things behave him-self as a faithfull Apprntice ought to do; And the said Master shall use his utmost en-deavour to teach or cause to be taught and instructed the said Apprentice in the trade and mystery of Shoe Making, give him one years schooling and at expiration of said term one suit of new cloaths; In Witness whereof the said parties have interchange-ably set their hands and seals hereunto dated the 24th day of October in year of our Lord one thousand seven hundred and Ninety four
Sealed and Delivered in presence of   GEORGE NORWOOD
        (no witnesses shown)   SUSANNA her mark X HUGHES
                                                  GEORGE his mark X HUGHES
   At a Court of Hustings held for the Town of Fredericksburg on Fryday the 24th day of October 1794   These Indentures of Apprenticeship between GEORGE NORWOOD and SUSANNAH HUGHS was acknowledged by the said parties and approved of by the Court and ordered to be recorded
Examd. & deld. Mr. G. NORWOOD   Teste JNO: CHEW, C.C.H.

pp.   KNOW ALL MEN by these presents that I RICH WILLIS of County of BERKELEY
14-   and State of Virginia for sum of Two hundred pounds current money of Virginia
15   by these presents do bargain and sell unto SARAH F. WILLIS & LEWIS WILLIS,
           the Son of said SARAH the following slaves (together with their future increase)

Vizt. Louis, Mary, Lucy, Polly, William, Rose, Henry & Joseph, To have and to hold the said slaves with their increase unto SARAH F. WILLIS and LEWIS WILLIS, And I said RICH WILLIS for myself my heirs do agree that I will ever warrant and defend the said slaves & their increase against any person who may claim under me; In Witness where- of I have hereunto subscribed my hand & seal this Sixth day of February 1795
Sealed & Delivered in presence of
    ROBERT MERCER,   RICH WILLIS
    WM. PROCTOR, ANN WILLIS
    At a Court of Hustings held for the Town & Corporation of Fredericksburg the 27th day of February 1795   This Bill of Sale from RICH WILLIS to SARAH F. WILLIS &c. was proved by the oaths of three witnesses thereto & together with the Receipt endorsed which was proved by the Witness thereto were ordered to be recorded
Examd. & deld. Colo. L. WILLIS for Mrs. WILLIS   Teste   JNO: CHEW, C. C. H.

pp.   ARTICLES of AGREEMENT entered into between JOHN FARNEHOUGH of Town of
15-   Fredericksburg and ROBERT MERCER of aforesaid Town. Whereas said FARNE-
16   HOUGH has belonging to him a Negro slave named Charles, a Wheelright by
           Trade, and is desirous of stimulating him to a faithfull discharge of his duty as his slave for twelve years ensuing the date hereof, and the said Charles upon condition that he shall be emancipated at the expiration of the twelve years promises to be a faithful sober industrious tradesman, the said JOHN FARNEHOUGH in consideration of the premises & five shillings to him in hand paid by ROBERT MERCER, doth covenant with ROBERT MERCER that if said Charles shall demean himself as a faithfull sober industrious tradesman during twelve years ensuing the date hereof said JOHN FARNE- HOUGH his heirs at the expiration of said twelve years will do and execute every act whatsoever required by the Laws of this Country for the Emancipation of the said slave Charles; In Witness whereof said JOHN FARNEHOUGH hath hereunto affixed his hand and seal the first day of January Anno Domini one thousand seven hundred ninety five
Teste JOHN T. BROOKE,   JOHN FERNEYHOUGH
    At a Court of Hustings held for the Town & Corporation of Fredericksburg the 27th day of February 1795   These Articles of Agreement were acknowledged by JOHN FERNEYHOUGH & ordered to be recorded
Examd. & Deld. Charles   Teste   JNO: CHEW, C. C. H.

pp.   KNOW ALL MEN by these presents that I THOMAS VOULS of the Corporation of
16-   of Fredericksburg for sum of Nineteen pounds seventeen shillings and four
18   pence current money to me in hand paid by JAMES SOMERVILLE of said place,
           Merchant, by these presents do bargain and sell unto JAMES SOMERVILLE one Negroe slave named Betty about seventeen years old; To have and to hold said slave Betty with her future increase unto JAMES SOMERVILLE his heirs and THOMAS VOULS for himself his heirs do warrant the said slave Betty unto JAMES SOMERVILLE his heirs against all persons; In Witness whereof I have hereunto sett my hand & seal this Eighteenth day of April, one thousand seven hundred and Ninety five
Signed sealed & delivered in the presence of
    JOHN DARE, DANIEL GRINNAN JUNR.   THOS: VOWLES
    JAMES SOMERVILLE JUNR.
    N. B. In case the within named THOMAS VOULS or any person for him pay to said SOMERVILLE the sum of Nineteen pounds seventeen shillings & four pence with in- terest thereon before the first day of October next, the within named slave Betty to be his property; Witness our hands this twenty third day of February 1793

Teste JOHN DARE;   THOS: VOWLES
      JAMES SOMERVILLE JUNR.   JAMES SOMERVILLE
   At a Court of Hustings held for the Town and Corpo: of Fredericksburg 20th June 1795
This Bill of Sale was proved by the oath of two of the witnesses thereto & ordered to be
recorded

pp.   THIS INDENTURE made this twenty fourth day of June in year of our Lord one
19-   thousand seven hundred and Ninety five Between BENJAMIN HAZLEGROVE of
22   Town of PORT ROYAL of one part and ADAM DARBY of Town of Fredericksburg
        of other part; Witnesseth that BENJAMIN HAZLEGROVE hath bargained sold and
delivered unto ADAM DARBY his heirs that part of the lott lying in Town of Fredericksburg numbered Fifty three containing by estimation Two thousand four hundred and
fifty five 5/9 square yards be the same more or less for sum of One hundred and seventy five pounds current money of Virginia, bounded, beginning at the lower corner of
said lott bounded by PRINCES ANN and WOLF STREETs, from thence runing up said
PRINCES ANN STREET one hundred feet to the boundary line of that part of said lott now
the property of DAVID BLAIR, from thence at right angles along said boundary line two
hundred and twenty one feet to the boundary line of that part of said lott the property
of REUBEN DIXON (a Free Negroe) from thence at right angles along the last mentioned
boundary line across to WOLF STREET and from thence at right angles along said WOLF
STREET to the begining, To have and to hold the bargained premises unto ADAM DARBY
his heirs free and clear of all manner of incumbrances; and BENJAMIN HAZLEGROVE
against the lawfull claims of any person to warrant and defend by these presents; In
Witness whereof BENJAMIN HAZLEGROVE hath hereunto set his hand and seal the day
and year first within written
Signed Sealed Acknowledged & delivered in the presents of
    DANIEL GRINNAN JUNR., JAMES NEWBY,   BENJN: HAZLEGROVE
    THOMAS SEDDON JUNR., JAMES SOMERVILLE JUNR.
   At a Court of Hustings held for the Town and Corpo: of Fredericksburg the 20th day of
June 1795   This Indenture for Lott from BENJAMIN HAZLEGROVE to ADAM DARBY
was proved by the oaths of three of the witnesses thereto & ordered to be recorded
Examd. & Deld. Mr. A. DARBY   Teste   JNO: CHEW, C. C. H.

pp.   THIS INDENTURE made this fourteenth day of March Anno Domini one thousand
22-   seven hundred and Ninety five Between TIMOTHY McCARTHY and SUSANNAH his
24   Wife of Town of Fredericksburg of one part and JAMES FURGUSON of same Town
        of second part, Witnesseth that said TIMOTHY and SUSANNAH his Wife for sum of
Thirty pounds to them in hand paid by JAMES FURGUSON by these presents do bargain &
sell unto JAMES FURGUSON and his heirs all that lott of ground in Town of Fredericksburg known by the number Two hundred and four; Begining at the corner joining
PRINCES MARY STREET & PRINCES ELIZABETH STREET, thence binding on PRINCES
ELIZABETH STREET one hundred and thirty two feet, thence parrellel with PRINCES
MARY STREET ten pole, thence parrellel with PRINCES ELIZABETH STREET to COLO.
WILLIS's Line, and with the same to PRINCESS MARY STREET and binding on the same to
the begining; and all houses profits commodities & appurtenances belonging; To have
and to hold the said lott unto JAMES FURGUSON his heirs and TIMOTHY McCARTHY and
SUSANNAH his Wife for themselves and their heirs the said lott will warrant and forever defend by these presents; In Testimony whereof the said TIMOTHY and SUSANNAH
his Wife have hereunto put their hands and seals this the same day day and year above
mentioned

Signed sealed & delivered in the presence of
THOMAS WEST,   TIMTH: McCARTHY
WILLIAM ELLIS, JOHN S. FARISH   SUSANNAH her mark X McCARTHY
At a Court of Hustings held for the Town and Corpo: of Fredericksburg 20th June 1795 This Indenture was proved by the oaths of two of the witnesses thereto & ordered to be recorded
Examd. & deld. JAS: FERGUSON   Teste JNO: CHEW, C.C.H.

pp. 24-27   THIS INDENTURE made this Twenty fourth day of September in year of our Lord one thousand seven hundred and ninety four Between WILLIAM GLASSELL of one part and FRANCIS TUPMAN of other part; Witnesseth that WILLIAM GLAS-SELL for sum of Two hundred pounds to him in hand paid by FRANCIS TUPMAN by these presents do bargain and sell unto FRANCIS TUPMAN all that parcel of land in Town of Fredericksburg lying on CAROLINE STREET and bounded, Begining at the uper corner of the land leased by WILLIAM JACKSON and runing thence up said CAROLINE STREET twenty eight feet to the lower corner of the lott purchased by DAVID COYLEY of ROGER DIXON (reserving a right of way of four feet between the lotts herein sold and that purchased by DAVID COYLEY), runing thence by a straight line at right angles with CAROLINE STREET the whole depth of the Lott No. 16, (of which this is a part) one hundred and thirty two feet from thence by a right line parrellel with CAROLINE STREET one hundred and thirty two feet and thence by a right line to the begining, Together with all appurtenances thereunto belonging; To have and to hold the said lott of ground unto FRANCIS TUPMAN his heirs and WILLIAM GLASSELL his heirs unto FRANCIS TUPMAN his heirs will warrant and forever defend by these presents; In Witness whereof WILLIAM GLASSELL have hereunto set his hand and affixed his seal the day and year first above written
Signed sealed and delivered in the presence of
WILLIAM HARVEY,   WM. GLASSELL
ALEX: REDDICK, ROBT. G. LEEKIE
At a Court of Hustings held for the Town & Corporation of Fredericksburg the 24th June 1795 This Indenture was acknowledged by the said WILLIAM GLASSELL and ordered to be recorded   Teste JNO: CHEW, C.C.H.

pp. 27-28   TO ALL TO WHOM these presents shall come, Know ye that by these presents for the sum of Twenty pounds do set free and emancipate a Negroe boy named Jack and do by these presents release and give up all right title & claim to said boy Jack; In Witness whereof I have hereunto set my hand and seal this 14th day of August 1794
Signed & Sealed in presence of
Test JOHN RICHARDS,   CONRAD HANSBURGER
THOMAS WEST, BEV: CHEW
At a Court of Hustings held for Town & Corporation of Fredericksburg the 24th July 1795 This Writing from the hand of CONROD HANSBURGER for the Emancipation of Negroe Jack was proved by the oaths of JOHN RICHARDS and BEVERLEY CHEW, two of the witnesses thereto and ordered to be recorded
Exd. & deld. Kippin, Father to Jack   Teste JNO: CHEW, C.C.H.

pp. 28-29   KNOW ALL TO WHOM THESE PRESENCE shall come Greeting. Know ye that I WALKER RANDOLPH CARTER formerly of Town of Fredericksburg for good causes me thereunto moving by these presents do appoint FONTAINE MAURY Esquire of Town of Fredericksburg my true and lawfull Attorney for me and in

my name to sell and dispose of all the slaves conveyed to me by my Mother, Mrs. ELIZA-
BETH CARTER of the Town of Fredericksburg, and make all conveyances of said slaves to
persons becoming purchasers thereof; hereby ratifying all my said Attorney shall do
according to the true intent of these presents; In Witness whereof I the said WALKER
RANDOLPH CARTER have hereunto subscribed my hand and affixed my seal this Eigh-
teenth day of March in year of our Lord one thousand seven hundred and ninety four
Teste W. S. STONE,   W. R. CARTER
      DAVID HENDERSON
  At a Court of Hustigns held for the Corpo: of Fredsbg. the 25th day of Septr: 1795
This Letter of Attorney was acknowledged by the said CARTER & ordered to be recorded
Examd. & sent Mr. T. MAURY p. L. H. MAURY   Teste JNO: CHEW C. C. H.

pp.   KNOW ALL MEN by these presents that I WALKER RANDOLPH CARTER formerly
30-   of Town of Fredericksburg and now of the City of PHILADELPHIA by these pre-
31   sents appoint FONTAIN MAURY Esquire of the Town aforesaid my true and law-
      full Attorney for me to sell and dispose of sundry Negroes in the State of Vir-
ginia being all those whereto I became entitled by the Bequest of MRS. JUDITH BANKS
deceased, Except Moses, Ned, Hary, George & James, part of the Bequest and now in the
possession of my Father, CHARLES CARTER of Town of Fredericksburg, and execute to
the purchasers a Bill of Sale; In Witness whereof I have hereunto set my hand and
affixed my seal this sixth day of February in year of our Lord one thousand seven hundred and ninety four
Signed sealed & Delivered in presence of
     WILLIAM GATT, CHAS. L. CARTER,   W. R. CARTER
     CHS. HEINEKE, W. F. STONE, B. W. HOBE,
     JAN HENA. DAVID HENDERSON
  At a Court of Hustings held for the Town and Corpo: of Fredericksburg 25th September
1795; This Letter of Attorney was acknowledged by the within named WALKER R.
CARTER and ordered to be recorded
Examd. & sent Mr. MAURY p. Mr. L. H. MAURY   Teste JNO: CHEW, C. C. H.

pp.   THIS INDENTURE made this twentieth and third day of June in year of our Lord
31-   one thousand seven hundred and ninety four Between WALKER RANDOLPH
36   CARTER of Town of Fredericksburg of one part and JOHN FERNEYHOUGH of same
      Town of other part; Witnesseth that WALKER R. CARTER for sum of Seven hun-
dred & seventy three pounds six shillings and eight pence to him in hand paid do bargain & sell unto JOHN FERNEYHOUGH three parcels of land lying in Town aforesaid and
known by lotts No. 68, 69 & 70; and connected as follows, to wit, Lott No. 68 on the North
by HAWKE STREET, on the East by RAPPAHANNOCK RIVER, on the South by Lott No. 67,
and on the West by SOPHIA STREET, and the Lotts No. 69 & 70 are bounded by PITT STREET
SOPHIA STREET and HAWKE STREET, said three lotts being the same whereon said JOHN
FERNEYHOUGH has resided and carried on his business, one which he purchased of
JOHN LEWIS and MARY ANNE his Wife as by their Deed bearing date the one the 1st day
of January 1788 and the other on the 22d. day of November 1791, both of Record in the
Court of the Corpo: of Fredericksburg have been by JOHN FERNEYHOUGH sold and
conveyed to said WALKER R. CARTER with the remainder, reversion and every the ap-
purtenances to the three lotts belonging; To have and to hold the lotts of land unto
JOHN FERNEYHOUGH his heirs, Provided always that if WALKER R. CARTER his heirs well
and truly pay or cause to be paid unto JOHN FERNEYHOUGH or assigns the full sum of
Three hundred and eighty five pounds thirteen shillings and four pence upon the

23rd of June next ensuing and also the further sum of Three hundred and eighty six pounds thirteen shillings & six pence in and upon the 23rd day of June which shall be in the year one thousand seven hundred and Ninety six, without any deduction or abatement for Taxes assignments or any other impositions according to the several bonds wherein WALKER RANDOLPH CARTER is bound to JOHN FERNEYHOUGH in the penal sum in each bond of seven hundred and seventy three pounds two shillings and eight pence, and until default shall be made WALKER R. CARTER his heirs may hold the said premises and receive the rents issue and profits thereof to his own benefit, In Witness whereof the parties have hereunto set their hands and seals the day and year above written

Signed sealed & Delivered in the presence of
        JOHN T. BROOKE,   W. R. CARTER
        FRANCIS BROOKE, ROBERT MERCER
This Deed was executed on the 23rd of June 1794.
  12th February 1795. For value received, I assign the within Mortgage to JOHN LEWIS
Teste JOHN T. BROOKE   JOHN FERNEYHOUGH
  At a Court of Hustings held for Town and Corporation of Fredericksburg the 25th Septr. 1795.   This Deed of Mortgage from WALKER R. CARTER to JOHN FERNEYHOUGH was ack-nowledged by said CARTER & ordered to be recorded
Exd. and deld. JNO: MERCER Esqr. Attorney for JNO: LEWIS   Teste JNO: CHEW C. C. H.

pp.   THIS INDENTURE made this fifth day of October 1795 Between WILLIAM SMITH
36-   and ANN his Wife and CHARLES A. LEWIS, Attorney in fact for EBENEZER
41   HAZARD late Post Master General of North America and Mortagee of said WIL-
           LIAM SMITH and ANN his Wife of one part and GEORGE MURRAY, Merchant, of
Town of Fredericksburg of other part; Witnesseth that WILLIAM SMITH and ANN his
Wife and CHARLES A. LEWIS, Attorney in fact as aforesaid, for sum of Two hundred and
Sixty nine pounds nineteen shillings to them in hand paid by GEORGE MURRAY by
these presents hath bargained and sold unto GEORGE MURRAY his heirs all that parcel
of ground lying in Town of Fredericksburg and bounded, Begining at the Corner of
COLIN & JAMES ROSS's Lott on the Main Street called CAROLINE STREET being seventy
one feet from LEWIS's STREET, from thence up the said Main Street sixty one and a half
feet to the corner of GEORGE MURRAY's Lott and from thence across Lott No. 72 one
hundred and thirty two feet parrellel to the Cross Street called LEWIS's STREET, from
thence up the back of GEORGE MURRAY's Lott adjoining Lott No. 71 thirty two feet and a
half to Mr. BROWN's Lott and from thence down to the Back Street parrellel to the Cross
Street one hundred and thirty two feet and from thence along the said Back Street
called SOPHIA STREET ninety four feet to the corner of COLIN and JAMES ROSS's Lott and
from thence up crossing lots No. 71 & No. 72 two hundred and sixty four feet to the begining; To have & to hold unto GEORGE MURRAY his heirs and WILLIAM SMITH and ANN
his Wife for themselves and their heirs against the claims of all persons will warrent
and forever defend by these presents and CHARLES A. LEWIS, Attorney in fact for
EBENEZER HAZARD, late Postmaster General of North America, do by these present warrent and defend to said GEORGE MURRAY his heirs by virtue of his power; In Witness
whereof they have hereunto signed their named & affixed their seals the day & year
above written
Signed sealed and Delivered in presence of
        RICHD. JOHNSTON JUNR., WM. TAYLOR,   WILLM. SMITH
        JNO: HARDIA, JNO: THOMPSON, THO: WARE,   ANN SMITH
        SAM: RODDEY, THOS: R. ROOTES   CHAS. A. LEWIS
   The Commonwealth of Virginia to GEO: W. B. SPOONER and WM. HARVEY & also ELISHA

HALL Gentlemen Greeting, Whereas (the Commission for the privy Examination of ANN, the Wife of WILLIAM SMITH); Witness JOHN CHEW, Clerk of our said Hustings Court the fifth day of October 1795 and in the 20th year of the Commonwealth   JNO: CHEW

Corporation of Fredsby. Sct. Pursuant to the within Commission to us directed (the return of the execution of the examination of ANN SMITH); Given under our hands & seals this 5th day of October 1795   GEO: W. B. SPOONER
                                                                 WILLIAM HARVEY

At a Court of Hustings held for the Town & Corporation of Fredericksburg 23rd October 1795   This Indenture was proved by the oaths of JOHN HARDIA, THOMAS WARE and THOMAS R. ROOTES, three witnesses as to the Execution of CHARLES A. LEWIS, which is ordered to be recorded as to him, and was further proved by the oaths of JOHN THOMPSON and RICHARD JOHNSTON JUNR., two witnesses as to the execution of WILLIAM SMITH & ordred to be certfied as to him

pp.   THIS INDENTURE made this fifth day of October 1795 Between WILLIAM SMITH
41-   and ANN his Wife and CHARLES A. LEWIS, Attorney in fact for EBENEZER HAZARD
47   late Postmaster General of North America and Mortgagee of said WILLIAM
        SMITH and ANN his Wife of one part and COLIN & JAMES ROSS, Merchants of Fredericksburg of other part; Witnesseth that WILLIAM SMITH and Ann his Wife and CHARLES A. LEWIS, attorney in fact, for sum of Three hundred and seven pounds two shillings and eight pence current money of Virginia to them in hand paid by COLIN & JAMES ROSS, have bargained and sold unto COLIN & JAMES ROSS theirheirs all that parcel of ground lying in Town of Fredericksburg bounded, Beginning on LEWIS STREET at the Corner of Lott No. 71, being one hundred and thirty two feet from SOPHIA STREET and the same from CAROLINE STREET, thence up Lot No. 71 seventy one feet parrellel to SOPHIA STREET, from thence across Lot No. 71 one hundred and thirty two feet to the Back Street called SOPHIA STREET and parallel to LEWIS STREET and from thence down SOPHIA STREET seventy one feet to the corner of Lot No. 71 and from thence to the begining; To have & to hold the premises unto COLIN & JAMES ROSS , and WILLIAM SMITH and ANN his Wife their heirs against the claim of themselves & their heirs and every other person shall forever warrent and defend by these presents, and CHARLES A. LEWIS, Attorney in fact for EBENEZER HAZARD, late Postmaster General of North America, doth by these presents warrent and defend to said COLIN & JAMES ROSS their heirs by virtue of his power; In Witness whereof they have hereunto signed their names and affixed their seals the day and year above written
Signed Sealed & Delivered in presence of
     RICHARD JOHNSON JUNR.,   )   WILLM. SMITH
     JNO: THOMPSON   ) as to W.S.   ANN SMITH
     SAM: RODDEY   )   CHAS. A. LEWIS
     WILLIAM TAYLOR,
     JOHN HARDIA, THOMAS WARE, THOS: R. ROOTES as to C.A.S.
The Commonwealth of Virginia to GEO: W. B. SPOONER and WILLIAM HARVEY also to ELISHA HALL Gentlemen Greeting, Whereas (the Commission for the privy Examination of ANN the Wife of WILLIAM SMITH); Witness JOHN CHEW, Clerk of our said Hustings Court the 5th day of October 1795 in the 20th year of the Commonwealth   JNO: CHEW

Corporation of Fredericksburg Vizt. By virtue of the within Commission we the Subscribers did on the fifth day of October 1795 go to the within named ANN (the return of the execution of the examination of ANN SMITH); Witness our hands and seals the day and year above written   GEO: W. B. SPOONER
                                                                 WILLIAM HARVEY

At a Court of Hustings held for the Town & Corporation of Fredericksburg the 23rd Octr. 1795; This Indenture was proved by the oaths of JOHN HARDIA, THOMAS WARE & THOMAS R. ROOTES three witnesses as to the execution of CHARLES A. LEWIS, which is ordered to be recorded as to him; And was further proved by the oaths of JOHN THOMPSON and RICHARD JOHNSON JR. two witnesses as to the execution of WILLIAM SMITH & ordered to be recorded   Teste JNO: CHEW, C. C. H.

At a Court of Hustings held for the Town & Corporaltion of Fredericksburg the 25th day of December 1795   This Indenture was further proved by the oath of WM. TAYLOR, a witness thereto, as to the execution thereof by WM. SMITH & together with the Commission annexed and the Certificate of Execution thereof Indorsed, were ordered to be recorded

Exd. & deld. JAS. ROSS   Teste JNO: CHEW, C. C. H.

pp. THIS INDENTURE made this Fifth day of October 1795 Between WILLIAM SMITH
47- and ANN his Wife of one part and COLIN & JAMES ROSS, Merchants of Fredericks-
51 burg of other part; Witnesseth that WILLIAM SMITH and ANN his Wife for sum of Two hundred and thirty two pounds, seventeen shillings & four pence to them in hand paid by COLIN & JAMES ROSS, have bargained and sold unto COLIN & JAMES ROSS their heirs all that lot of ground lying in Town of Fredericksburg and bounded, Begining from the corner of Lot No. 72 formed by the Cross Street called LEWIS STREET and the Main Street called CAROLINE STREET from this begining up said Main Street seventy one feet from thence down said Lot one hundred and thirty two feet being parellel to the Cross Street called LEWIS STREET from thence seventy one feet parrellel to the Front Street till it intersects said LEWIS STREET, from thence to the begining; To have and to hold the said premises unto COLIN & JAMES ROSS their heirs and WILLIAM SMITH and ANN his Wife for themselves and their heirs this parcel of land against the claim of every person will warrant and defend by these presents; In Witness whereof the parties have hereunto signed their names and affixed their seals the day and year above written

Signed Sealed & Delivered in the presents of
   JOHN THOMPSON, RICHARD JOHNSON JUNR.,   WILLIAM SMITH
   SAM: RODDEY, WILLIAM TAYLOR   ANN SMITH

The Commonwealth of Virginia to GEO: W. B. SPOONER, WILLIAM HARVEY also Doctr. ELISHA HALL Gentlemen Greeting, Whereas (the Commission for the privy Examination of ANN, the Wife of WILLIAM SMITH); Witness JOHN CHEW Clerk of our said Hustings Court the fifth of October 1795 and in the 20th year of the Commonwealth   JNO: CHEW

Corporation of Fredericksburg, By virtue of the within Commission, we the Subscribers did on the fifth day of October 1795 go to the within named ANN (the return of the Execution of the privy Examination of ANN SMITH); Witness our hands & seals the day and year above written   GEO: W. B. SPOONER
               WM. HARVEY

At a Court of Hustings held for the Town and Corporation of Fredericksburg the 23rd day of October 1795   This Indenture for Lotts from WILLIAM SMITH to COLIN & JAMES ROSS was proved by the oaths of JOHN THOMPSON & RICHARD JOHNSTON JUNR. two witnesses thereto and ordered to be certified

At a Court of Hustings held for the Town and Corporation of Fredg. the 25th Decr. 1795 This Indenture was further proved by the oath of WM. TAYLOR, a Witness thereto, & together with the Commission annexed & the Certificate of Execution thereof indorsed, were ordered to be recorded

Examd. & Deld. JAS. ROSS   Teste JNO: CHEW, C. C. H.

pp.   THIS INDENTURE made this 30th day of May in year of our Lord one thousand
51-   seven hundred and Ninety five Between THOMAS VOWLES of Town of Fredg. of
53   one part and JAMES BLAIR & JAMES SUMMERVILLE, Acting Executors of HENRY
MITCHELL deceased, of the other part; Witnesseth that THOMAS VOWLES for the
sum of Five shillings by JAMES BLAIR and JAMES SUMMERVILLE to him in hand paid
and in consideration of the causes hereafter expressed by these presents doth bargain
& sell to JAMES BLAIR & JAMES SOMERVILLE one Negroe Woman named Rebecca together with her future increase, one bed and furniture; and all the Tools and materials
for turning now belonging to THOMAS VOWLES, To have and tohold the said slave and
her future increase and all other the property hereby conveyed to JAMES BLAIR and
JAMES SUMMERVILLE or the Survivor in Trust, that is to say, First that JAMES BLAIR
and JAMES SOMERVILLE or the Survivor shall apply so much of the aforesaid property
as will discharge the ballance of the account due the said VOWLES to the Estate of HENRY
MITCHELL amounting to the sum of Twenty two pounds five shillings and eleven pence
together with all Interest due; Secondly, in trust to the use of such persons as said
VOWLES shall bequeath or devise the remainder of the property after discharging the
aforesaid Account, Interest and costs; In Witness whereof THOMAS VOWLES hath hereunto subscribed his name and affixed his seal the day and year first above written
Signed sealed and delivered in presence of
     ALEXR. RIDDICK,   THOS: VOWLES
     ROBERT STRINGFELLOW JUNR.,
     W. FLETCHER,   ROBERT WALKER
    At a Court of Hustings held for the Town and Corporation of Fredericksburg on Friday
the 25th day of Decr. 1795;   This Deed of Trust was proved by three of the witnesses
thereto and ordered to be recorded
Exd. & deld. A. BUCK   Teste   JNO: CHEW, C. C. H.

pp.   THIS INDENTURE made this twenty seventh day of May in year of our Lord one
54-   thousand seven hundred and Ninety five Between THOMAS VOWLES of Town of
56   Fredericksburg of one part and DAVID & JAMES BLAIR, Merchants, of the same
place of other part; Witnesseth that THOMAS VOWLES for sum of Five shillings
by DAVID & JAMES BLAIR to him in hand paid doth by these presents grant & sell to
DAVID & JAMES BLAIR, One Negro woman named Rebecca together with her future
increase, one bed and furniture and all the Tools and other materials for turning now
belonging to said VOWLES, To have and to hold to DAVID and JAMES BLAIR or the Survivor of them in Trust, that is to say, DAVID & JAMES BLAIR or the Survivor shall apply so
much of the aforementioned property to the payment of two Judgments obtained
against said VOWLES in Court of Hustings held for the said Town, one Judgment being
for Four pounds eight shillings and five pence 1/2, and two dollars and forty two cents
for costs obtained September 1793; and the other for Twelve pounds fourteen shillings
and six pence and Five dollars & fifty four cents for costs obtained March 1794 as will
discharge the same together with legal Interest upon the whole amount untill it shall
be paid; In Witness whereof THOMAS VOWLES hath hereunto subscribed his name and
affixed his seal the day and year first above written
Signed Sealed and Delivered in the presence of
     ALEXR. RIDDICK,   THOS: VOWLES
     ROBERT STRINGFELLOW JUNR.
     H. FLETCHER, ROBT. WALKER
    At a Court of Hustings held for the Town & Corporation of Fredericksburg on Friday
the 25th day of December 1795   This Deed of Trust was proved by three of the witnesses thereto and ordered to be recorded

pp,   THIS INDNETURE made this Sixth day of March Anno Domini one thousand
57-   seven hundred and Ninety five Between JAMES SOMERVILLE, as Survivor of
60   ARCHIBALD RITCHIE, ROBERT GILCHRIST, JOHN GRAY and JAMES SOMERVILLE,
          who were Trustees of MITCHELL, LENOX & SCOTT of the first part and THOMAS
RYAN of the other part. Whereas a certain JOHN ALLAN (as factor for BUCHANAN and
HAMILTON) being seized in fee of & in a certain lott of ground in Town of Fredericksburg, and numbered Six, bounded by AMELIA, SOPHIA and WILLIAM STREETs & the
RIVER RAPPAHANNOCK and by his last Will and Testament impowered his Executors to
dispose of all his Estate both real & personal in order to fulfill his Will which said lott
was afterwards by Deed bearing date the first day of October Anno Domini one thousand
seven hundred and sixty two and recorded in the General Court, conveyed by JAMES
HUNTER as Executor of JOHN ALLEN & SAMUEL RICHARDS, ISRAEL MORDUIT, ARCHI-
BALD McCLANE, EDMUND LARDNER & WILLIAM COOKE, assinees of said BUCHANAN &
HAMILTON to MITCHELL LENOX and SCOTT for a valuable considertion; And Whereas by
Deed bearing date the twenty fifth day of October one thousand seven hundred & seven-
ty three and recorded in the General Court, JOHN MITCHELL as surviving partner of
MITCHELL, LENOX & SCOTT, did convey among other property the aforesaid lott of land
unto JOHN GRAY, ARCHIBALD RITCHIE, ROBERT GILCHRIST and JAMES SOMERVILLE &
their heirs in Trust for certain purposes in said Deed expressed; of which Trustees
JAMES SOMERVILLE is the only Survivor and as such and for the fulfilment of the said
Trust hath sold one half of said Lott number six and bounded begining at the corner of
said lott on AMELIA & SOPHIA STREETs, down SOPHIA STREET one hundred and sixty five
feet or to the corner of the Lott now occupied by FIELDING LUCAS, thence with his line
to the said River, thence up the River to the corner of AMELIA STREET, from thence to
the begining unto the said THOMAS RYAN for the sum of Fifty four pounds curry., for
the more perfect conveying and assuring said lott, This Indenture Witnesseth that
JAMES SOMERVILLE for sum of Fifty four pounds to him in hand paid by THOMAS RYAN
by these presents doth bargain & sell unto THOMAS RYAN the one half of said lott of
ground together with all ways profits commodities and appertenances belonging; To
have and to hold said parcel of land unto THOMAS RYAN his heirs, And JAMES SOMER-
VILLE for himself his heirs the said lott of land against the claims of every person shall
truly defend & warrant; In Witness whereof JAMES SOMERVILLE hath set his hand and
afixed his seal the day & year first above written
Sealed & Delivered in presence of
        G. NORWOOD, DANIEL GRINNAN JUNR.   JAMES SOMERVILLE
        JAMES SOMERVILLE JUNR.
    At a Court of Hustings held for the Town & Corporation of Fredericksburg the 25th day
of Decr. 1795; This Indenture was acknowledged by the said JAMES SOMERVILLE &
ordered to be recorded
Exd. & Deld. THOS: RYAN   Teste   JNO: CHEW, C. C. H.

pp.   THIS INDENTURE made the 25th day of December Anno Domini one thousand
60-   seven hundred and Ninety five Between PHILIP LIPSCOMB of the Corporation of
62   Fredericksburg of one part and JAMES BROWN of the Corporation aforesaid of
          the other part; Witnesseth that PHILIP LIPSCOMB for sum of One hundred and
forty seven pounds Nine shillings and Five pence specie to him in hand paid by these
presents do bargain & sell unto JAMES BROWN his heirs all that Tenement leased by said
PHILIP to a certain GEORGE McCUTCHEN for the term of Twelve years commencing in
the year of our Lord one thousand seven hundred and eighty seven; and bound, begining on the North end of CAROLINE STREET and joining the said PHILIPs Lot in which
he then lived, thence North East 58 feet, thence South East 132 feet, thence S. W. 58 feet,

thence N. W. to the begining; To have and to hold the Tenement with the apperternances unto JAMES BROWN his heirs; Provided always that if said PHILIP his heirs shall pay unto JAMES BROWN or assigns the full sum of One hundred & forty seven pounds, Nine shillings & Five pence with Interest from the sixteenth day of July Anno Domini one thousand seven hundred and ninety one untill paid then these presents t be void; In Witness whereof the parties have hereunto affixed their hands and seals the day and year first above written   PHILIP LIPSCOMB

 At a Court of Hustigns held for the Town and Corporation of Fredericksburg December the 25th 1795 This Indenture was acknowledged by the said PHILIP LIPSCOMB and ordered to be recorded

Exd. & deld Mr. JAS: BROWN   Teste JNO: CHEW, C. C. H.

pp,   THIS INDENTURE made the twenty eighth day of November one thousand seven
62-   hundred and Ninety five Between CHARLES MORTIMER, GEORGE FRENCH, WIL-
63   LIAM HARVEY, BENJAMIN DAY & STEVEN LaCOSTE, Trustees to the Estate of
         SAMUEL ABBETT deced., of one part and DAVID OLIVIER of Town of Fredericks-
burg of other part; Witnesseth that the (Trustees) by virtue of an Act of Assembly passed the Eleventh day of December one thousand seven hundred and Eighty nine and for Two hundred and seventy five pounds current money of Virginia to them in hand paid do by virtue of said Act of Assembly bargain and sell unto DAVID OLIVIER and his heirs one lott of Land in Town of Fredericksburg known by number 257 bounded West by CAROLINE STREET, North by PRUSSIA STREET, on the East by JAMES HUNTER's Lott and the South by JAMES HEATH's Lott, of which Lott SAMUEL ABBOTT died seized, together with all appurtenances; To have and to hold the said lott No. 257 to DAVID OLIVIER his heirs And the said Trustees from the authority vested in them by said Act of Assembly will forever warrant & defend; In Witness whereof the said Trustees have hereunto subscribed their names and affixed their seals the 28th November 1795
Signed sealed and Delivered in the presence of
          WILLIAM TAYLOR,   CHS: MORTIMER
          THOMAS SEDDON JR.   GEO: FRENCH
          JAMES NEWBY   WILLIAM HARVEY
                                       BENJN: DAY

 At a Court of Hustings held for the Town & Corporation of Fredericksburg December 25th 1795   This Indenture was proved by three of the witnesses thereto and ordered to be recorded

pp.   THIS INDENTURE made this twenty fourth of December one thousand seven
64-   hundred and Ninety five Between DAVID OLIVIER of Town of Fredericksburg of
65   one part and JAMES SOMERVILLE of said place of other part; Witnesseth that
         DAVID OLIVIER for sum of Two hundred & fifty pounds current money to him in
hand paid by JAMES SOMERVILLE, hath bargains sold and delivered to JAMES SOMER-
VILLE his heirs a certain lott of land in said Town known by the number 257 bounded West by CAROLINE STREET, North by PRUSSIA STREET, on the East by said SOMERVILLE and the South by JAMES HEATHs lott, together with all houses and appurtenances be-longing; To have and to hold unto JAMES SOMERVILLE his heirs freed and discharged from all incumbrances suffered by DAVID OLIVIER; and DAVID OLIVER his heirs will warrant & forever defend by these presents; In Witness whereof DAVID OLIVIER hath hereunto set his hand and seal the day and year above written
Sealed & Delivered in presence of
          (no witnesses shown)   DAVID OLIVIER

At a Court of Hustings held for the Town & Corporation of Fredericksburg December
25th 1795   This Indenture was acknowledged by the said DAVID OLIVIER & ordered
to be recorded

pp.   KNOW ALL MEN by these presents that I LUCY DIXON, Relict of ROGER DIXON
66-   deceased for sum of Ten pounds to me in hand paid by RICHARD PEACOCK have
67   sold to said PEACOCK & his heirs a parcel of ground Sixteen feet in front situate
           on North East side of CAROLINE STREET and adjoining or part of lot No. 258,
which parcel of ground I do for myself my heirs warrant & defend to said PEACOCK and
his heirs; And it is further my desire that my Son, ROGER DIXON, shall at any time hereafter if requested make any right that may be vested in him to said PEACOCK; In Witness whereof I have hereunto set my hand & seal this Eighth day of September one
thousand seven hundred and Ninety five
Testes JAMES NEWBY,   LUCY DIXON
       GEORGE LAFONG,   WILLIAM TAYLOR
   At a Court of Hustings held for the Town & Corporation of Fredericksburg December
25th 1795   This Deed was proved by three of the witnesses thereto and ordered to be
recorded

pp.   THIS INDENTURE made the twelfth day of August one thousand seven hundred
67-   and Ninety five Between MARY SULLIVAN and LUCY DIXON of Town of
69   Fredericksburg of one part and RICHARD PEACOCK of Fredericksburg of other
           part; Witnesseth that MARY SULLIVAN and LUCY DIXON for sum of Four hun-
dred and forty pounds current money of Virginia to them in hand paid do bargain sell
& deliver unto RICHARD PEACOCK his heirs one part of a lott of ground lying in Town of
Fredericksburg number 258 and bounded, begining on CAROLINE STREET at the Lott belonging to the Estate of EDWARD ROSS deced., thence runing down CAROLINE STREET to
the part of Lott lately purchased by said PEACOCK of J. HUNTERs Exors., being seventy
two feet more or less, thence Eastwardly parrellel with PRUSSIA STREET to the full
debth of said Lott No. 258; thence Northwardly and parrellel with CAROLINE STREET to
the aforesaid Lott belonging to the Estate of EDWARD ROSS deceased and from thence to
the begining on CAROLINE STREET; together with all appurtenances; To have and to
hold the part of lott with its appurtenances unto RICHARD PEACOCK his heirs, And
MARY SULLIVAN and LUCY DIXON for themselves and their heirs the said part of a lott
unto RICHARD PEACOCK his heirs against all persons will forever warrant & defend; In
Witness whereof MARY SULLIVAN and LUCY DIXON have hereunto their hands & seals
the day and year first above written
Signed Sealed & Delivered in the presence of
       JAMES NEWBY,   MARY SULLIVAN her mark
       JAMES RIDLEY, GEORGE LAFONG   LUCY DIXON
   At a Court of Hustings held for the Town & Corporation of Fredericksburg December
25th 1795   This Indenture was proved by three of the witnesses thereto & ordered to
be recorded
Exd. & deld. RD. PEACOCK's Son   Teste   JNO: CHEW C. C. H.

pp.   TO ALL TO WHOM THESE PRESENTS shall come, Whereas WILLIAM SMITH, late
69-   Postmaster of the Town of Fredericksburg and ANN SMITH his Wife by an In-
74   denture dated the twenty third day of May one thousand seven hundred and
           eighty nine (duly proved assented to and recorded in the Court of Hustings of
said Corporation) did bargain sell and confirm unto EBENEZOR HAZARD, then Postmaster General of the United States of North America and to his heirs certain lots of land

which in said Indenture are described in these words; Vizt. all that parcel of ground
being part of Lot No. 72 containing sixty one and an half feet front on CAROLINE STREET
thence down the said lot adjoining Lot No. 71, one hundred and thirty two feet, thence
up said lot sixty one and a half feet parallel to CAROLINE thence one hundred and thirty two feet to the begining; (on this lit is a convenient warehouse 40 by 20 feet in good
repair with a good cellar under the whole on CAROLINE STREET, also the lot of ground
No. 71 containing half an acre adjoining Lot No. 72 both which lots are situate in Town
of Fredericksburg, with proviso that if WILLIAM SMITH should pay EBENEZER HAZARD
or his certain Attorney the sum of Five hundred and seven pounds nine shillings and
five pence 5/8ths. current money of Virginia on or before the first day of July then
next following with lawfull interest from the Eleventh day of November one thousand
seven hundred and eighty eight the said Indenture should be void; Now Know ye that
said EBENEZER HAZARD (the said sum & interest not having been paid) do constitute
CHARLES LEWIS of Fredericksburg my true and lawfull attorney in the premises and
also the true and lawfull attorney of said WILLIAM SMITH and ANN his Wife with full
power to sell the two lots of land afore described; Given under my hand and seal this
25th day of February in year of our Lord one thousand seven hundred and ninety two
Signed sealed and delivered in the presence of
    OLIV: WOLCOTT JR.   EBEN: HAZARD   -
    WILLIAM CLARKSON, MICHL: REYNOLDS
CITY of PHILADELPHIA Sct. Before me, JOHN BARCLAY, Esqr., Mayor of the City of
PHILADELPHIA in the State of PENNSYLVANIA personally appeared EBENEZER HAZARD
of said City and acknowledged the annexed Power of Attorney to be his act and deed and
desired the same may be recorded according to the Laws of the Commonwealth of the
State of Virginia. In Testimony wherof I the said Mayor have hereunto set my hand and
caused the Seal of the Mayoralty to be affixed the 25th of February Anno Domini 1792
                                 JOHN BARCLAY
    At a Court of Hustings continued and held for the Town and Corporation of Fredericks-
burg December 26th 1796   This Letter of Attorney from EBENEZER HAZARD to
CHARLES LEWIS and the Certificate of the Lord Mayor of the City of PHILADELPHIA
hereto annexed are on motion of CHARLES LEWIS ordered to be recorded

pp.   THIS INDENTURE made the Sixteenth day of February Anno Domini one thou-
74-   sand seven hundred and Ninety Six Between WILLIAM GLASSELL and SARAH his
79   Wife of Town of Fredericksburg of one part and JACOB KUHN of same Town of
        other part; Whereas by Deed indented bearing date the twenty first day of June
one thousand seven hundred and Ninety four Between said JACOB KUHN of one part and
WILLIAM GLASSELL of other part said JACOB KUHN did for the consideration therein
expressed bargain and sell unto WILLIAM GLASSELL a certain lott of ground situate on
CAROLINE STREE between the lotts of WALTER GREGORY and WILLIAM DRUMMOND
bounded, Begining at the lower corner of lott number twenty eight on CAROLINE
STREET thence up and along said Street thirty feet, thence at right angles with said
Street one hundred feet Eastward, thence parellel with CAROLINE STREET thirty feet to
the lower line of said lott and from thence along the lower line to the begining, together with all houses and appurtenaces to said lott belonging; Also the upper moiety of a
lott number Five bounded, by WILLIAM STREET on the North West, by SOPHIA STREET on
the South West, Lott No. Twenty three being opposite the same & on the South East by
one other prt of Lott No. five, and on the North East on the River RAPPAHANNOCK containing one quarter of an acre with all its appurtenances; Also seven parcels of land in
the County of GREENBRIER containg Seven thousand acres be the same more or less as
described by a Deed of Bargain and Sale from WILLIAM HANCHER and ANN his Wife to

said KUHN bearing date the twentieth of February 1790 now of record in the County of GREENBRIER; To have and to hold the said lotts land and all the premises unto WILLIAM GLASSELL his heirs with the proviso that if JACOB KUHN his heirs should pay unto said WILLIAM the sum of Fourteen hundred pounds at three equal payments the said Indenture to be void; NOW THIS INDENTURE Witnesseth that WILLIAM GLASSELL and SARAH his Wife in consideration of the premises and sum of Five shillings to them in hand paid by JACOB KUHN do by these presents bargain sell and release unto JACOB KUHN his heirs all the lands and premises in said recited Indenture mentioned; In Witness whereof WILLIAM GLASSELL & SARAH his Wife have hereunto set their hands and affixed their seals the day & year first above written
Signed sealed and Delivered in the presence of

ALEX. RIDDICK,	WILLIAM GLASSELL
GEO: THORNTON, BALDWIN TALIAFERRO,	SARAH GLASSELL
WM. HARVEY, WM. HERNDON	

The Commonwealth of Virginia to WILLIAM HARVEY, FONTAIN MAURY & WILLIAM HERNDON Gent., Greeting; Whereas (the Commission for the privy Examination of SARAH, the Wife of WILLIAM GLASSELL); Witness JOHN CHEW Clerk of our said Hustings Court the 17th day of February 1796 and in the 20th year of the Commonwealth

Corporation of Fredericksburg to wit; In obedience to the within Commission to us directed (the return of the execution of the privy Examination of SARAH GLASSELL); Given under our hands and seals the 20th day of February 1796   WM. HARVEY
                                                                                                                                          WM. HERNDON

At a Court of Hustings held for the Town and Corporation of Fredericksburg the 27th February 1796   This Indenture for Land and Release of a Mortgage from WM. GLASSELL & SARAH his Wife to JACOB KUHN was acknowledged by the said GLASSELL and together with the Commission annexed & Certificate of the execution thereo indorsed were ordered to be recorded

pp.   THIS INDENTURE made the twenty fifth day of February in year one thousand
79-   seven hundred and Ninety six Between JACOB KUHN of Town of Fredericksburg
80   of one part & THOMAS SYDNOR of Fredericksburg of other part; Witnesseth
             that JACOB KUHN for Five pounds current money of Virginia to him in hand paid
do bargain and sell unto THOMAS SYDNOR & his heirs a certain parcel of ground lying in said Town on CAROLINE STREET between the lott of ground the property of WALTER GREGORY and that piece now holden by Docter ELISHA HALL and is bounded; Begining at the lower corner of Lott No.28 on CAROLINE STREET thence up said Street and along it thirty feet, thence at right angles with said Street one hundred feet Eastwardly, thence parellel with CAROLINE STREET thirty feet to the lower line of said Lott and from thence along said lower line to the begining on CAROLINE STREET, including an oblong or area of one hundred feet by thirty; Together with the two story dwelling house, kitchen, out houses and all appurtenances thereunto belonging; To have & to hold unto THOMAS SYDNOR and his heirs, And JACOB KUHN and his heirs will forever warrant and defend; In Witness whereof JACOB KUHN hath hereunto set his hand and seal the day and year above written
Signed Sealed and Delivered in the presence of us
          (no witnesses shown)   JACOB KUHN
At a Court of Husting held for the Town & Corpo: of Fredg. 27th February 1796
This Indenture for a Lott from JACOB KUHN to THOMAS SYDNOR was acknowledged by said JACOB KUHN and ordered to be recorded
Examd. & deld. J. ROSS p. order filed   Teste JNO: CHEW, C.C.H.

pp.   THIS INDENTURE made the Twenty fifth day of February one thousand seven
81-   hundred and ninety six Between JACOB KUHN of Town of Fredericksburg of one
82   part and THOMAS SYDNOR of said Town of other part; Witnesseth that JACOB
KUHN for sum of Five pounds current money of Virginia to him in hand paid do
bargin and sell unto THOMAS SYDNOR and his heirs part of a Lott of ground in afsd.
Town being the upper moiety of a lott known by number Five and bounded by WILLIAM
STREET on the Northwest, by SOPHIA STREET on the Southwest and extending along
SOPHIA STREET as far as Lott number Twenty three bieng opposite the same and on the
Southeast by one other part of said Lott number Five and on the Northeast by the River
RAPPAHANNOCK, containing one quarter of an acre, together with a two story Ware-
house and all other appurtenances thereto belonging; To have and to hold said part of a
lott to THOMAS SYDNOR and his heirs and JACOB KUHN his heirs will warrant and defend
In Witness whereof JACOB KUHN hath hereunto set his hand and seal the day and year
first above written
Signed sealed & delivered in the presence of us
        (no witnesses shown)   JACOB KUHN
   At a Court of Hustings held for the Town & Corpo: of Fredericksburg the 27th day of
February 1796   This Indenture for a Lott from JACOB KUHN to THOMAS SYDNOR
was acknowledged by the said JACOB KUHN and ordered to be recorded
Examd. & deld. J. ROSS, p. ord. filed   Teste JNO: CHEW, C. C. H.

pp.   THIS INDENTURE made this 22nd day of July Anno Domini one thousand seven
82-   hundred and ninety five Between LARKIN SMITH and (blank) his Wife of City of
85   RICHMOND of one part and ELISHA HALL of Town of Fredericksburg of other
        part; Witnesseth that LARKIN SMITH and MARY ELEANOR his Wife for sum of Six
hundred pounds to them in hand paid by ELISHA HALL by these presents do bargain
sell & confirm unto ELISHA HALL his heirs, a certain lott of ground lying in said Town
and known by the number Forty three purchased by LARKIN SMITH of JOHN ATKINSON
and by him purchased of GEORGE MITCHELL; and is bounded begining at the lower
Southeast corner of the second Lott on CAROLINE STREET being the uper corner of a Lott
formerly the LONG ORDINARY LOTT, thence with the same Westward 132 feet to the lotts
called the COURT HOUSE LOTTS, thence with the same 37 1/2 feet, thence in a direction
nearly parellel with the COURT HOUSE abovementioned to CAROLINE STREET so as to
make the last course upon and along the said Street to the begining a distance of 33 feet
with all profits commodities & appurtenances belonging; To have and to hold the lott of
ground unto ELISHA HALL his heirs and LARKIN SMITH and MARY ELEANOR his Wife
for themselves their heirs the lott of ground to said ELISHA HALL hisheirs will warrant
and forever defend by these presents; In Witness whereof the parties have hereunto
set their hands and affixed their seals the day & year first above written
Signed sealed and delivered in presence of
     JOHN THOMPSON, WM. GARNER,   LARKIN SMITH
     JAMES HEATH, GO: LEWIS, SIMON SEXSMITH
   At a Court of Hustings held for the Town & Corporation of Fredericksburg 27th February 1796;   This Indenture for a Lott of Land from LARKIN SMITH to ELISHA HALL
was proved by the oaths of three of the witnesses thereto & ordered to be recorded

pp.   THIS INDENTURE made &c. Between CHAS. JULIAN of Corporation of Fredericks-
85-   burg of one part and JOSEPH CHRISTY of said Corporation of other part; Witnes-
87   that CHARLES JULIAN for sum of 288 L. 17 shillings to him in hand paid by
        JOSEPH CHRISTY by these presents doth bargain and sell unto JOSEPH CHRISTY
two lott on the back street of Fredg., comonly caled WATER STREET, Vizt. Lott No. 31,

begining at WATER STREET and runing in a straight line to a corner of Mr. JAMES
SUMERVALs Lott & thence along said SOMERVALs lott makes a corner at Mr. JOHN CHEWs
Lott and along said CHEWs lott and a lott of above JAMES SUMERVALs to said WATER
STREET and along said Street to the begining: And Lott No. 8 begining at said WATER
STREET and runing in a straight line to RAPPAHANNOCK RIVER all along the lott of MR.
GODLOVE HIESKELs & taking in nere 1/3 of a large old House, the property of said HEIS-
IELL and thence runing along the River to a corner on a Cross Street caled LEWIS
STREET and along said Street to WATER STREET & along WATER STREET to the begining,
To have and to hold said lotts houses improvements &c. &c., unto JOSEPH CHRISTY his
heirs and CHARLES JULIAN and his heirs to said JOSEPH CHRISTY his heirs will warrant
& forever defend by these presents; In Witness whereof CHARLES JULIAN hath afixed
his hand and seal this 12th day of February one thousand seven hundred ninety six
Witness ROBERT WALKER,   CHARLES JULIAN
      SAMUEL SCOTT, SAMUEL CHEWNING
    At a Court of Hustings held for the Town & Corpo: of Fredg., 27th february 1796
This Indenture for Lotts from CHARLES JULIAN to JOSEPH CHRISTY was acknowledged
by the said CHARLES JULIAN and ordered to be recorded
Exd. & Deld. JOS: CHRISTY   Teste   JNO: CHEW, C. C. H.

pp.   THIS INDENTURE made the twenty sixth day of December in year of our Lord
87-   one thousand seven hundred and ninety five Between RICHARD S. HACKLEY of
92   Town of Fredericksburg and ANN his Wife of one part and JAMES NEWBY of said
         Town of other part; Witnesseth that for sum of four hundred and twenty five
pounds current money of Virginia to be paid them, that is to say, One hundred and six
pounds Five shillings on or before the 25th Instant, one hundred & six pounds Five
shillings on or before the 25th day of December one thousand seven hundred and ninety six, One hundred and six pounds Five shillings on or before the twenty fifth day of
December one thousand seven hundred and Ninety seven and One hundred and six
pounds and five shillings on or before the twenty fifth day of December one thousand
seven hundred and ninety eight by these presents do bargain sell and confirm unto
JAMES NEWBY his heirs part of a lott lying in Town of Fredericksburg know by No.
15.15; and bounded, Begining on the Main or CAROLINE STREET at the corner of WOLF
STREET and runing down and along CAROLINE STREET one hundred and ten feet three
inches, thence Westwardly and parrellel with WOLF STREET one hundred and thirty two
feet, thence Northwardly parellel with CAROLINE or the Main Street one hundred & ten
feet three inches to WOLF STREET, thence Eastwardly along WOLF STREET one hundred
and thirty two feet to the begining, togehter with all houses and buildings erected
thereon; To have and to hold the part of a lott of land unto JAMES NEWBEY his heirs and
the said RICHARD and ANN his Wife & their heirs shall warrant & ever defend by these
presents; In Witness whereof the said RICHARD and ANNE his Wife have hereunto
affixed their hands & seals this day and year first above written
Signed sealed and acknowledged in the presence of
      JAMES J. GARNETT,   RICHARD S. HACKLEY
      GEO: S. HACKLEY,   ANN HACKLEY
      WM. DRUMMOND, JAMES ROSS
   Received One hundred and six pounds five shillings in full of the first payment for the
within Lott and four pounds seven & six pence on account of second payment & four
pounds seven shillings and six pence on account of third payment & four pounds seven
shillings & six pence on accunt of the fourth payment
Test RICHARD PEACOCK   RICHARD S. HACKLEY
   The Commonwealth of Virginia to WM. HARVEY, ELISHA HALL & FONTAINE MAURY

Gentlemen Greeting; Whereas (the Commission for the privy Examination of ANN, the Wife of
RICHARD S. HACKLEY); Witness JOHN CHEW Clerk of our said Hustings Court the 18th day of
January 1796 and in the 20th year of the Commonwealth   JNO: CHEW
 Corporation of Fredericksburg Sct. In Obedience to the within Commission to us
directed we this day (the return of the execution of the privy Examination of ANN HACKLEY);
Given under our hands & seals this 10th day of February 1796   WILLIAM HARVEY
                                                                 ELISHA HALL
    At a Court of Hustings held for the Town & Corpo: of Fredg. the 27th day of February
1796   This Indenture from RICHARD S. HACKLEY & ANN his Wife to JAMES NEWBY was
acknowledged by the said RICHARD S. HACKLEY and together with the Commission annexed and Certificate of the execution thereof indorsed are ordered to be recorded
Examd. & deld. JAS: NEWBY   Teste   JNO: CHEW, C. C. H.

pp.   THIS INDENTURE made and entered into this 27th day of December in year of
93-   our Lord one thousand seven hundred and Ninety five Between JAMES NEWBY
96   of Town of Fredbg. of one part and RICHARDS S. HACKLEY of same place of other
           part; Witnesseth that JAMES NEWBY for sum of four hundred and twenty five
pounds lawfull money of Virginia by these presents doth bargain and sell unto said
RICHARD S. HACKLEY a part of a lott lying in said Town and known by No. 15.15; and
bounded, Begining on the Main or CAROLINE STREET at the corner of WOLF STREET and
runing down CAROLINE STREET one hundred and ten feet three inches, thence Westwardly and parellel with WOLF STREET one hundred and thirty feet, thence Northwardly parellel with CAROLINE STREET one hundred and ten feet three inches to WOLF
STREET, thence Eastwardly along WOLF STRETT one hundred & thirty two feet to the begining; To have and to hold the part of a lott unto RICHARD S. HACKLEY and assigns
during the Term of Five hundred years paying therefor yearly one Shilling if de-
manded, provided always & upon condition that if JAMES NEWBY his heirs pay RICHARD
S. HACKLEY or assigns the full sum before the 25th day of December one thousand
seven hundred and Ninety Eight (the payments as set out above are repeated in this Indenture)
In Witness whereof JAMES NEWBY hath hereunto set his hand and seal the day and year
first above written
Signed Sealed & Delivered in presence of
    ROBERT PEACOCK   JAMES NEWBY
    At a Court of Hustings held for the Town and Corporation of Fredericksburg the 27th
February 1796   This Deed of Mortgage from JAMES NEWBY to RICHD. S. HACKLEY
was acknowledged by the said JAMES NEWBY and ordered to be recorded
Examined and Delivered THOMAS R. ROOTES   Teste JNO: CHEW, C. C. H.

pp.   THIS INDENTURE made this (blank) day of Octr. Anno Domini one thousand seven
97-   hundred and ninety five Between JOHN TALIAFERRO BROOKE & JAMES MERCER
99   GARNET, Admors. with the Will annexed of the late JAMES MERCER deced., of one
           part and JOHN LEGG of other part; Witnesseth that whereas JAMES MERCER did
by his last Will and Testament bearing date the 26th of May one thousand seven hundred and ninety one and recorded in County Court of Spotsylvania among other things
devise that all his property in the Town of Fredbg. should be sold by his Executors, Mr.
MUSCOE GARNETT of ESSEX, & Mr. BENJA: HARRISON of HENRICO for the purpose of
paying his just debts & other purposes & said MUSCOE GARNETT & BENJAMIN HARRISON
having been summoned to the County Court of Spotsylvania and having refused to execute the said Will and by virtue of an Act of Assembly passed the 13th day of December
Anno Domini one thousand seven hundred and ninety two the power of selling the said

property has devolved on the Administrators, the said JOHN TALIAFERRO BROOKE &
JAMES MERCER GARNETT for sum of One hundred and thirty one pounds Virginia Currency to them in hand paid by JOHN LEGG, do bargain and sell unto JOHN LEGG his heirs
four Lotts in the Town of Fredericksburg numbered one hundred & fifteen, one hundred and sixteen, one hundred seventeen, one hundred and eighteen, and bounded on
the North by PITT STREET, on the South by HAWKE STREET, on the West by PRINCE
EDWARD & on the East by CHARLES STREET with all the trees profits commodities &
hereditaments to said lotts belonging; To have and to hold the said lotts with the appurtenances unto said JOHN LEGG his heirs, In Witness whereof the parties have hereunto
affixed their hands and seals the day and year above written
Sealed & Delivered in presence of
          GEO: BAGGOT as to Mr. GARNETT   J. MERCER GARNETT
          JOSA INGRAM, JOHN VICTOR)   JOHN T. BROOKE
          GEO: NORWOOD   ) as to Mr. Garnett
     At a Court of Hustings held for the Town & Corporation of Fredericksburg 27th Febru-
ary 1796. This Indenture for Lotts from JOHN T. BROOKE and JAMES M. GARNETT, Ad-
ministers of JAMES MERCER deced., to JOHN LEGG was acknowledged by the said JOHN T.
BROOKE and proved by the oaths of four Witnesses as to the exectuion of the said JAMES
M. GARNETT & ordered to be recorded
Examd. & Deld THOS· LEGG, Son of JNO: LEGG   Teste   JNO: CHEW C. C. H.

pp.   THIS INDENTURE made this 24th day of November in year of our Lord one thou-
99-   sand seven hundred and ninety five Between JOHN LEWIS of Corporation of
101   Fredericksburg of one part and GUSTAVUS BROWN WALLACE of the Corporation
           aforesaid of other part; That in consideration of sum of Forty pounds in hand
paid said JOHN LEWIS by these presents doth bargain and sell unto GUSTAVUS BROWN
WALLACE his heirs a certain Water Lott situated on the River in Town of Fredericksburg and known by number Sixty six adjoining Lott number Sixty five on one side,
SOPHIA & FAUQUIER STREETs on two other sides and the RIVER RAPPAHANNOCK on the
other side Eastward, together with all appurtenances thereunto belonging; To have and
to hold the said lott of land unto GUSTAVUS BROWN WALLACE his heirs; In Witness
whereof he hath hereunto affixed his Seal & set his hand the day & year above written
                                                  JOHN LEWIS
     At a Court of Hustings held for Town & Corpo: of Fredericksburg the 23rd day of April
1796,   This Indenture from JOHN LEWIS to GUSTAVUS BROWN WALLACE was acknow-
leged by said JOHN LEWIS & ordered to be recorded

pp.   THIS INDENTURE made the 14th day of March one thousand seven hundred and
101-   ninety six Between CHARLES MORTIMER and SARAH his Wife of Town and Cor-
102   poration of Fredericksburg of one part and BARTHOLOMEW FULLER of said Town
           & Corpo. of other part; Witnesseth that CHARLES MORTIMER and SARAH his Wife
for thirty pounds current money to them in hand paid by BARTHOLOMEW FULLER by
these presents bargain and sell unto BARTHO: FULLER one parcel of ground situate in
County of Spotsylvania and within the limits & jurisdiction of the Corpo: of Fredsbg.,
being a part of a survey laid out by Mr. JAMES TUTT, Surveyr:, at the reqeust of said
CHARLES MORTIMER into several lotts agreeable to such a survey is numbered one and
contains about one acre more or less; To have and to hold the land unto BARTHO: FULLER
his heirs. And CHARLES MORTIMER and SARAH his Wife will forever warrant & defend
the title of the said land; In Witness whereof CHARLES MORTIMER and SARAH his Wife
have hereunto set their hands and seals the day and year above written

Signed Sealed acknowledged and   CHS. MORTIMER
  delivered in presene of (no witnesses shown)   SARAH MORTIMER
  At a Court of Hustings held for the town & Corporation of Fredericksburg the 23rd day
of April 1796   This Indenture was acknowledged by CHARLES MORTIMER and ordered to
be recorded
Exd. & Deld. B. FULLER   Teste JNO: CHEW C. H. C.

pp,   THIS INDENTURE made the second day of January in year of our Lord one thou-
103-   sand seven hundred and Ninety six Between JAMES SMOCK of Corpo. of Fredbg.,
107   & SARAH his Wife of one part and THOMAS COLSON of County of Spotslylvania of
        other part; Whereas JAMES SMOCK by his bond or obligation dated the first day
of October one thousand seven hundred and ninety five became bound to said THOMAS
COLSON in the penal sum of Two thousand pounds gold or silver coin or Spanish milled
dollars at the rate of six shillings per dollar & all other gold and silver at the same proportion with a condition thereunder written that if JAMES SMOCK should pay to THOMAS
COLSON the just sum of One thousand pounds reckoning the value thereof as is herein
mentioned together with legal interest thereon from the first day of November last past
annually which was explained by a memorandum in writing on the back of said Bond,
then the Bond to be void which memorandum is according to the following tenor; That
no suit shall be commenced on the same in less time then ten years from the date of said
Bond provided JAMES SMOCK should pay the legal interest and one hundred pounds of
the principal sum as it annually becomes due, the first of which annual payments becomes due and payable the first day of November one thousand seven hundred & ninety
six; Now This Indenture Witnesseth that JAMES SMOCK and SARAH his Wife as well for
the better securing the payment of said sum and in consideration of sum of Five shillings to JAMES SMOCK in hand, said JAMES SMOCK and SARAH his Wife by these presents
do bargain and sell unto THOMAS COLSON his heirs one lott of ground situate on the
Main Street in the Town of Fredericksburg and is part of the CHURCH LOTT sold by an
Act of General Assembly for the benefit of the Parish of St. George and contains fifty
feet five inches in front on CAROLINE STREET and runs One hundred and thirty two feet
back as by a plott thereof hereto annexed; Together with all Improvements to the same
belonging; To have and to hold the parcel of land unto THOMAS COLSON his heirs, Provided always that if JAMES SMOCK his heirs shall pay the aforementioned sum with the
legal Interest then this writing to be void; In Witness whereof JAMES SMOCK and
SARAH his Wife have hereunto set their hands and affixed their seals the day and year
first afore written
Sealed & Delivered in presence of
     RICHD: S: HACKLEY   JAMES SMOCK
     ALEXR. NAIRNE, G., HEISKILL   SARAH SMOCK
  The Commonwealth of Virginia to WILLIAM HARVEY, FONTAINE MAURY & ELISHA
HALL Gentlemen Greeting; Whereas (the Commission for the privy Examination of SARAH, Wife
of JAMES SMOCK); Witness JOHN CHEW Clerk of ur said Hustings Court the 4th day of January 1796 and in the 20th year of the Commonwealth   JNO: CHEW
  Corporation of Fredericksburg; Pursuant to the within Commission, we the Subscribers
(the return of the execution of the privy Examination of SARAH SMOCK); Certified under our
hands and seals the fourth day of January 1796   WILLIAM HARVEY
                                                       ELISHA HALL

  At a Court of Hustings held for the Town and Corporation of Freds:burg the 25th day of
June 1796   This Indenture of Mortgage from JAMES SMOCK to THOMAS COLSON was
acknowledged by the said JAMES SMOCK and together with the Commission annexed and

Certificate of Execution thereof Indorsed, are ordered to be recorded
Exd. & Deld THOS: COLSON   Teste JNO: CHEW, C.C.H.

pp.   THIS INDENTURE made this the ninth day of March Anno Domini one thousand
107-   seven hundred and Ninety six Between ROBERT BROOKE of the City of RICHMOND
108   of one part and CHARLES MORTIMER of Town of Fredericksburg of other part;
          Witnesseth that ROBERT BROOKE for sum of Three hundred pounds to him in
hand paid, hath bargained and sold unto CHARLES MORTIMER his heirs the following
Negroes, to wit, King, Charles, Billy, John, Big Polly, & Criss; To have and to hold the
said Negroes unto CHARLES MORTIMER his heirs, Provided Always that if ROBERT
BROOKE his heirs truly pay unto CHARLES MORTIMER his heirs said sum of money with
interest from the 9th day of March 1790 without any deduction for Taxes then these
presence shall cease and be void; In Witness whereof ROBT. BROOKE has hereunto
affixed his hand and seal the day and year first above written
Signed sealed & Delivered in presence of
        FONTAINE MAURY,   ROBT. BROOKE
        RICHD. KENNY
I assign the within Mortgage to FRANCIS T. BROOKE & FONTAINE MAURY, they
engaging to have no recourse against me in case of accident
        ABRAHAM CARTER   CHAS. MORTIMER
    At a Court of Hustings held for the Town and Corporation of Fredericksburg the 25th
day of June 1796   This Indenture of Mortgage from ROBT. BROOKE Esqr. to CHARLES
MORTIMER was proved by two of the witnesses thereto & ordered to be recorded
Exd. & Deld. C. MORTIMER   Teste JNO: CHEW, C. H. C.

pp.   THIS INDENTURE made the fifth day of April one thousand seven hundred and
109-   ninety six Between WILLIAM REAT of Town of Fredericksburg of one part and
111   ALEXANDER NAIRNE of same Town of second part; Whereas JAMES HEATH &
          SUSANNAH HEATH did by Lease bearing date the fifteenth day of February one
thousand seven hundred and ninety demise & grant unto WM. REAT his heirs a part of a
lott of ground lying in Town of Fredericksburg No. 20, bounded as in said Lease will
more fully appear, And Whereas WM. REAT did by said demise covenant to pay for the
same on the Fifteenth day of February yearly the rent of Fourteen pounds Six shillings
current money of Virginia, Now This Indenture Witnesseth that WM. REAT in consideration of the Rents & agreements in this Indenture contained on part of ALEXANDER
NAIRNE to be paid and performed doth bargain & sell unto ALEXANDER NAIRNE his
heirs said part of lott; To have and to hold to said ALEXANDER NAIRNE his heirs and as a
further consideration the said ALEXANDER NAIRNE has paid to WILLIAM REAT the sum
of Six hundred pounds and doth agree that he will pay unto JAMES HEATH & SUSANNAH
HEATH their heirs the said Rent mentioned in the said lease; In Witness whereof said
parties have hereunto put their hands & affixed their seals day and year above written
Signed sealed & Delivered in presence of
        HENRY WHITE,   WILLIAM REAT
        GEORGE SMITH, PETER R. JOHNSON   ALEXANDER NAIRNE
    At a Court of Hustings held for the Town & Corporation of Fredericksburg the 25th day
of June 1796   This Indenture of Lease between WM. REAT and ALEXANDER NAIRNE was
acknowledged by the parties & ordered to be recorded
Examd. & deld. ALEXR. NAIRNE   Teste JNO: CHEW, C.C.H.

pp.   THIS INDENTURE made the 2nd day of Janry. in year of our Lord one thousand
111-   seven hundred & ninety six Between CHARLES WARDELL of Corporation of
116   Fredericksburg and SARAH his Wife of one part and THOMAS COLSON of County
       of Spotsylvania of other part. Whereas CHARLES WARDELL by his Bond dated 23
day of Octr. one thousand seven hundred and ninety five became bound in the penal
sum of Two thousand pounds Gold and Silver coin reckoning Spanish Milled Dollars at
the rate of Six Shillings p Dollar and all other Gold & Silver at the same proportion with
a condition thereunder written that if CHARLES WARDELL shall pay to THOMAS COLSON
the just sum of One thousand pounds Gold & Silver coins with legal interest from the
first day of Novr. last past annually as the same shall become due then said Bond to be
void; Now This Indenture Witnesseth that CHARLES WARDELL and SARAH his Wife as
well for the better securing the payment of sum of One thousand pounds in manner
aforesaid with legal interest on the same to THOMAS COLSON as also for sum of Five shillings to CHARLES WARDELL in hand paid by these presents doth bargain & sell THOS:
COLSON his heirs all that parcel of land in Town of Fredericksburg containing Forty one
feet six inches in front on CAROLINE STREET and one hundred & thirty two feet back, be
the same more or less, and is that part of the CHURCH LOTT sold by Act of Assembly for
the benefit of the Parish of Saint George and purchased by JOHN LEWIS, by him sold to
JOHN & ELIJAH CRAIGs, by them to EDWARD SIMPSON, by him to JOHN WELCH, and by
said WELCH to THOMAS COLSON, as also the same parcel of land sold by said THOMAS
COLSON & by FRANCES his Wife to said CHARLES WARDELL and conveyed by Indenture
bearing date the first day of January one thousand seven hundred and ninety six; To
have and to hold the above mentioned parcel of land unto THOMAS COLSON his heirs,
Provided always that if CHARLES WARDELL hisheirs shall pay the aforementioned sum
with legal interest thereon then this writing to be void; In Witness whereof CHARLES
WARDELL and SARAH his Wife have hereunto set their hands and affixed their seals the
day and year afore written
Sealed & Delivered in presence of
      RICHD. S. HACKLEY, G. HEISKILL   CHARLES WARDELL
      ALEXR. NAIRNE, GEO: ROTHROCK   SARAH WARDELL
      PHILLIP GLOVER, LAC. MACKENTOSHE
 The Commonwealth of Virginia to WILLIAM HARVEY, FONTAINE MAURY & ELISHA
HALL Gent., Greeting, Whereas (the Commission for the privy Examination of SARAH, the Wife
of CHARLES WARDELL), Witness JOHN CHEW Clerk of our said Hustings Court the 4th day of
January 1796 and in the 20th year of the Commonwealth   JNO: CHEW
 Corporation of Fredg.: Pursuant to the within Commission (the return of the execution of
the privy Examination of SARAH WARDELL) Certifyed under our hands and seals the Fourth
day of Jany. 1796   WM. HARVEY
                               ELISHA HALL
   At a Court of Hustings held for the Town & Corporation of Fredg. the 25th day of June
1796   This Indenture of Mortgage from CHARLES WARDELL to THOS: COLSON was
acknowledged by the said CHARLES WARDELL and together with the Commission
annexed and a Certificate of the Execution thereof Indorsed, are ordered to be recorded
Exd. & Deld. THOS: COLSON   Teste   JNO: CHEW, C. C. H.

pp.   THIS INDENTURE made this Nineteenth day of May in year of our Lord one
116-   thousand seven hundred and ninety six Between RICHARD L. HACKLEY and
119   ANNE his Wife of Town of Fredericksburg of one part and DAVID COYLE of same
       Town of other part; Whereas ROGER DIXON supposing that he was intitled to a
part of a lott number sixteen or 16.16 measuring thirty four feet front and extending
back to the division line of Lott No. 14.14 did by his Deed of Indenture bearing date the

7th day of March Anno Domini one thousand seven hundred & eighty nine convey the
same in fee simple to said DAVID COYLE and whereas it is found by a survey lately made
that the greatest part of the same belongs to RICHD. L. HACKLEY and ANNE his Wife
particularly the back part, And whereas said RICHD. L. HACKLEY and ANNE HACKLEY
his Wife are desirous of making a full and perfect title to said DAVID COYLE in the said
part; Now This Indenture Witnesseth that RICHD. L. HACKLEY & ANN his Wife for the
sum of Twenty six pounds ten shillings to them in hand paid by DAVID COYLE by these
presents do bargain & sell unto DAVID COYLE the aforementioned parcel of ground
being part of the said ground conveyed as aforesaid by ROGER DIXON to DAVID COYLE;
together with all profits commodities and appurtenances; To have and to hold the said
lands unto DAVID COYLE his heirs and RICHD. L. HACKLEY and ANNE HACKLEY for
themselves their heirs to DAVID COYLE his heirs will warrant and forever defend by
these presents; In Witness whereof RICHD. L. HACKLEY and ANNE his Wife have hereunto set their hands and affixed their seals the day and year above written
Signed Sealed and Delivered in presence of

JAMES MEGELLAVRAY,   RICHD. L. HACKLEY
GEO: S. HACKLEY   ANN HACKLEY

The Commonwealth of Virginia to FONTAINE MAURY, WM. HARVEY and ELISHA HALL
Gent., Greeting (the Commission for the privy Examination of ANN HACKLEY, Wife of RICHARD L.
HACKLEY) Witness JOHN CHEW Clerk of our said Court the 27th day of May 1796 and in the
20th year of the Commonwealth   JNO: CHEW

Corporation of Fredbg. Sc. In Obedience to the within Commission (the return of the execution of the privy Examination of ANN HACKLEY); Given under our hands and seals the 27th
May 1796   WM. HARVEY
                                                FONTAINE MAURY

At a Court of Hustings held for the Town and Corporation the 25th day of June 1796
This Indenture from RICHD. L. HACKLEY was acknowledged by the said RICHD. S. HACK-
LEY and together with the Commission annexed and the Certificate of Execution thereof
indorsed are ordered to be recorded
Exd. & deld. D. COYLE   Teste JNO: CHEW, C. C. H.

pp.   THIS INDENTURE made the 20th day of January Anno Domini one thousand
120-   seven hundred and Ninety six Between JAMES FISHER of Town of Fredericksburg
121   of one part and PETER GARTES of Town of BALTIMORE and State of MARYLAND of
          second part. Whereas the said FISHER about the 10th day of Octr. Anno Dom. one
thousand seven hundred & ninety five did purchase of said PETER GARTS a Billard Table
which now stands in the BILLARD HOUSE belonging to the lott which the said JAMES
rents of GUSTAVUS B. WALLACE in Town of Fredericksburg and for the same did agree to
pay said PETER the sum of Fifty six pounds Virginia Currency and in order now more
affectually to secure the payment of said sum so to be paid to PETER GARTS, This Indenture Witnesseth that JAMES FISHER in consideration of the premises and also the sum of
Fifty six pounds in hand paid to said JAMES by said PETER by these presents doth bargain and sell unto PETER GARTS & assigns the above described BILLARD TABLE together
with all its appurtenances; To have and to hold the said Billard Table to PETER GARTS
and assigns. It is provided however and the condition of these presents that if JAMES
FISHER and assigns shall truly pay the sum of Fifty six pounds Virginia currency to
PETER GARTS then the above obligation to be void; In Testimony whereof said JAMES
FISHER hath hereunto put his hand and affixed his seal the day and year above written
Signed sealed & delivered in the presence of

JAMES H. C. JOHNSTON,   JAMES FISHER
JOHN DAY

At a Court of Hustings held for the Town and Corporation of Fredg., on Saturday 23rd of July 1796   This Indenture Mortgage from JAMES FISHER to PETER GARTS was proved by the oaths of two of the witnesses thereto and ordered to be recorded

pp.
122-
124
THIS INDENTURE made the 21st day of June in year of our Lord one thousand seven hundred and Ninety six Between JOHN LEWIS and MARY ANN his Wife of Town of Fredericksburg in the County of Spotsylvania of one part and DANIEL STARKS of the County aforesaid of other part; Witnesseth that JNO: LEWIS for the sum of Forty pounds current money of Virginia to him in hand paid by DANIEL STARKS by these presents doth bargain and sell unto DANIEL STARKS his heirs a lott of ground lying in Town of Fredericksburg known by the Lott No. 105; and bounded on the North by PITT STREET, on the East by PRINCESS ANN STREET, on the South bot Lot No. 103; and on the West by Lot No. 106; containing half an acre together with all profits advantages and appurtenances belonging; To have and to hold the said lott with the appurtenances unto DANIEL STARKS his heirs, And JNO. LEWIS for himself his heirs the premises will warrant and forever defend by these presents; In Witness whereof said JOHN LEWIS and MARY ANN his Wife have interchangeably set their hands and affixed their seals the day & year first above written
Sealed & Delivered in presence of
    WILLIAM WIATT,   JOHN LEWIS
    JOHN COAKLEY, WM. SMITH   MARY A. LEWIS
  At a Court of Hustings held for Town and Corporaltion of Fredericksburg on Saturday 23rd July 1796   This Indenture from JNO: LEWIS to DANIEL STARKS was proved by the oaths of the three witnesses thereto and ordered to be recorded

pp.
124-
127
THIS INDENTURE made this 21st day of March Anno Domini one thousand seven hundred and Ninety six Between the Mayor and Commonality of Town of Fredericksburg, to wit, WILLIAM HARVEY Mayor; FONTAINE MAURY Recorder; ELISHA HALL, GEO: W. B. SPOONER, ZACH: LUCAS and WILLIAM HERNDON, Aldermen, and JAMES BROWN, RICHARD PEACOCK, WILLIAM PEARSON, FIELDING LUCAS, JOHN BENSON and RICHARD S. HACKNEY of the Common Council of the one part and WILLIAM HARVEY of the Town aforesaid of other part; Whereas by an Act of the Legislature of Virginia passed on the (blank) day of December Anno Domini 1789, it is enacted that it shall be lawfull for the Mayor and Commonalty of the Town of Fredg. and they are hereby impowered to Lease for three lives for Twenty one years or for any lesser Estate therein such unimproved part of the MARKETT HOUSE LOTT as to them shall seem most proper and apply the rents issuing therefrom for the Benefit of said Corporation and the said Mayor and Commonalty after advertizing in the FREDG. HERALD for a considerable time a part of said MARKETT HOUSE LOTT, to be rented in manner aforesaid did on the (blank) day of March 1796 set up to be rented as aforesaid a part of the said MARKETT HOUSE LOTTS known by numbers one & two and the said WILLIAM HARVEY became the purchaser of said lotts No. 1 & No. 2; Now this Indenture witnesseth that the Mayor and Commonalty in consideration of the Rents and Covenants by WILLIAM HARVEY to be paid and performed by these presents do bargain and sell unto WILLIAM HARVEY his heirs all of Lotts No. 1 & 2, with all advantages and commodities belonging, for Lott No. 1 during the natural lives of Doctor DAVID CORBIN KER; CHARLES and DAVID BENSON Sons of JOHN or during the natural life of the longest liver of them; and for Lott No. 2 during the natural life of Doctor DAVID CORBIN KER, WILLIAM & JAMES BENSON, Sons of JOHN BENSON of Fredericksburg or survivor of them, said WM. HARVEY his heirs paying on the twenty first day of March next ensuing the date of these presence for Lott No. one seven pounds fourteen shillings and for Lott No. two four pounds

two shillings currency of Virginia and yearly during the said term to the said Mayor and Commonalty and their successors, And WILLIAM HARVEY for himself his heirs doth covenant with the Mayor and Commonalty and their successors to build in a workman like manner two houses eighteen feet front and twenty eight feet deep at least and keep and deliver up the same in good repair at the expiration of the Lease; In Witness whereof the parties have hereunto affixed their hands and seals the day and year first mentioned

Signed Sealed & Delivered   WILLIAM HARVEY   FONTAINE MAURY
   in presence of us   ELISHA HALL   GEO: W. B. SPOONER
      (no witnesses shown)   ZACH: LUCAS   WM. HERNDON
                                   RICHARD PEACOCK   WM. PEARSON
                                   JOHN BENSON   FIELDING LUCAS
                                   RICHD. S. HACKLEY   WILLIAM HARVEY

At a Court of Hustings held for the Town and Corporation of Fredericksburg the 22nd day of October 1796   This Indenture of Lease from the Mayor and Commonalty of the Corporation of Fredericksburg to WILLIAM HARVEY was acknowledged by the parties and ordered to be recorded

Examd. & deld. WM. HARVEY   Teste   JNO: CHEW, C. C. H.

pp.   THIS INDENTURE made this 21st day of March Anno Domini one thousand seven
128-   hundred and ninety six Between the Mayor and Commonalty of the Town of
131   Fredericksburg being to wit, WILLIAM HARVEY Mayor, FONTAINE MAURY Re-
           corder, ELISHA HALL, GEO: W. B. SPOONER, ZACH, LUCAS and WILLIAM HERNDON
Aldermen and JAMES BENSON, RICHARD PEACOCK, WILLIAM PEARSON, FIELDING LUCAS
JOHN BENSON and RICHARD S. HACKLEY of the Common Council of the one part & JACOB
STYERS of Town and Corporation aforesaid of other part; Whereas (as in the foregoing Deed
the Act of Assembly regarding the MARKET HOUSE LOTT, is repeated); known by the number
three was struck down to said JACOB STYERS, Now This Indenture Witnesseth that the
Mayor and Commonalty for the rents and covenants herein after mentioned and by
JACOB STYERS to be paid and performed do bargain and sell unto JACOB STYERS his heirs
all of Lott number three with all advantages and commodites; To have and to hold lott
number three with appurtenances unto JACOB STYERS his heirs during the natural
lives of said JACOB STYERS, SARAH STYERS his Wife and GEORGE STYERS his Son, or
during the lives of the survivors of them; said JACOB STYERS paying on the twenty first
day of March next ensuing the date of these presents the sum of Four pounds Eight
Shillings Virginia Currency as an annual Rent to the Mayor & Commonalty and their
Successors, And the said JACOB STYERS his heirs will build in a workmanlike manner a
House Eighteen feet front and twenty eight feet deep on said Lot and keep & deliver up
the same in good repair at the expiration of the term of years aforesaid; In Witness
whereof the parties to these presents have hereunto affixed their hands & seals the day
and year first abovesaid

Signed Sealed & Delivered in presence of   (The same signatures as in the previous
      (no witnesses shown)   deed above except JACOB STYERS is listed)

At a Court of Hustings held for the Town & Corporation of Fredericksburg the 22d. day of October 1796.   This Indenture of Lease from the Mayor and Common Council of the Corporation of Fredericksburg to JACOB STYERS was acknowledged by the parties and ordered to be recorded

Examd. & Delivered JACOB STYERS   Teste   JNO: CHEW C. C. H.

pp.   THIS INDENTURE made the 21st day of March one thousand seven hundred and
131-   Ninety six Between the Mayor and Commonalty of Town of Fredericksburg (as
134   listed in the previous two deeds) and GENERAL THOMAS POSEY. Whereas (as in the
        foregoing two deeds, the Act of Assembly regarding the MARKET HOUSE LOTT is repeated),
lott Number Ten and said GENL. THOMAS POSEY being the highest bidder (runing twenty three feet in Front on CAROLINE STREET and Ninety six feet back) struck down to the
said THOMAS POSEY; Now This Indenture Witnesseth that the said Mayor and Commonalty in consideration of the rents and covenants herein after mentioned by said Genl.
THOMAS POSEY to be paid and performed by these presents do bargain and sell unto said
THOMAS POSEY his heirs all the afsd . number Ten with all advantages and commodities
belonging; To have and to hold Lott No. 10 unto THOMAS POSEY his heirs during the
natural lives of JOHN POSEY FAYETTE & LLOYD POSEY, Sons of said THOMAS POSEY or
during the natural life of the survivor of them sd. GENL. THOMAS POSEY his heirs
paying for the same on the twenty first day of March next ensuing the sum of Sixteen
pounds three shillings and eleven pence currency yearly; And said THOMAS POSEY his
heirs will build in a workman like manner a story house not less than eighteen feet
front and twenty eight feet deep and keep and deliver the same in good repair at the
expiration of the said Term; In Witness whereof the parties have hereunto set their
hands and seals the day and year first mentioned
Signed Sealed and Delivered in presence of
        JESSE WRIGHT,   JACOB KUHN,   (The same names as in the first Deed
        JOHN L. HAMILTON,   except THO: POSEY is listed at the end)
        ALEXANDER NAIRNE, PETER JOHNSTON
    At a Court of Hustings held for the Town and Corporation of Fredericksburg the 22nd
day of October 1796   This Indenture of Lease from the Mayor and Common Council of
the Corporation of Fredericksburg to THOMAS POSEY was acknowledged by the parties
and ordered to be recorded

pp.   THIS INDENTURE made this 21st day of March Anno Domini one thousand seven
135-   hundred and Ninety Six Between the Mayor and Commonalty of the Town of
138   Fredericksburg to wit: (as listed in the several other Deed above) of one part and
        THOMAS GOODWIN of the Town and Corporation aforesaid of other part; Whereas
(as in the foregoing Deeds, the Act of Assembly regarding the MARKET HOUSE LOTT is repeated);
Lott number Seven and said THOMAS GOODWIN became the purchaser: Now this Indenture Witnesseth that said Mayor & Commonalty in consideration of the rents and covenants herein after mentioned and by THOMAS GOODWIN to be payed and performed by
these presents do bargain and sell unto THOMAS GOODWIN his heirs all the Lott No.
seven with all advantages and commodities belonging; To have and to hold Lott No.
seven during the natural lives of ANN MARIA, WILLIAM P. and SARAH GOODWIN or
natural life of the survivor of them, said THOMAS GOODWIN paying yearly on the 21st
day of May the sum of Six pounds twelve shillings Virginia Currency, And THOMAS
GOODWIN his heirs will build in a workman like manner two houses Eighteen feet front
and twenty eight feet deep and keep and deliver up the same in good repair at the
expiration of the term afsd.,
Signed Sealed & Delivered in presence of
        (no witnesses shown)   (The same names as in the first Deed
                                             except THOMAS GOODWIN at the end.)
    At a Court of Hustings held for the Town and Corporation of Fredericksburg the 22nd
day of October 1796;   This Indenture of Lease from the Mayor and Common Council of
the Town and Corporation of Fredricksburg to THOS: GOODWIN was acknowledged by the
parties and ordered to be recorded

Exd. & Deld. THOS: GOODWIN   Teste JNO: CHEW, C.C.H.

pp.   THIS INDENTURE made this the 21st day of March Anno Domini one thousand
138-   seven hundred and Ninety six Between the Mayor and Commonalty of Town of
142   Fredericksburg, to wit, (the persons as listed in Deed above pages 124-127) of one part
       and WM. SMITH of the Town aforesaid of other part. Whereas by an Act of the
Legislature of Virginia passed on the seventh day of December Anno Domini one thousand seven hundred and Eighty nine (continues as in the Deed above pages 124-127) And the
said WILLIAM SMITH being the highest bidder the said Lot number nine was struck
down to the said WM. SMITH; Now This Indenture Witnesseth that the said Mayor and
Commonalty in consideration of the rents and covenants by WM. SMITH to be paid &
performed by these presents do bargain and sell unto said WM. SMITH his heirs all the
Lot No. nine with all advantages and commodities whatsoever belonging; To have and to
hold Lot number Nine with appurtenances unto WM. SMITH his heirs during the
natural lives of JESSE WRIGHT, MILIAN SMITH & JOHN BROWN, Son of JAMES BROWN,
Silver Smith of Fredericksburg) or the natural life of the survivor of them, said WM.
SMITH paying for the same on the 21st of March next ensuing the sum of Twenty four
pounds two shillings and eight pence Virginia currency yearly and will build in a
workman like manner a two story house eighteen feet front and twenty eight feet deep
at least and keep and deliver up the same in good repair at the expiration of the term,
In Witness whereof the parties have hereunto affixed their hands & seals the day and
year first mentioned
Signed sealed & delivered in presence of
       JOHN CHEW   WM. HARVEY, Mayor
       ROBERT S. CHEW,   FONTAINE MAURY, Recorder
       JAMES ALLAN JUNR.   ELISHA HALL, Alderman,
       BEV. C. STANARD   ZACH. LUCAS   do
                    GEO: W. B. SPOONER do; WM. HERNDON do; JOHN BENSON do;
                    JAMES BROWN do; RICHD. PEACOCK do; WM. PEARSON do;
                    FIELDING LUCAS do; RICHD. S. HACKLEY do; WM. SMITH.
   At a Court of Hustings held for the Town & Corporation of Fredericksburg the 22nd. day
of November 1796   This Indenture of Lease from the Mayor and Commonalty of the
Corporation of Fredg. to WM. SMITH was acknowledged by the parties and ordered to be
recorded
Exd. & deld. WM. SMITH   Teste JNO: CHEW, C.C.H.

pp.   THIS INDENTURE made this 21st day of March Anno Domini one thousand seven
143-   hundred and Ninety six Between the Mayor and Commonalty of the Town of
146   Fredg., to wit; (those listed in the Deed pages 124-127) of the one part and WILLIAM
       TAYLOR of Town of Fredericksburg of other part; Whereas by an Act of Assem-
bly (continues as in the Deed pages 124-127); Lott Number Six and WILLIAM TAYLOR became
the purchaser; Now This Indenture Witnesseth that the said Mayor and Commonalty in
consideration of the rents and covenants hereinafter mentioned and by WILLIAM
TAYLOR to be paid and performed by these presents do bargain and sell unto WILLIAM
TAYLOR his heirs all Lott No. six with all advantages and commodites belonging; To
have and to hold the Lott No. 6 unto WILLIAM TAYLOR his heirs during the natural life
of WILLIAM TAYLOR JUNR., Son of the afsd. WILLIAM TAYLOR, FONTAINE MAURY &
RICHARD TAYLOR, Son to the Camadore or during the natural life of the Survivor of the
said WILLIAM TAYLOR JUNR, ARCHD. & PHILIP TAYLOR, said WILLIAM TAYLOR his heirs
paying for the same on the twenty first day of March yearly the annual rent of four
pounds ten shilling Virginia Currency; And WILLIAM TAYLOR his heirs will build in a

workman like manner a house eighteen feet front and twenty eight feet deep and keep
and deliver up the same in good repair at the expiration of the term afsd., In Witness
whereof the parties have hereto affixed their hands & seals the day & year first above
mentioned

Signed sealed and delivered in presence of us   (The names of those as in the previous
          (no witnesses shown)   deeds, except WILIAM TAYLOR at the end)
    I do assign all my right and title to the property conveyed by this Deed to me to
FONTAINE MAURY his heirs as Witness my hand this 22nd day Octr. 1796
    At a Court of Hustings held for the Town and Corporation of Fredericksburg the 22nd
day of November 1796   This Indenture of Lease from the Mayor and Common Council
of the Corporation of Fredericksburg to WILLIAM TAYLOR was acknowledged by the
parties and ordered to be recorded
Examd. & deld. WM. DRUMMOND   Teste JNO: CHEW, C. C. H.

pp.   THIS INDENTURE made this twenty seventh day of Januray in year of our Lord
147-   one thousand seven hundred and Ninety eight Between ROBERT MERCER and
149   MILDRED his Wife of Town of Fredericksburg of one part and CHARLES CROUGH-
        TON of the same Town of other part; Witnesseth that ROBERT MERCER and MIL-
DRED his Wife for sum of Four hundred and fifty pounds, by these presents doth bargain and sell unto CHARLES CROUGHTON his heirs the lott numbered One hundred and
twenty seven situate in the aforesaid Town and bounded by the intersection of CHAS. &
WILLIAM STREETs, by Lotts number One hundred & seventy five and One hundred and
twenty eight being the same Lott that was conveyed to ROBERT MERCER by JAMES MON-
ROE and ELIZABETH his Wife and JOHN TALIAFERRO BROOKE as will more fully appear by
their Deed bearing date the 15th day of October one thousand seven hundred & ninety
two and duly recorded which Lott together with the Mansion or Dwelling House and all
houses and buildings thereon erected and all advantages and appurtenances to said
parcel of land belonging; To have and to hold the parcel of land hereby sold unto
CHARLES CROUGHTON his heirs and ROBERT MERCER and MILDRED his Wife their heirs
will warrant and forever defend by these presents; In Witness whereof the parties to
these presents have hereunto interchangeably set their hands & seals the day & year
first above written
Signed Sealed & Delivered in presence of
    THOMAS SEDDON JUNR.   ROBERT   MERCER
    CHARLES JULIAN, GEORGE MURRAY
    At a Court of Hustings held for the Town & Corporation of Fredericksburg the 22nd day
of April 1797 This Indenture from ROBERT MERCER to CHARLES CROUGHTON was proved
by three of the witnesses thereto and ordered to be recorded
Examd. & deld. C. CROUGHTON   Teste JNO: CHEW, C. C. H.
(Commission recorded fo. 233)

pp.   THIS INDENTURE made this Tenth day of May one thousand seven hundred and
149-   Ninety seven Between BIRKETT DAVENPORT of County of CULPEPER and State of
151   Virginia of one part and DAVID HENDERSON of Town of Fredericksburg of other
        part; Witnesses that whereas JAMES HACKLEY, late of Town of Fredericksburg
deceased did by his last Will & Testament bearing date the sixteenth day of July one
thousand seven hundred and eighty four and recorded in the Corporation Court of said
Town did make and constitute BIRKETT DAVENPORT one of the Executors of the said last
Will and Testament and by said Will directed that should ANN HACKLEY, Wife to the said
JAMES HACKLEY die without being married again then his Executors in the said Will
mentioned should sell the lotts & houses in the said Town belonging to JAMES HACKLEY

in such manner as the Executors might seem right; And whereas ANN HACKLEY died
without being married again, And Whereas said BIRKETT DAVENPORT hath alone qualified and acted as Executor of said last Will & Testament; NOW THIS INDENTURE further
WITNESSETH that BIRKETT DAVENPORT as Executor of JAMES HACKLEY for the sum of
Two hundred and ten pounds current money of Virginia by these presents in said
capacity doth bargain & sell unto DAVID HENDERSON his heirs all the right title and
interest said JAMES HACKLEY died possessed in the said lotts and houses lying in Town
of Fredericksburg opposite to ROYSTONs WAREHOUSEs and known by number Twenty
nine and bounded, Begining on AMELIA STREET at the corner of lott No. 30, thence with
the line of Lott No. 29 front thirty six feet, thence parallel with AMELIA STREET one
hundred and sixteen and a quarter feet, thence to the corner of DUNCANSONs part of
same lott and purchased of CHAS. COLSON, thence with the division line of Lotts No. 29
and 30 to the begining; together with all hereditaments and appurtenances belonging;
To have and to hold the lott and houses unto DAVID HENDERSON and his heirs; In Witness whereof he hath hereunto set his hand and seal this day & year first above written
Signed sealed & acknowledged in presence of

           DAVID WILLIAMSON, THOMAS ALLEN,   BIRKETT DAVENPORT
           GEO: T. TOD,   JOHN LATANE

 Fredsburg: 10th May 1797. Received Two hundred and ten pounds Virginia currency
being in full for the within consideration
Witness   GEO: MAURY,   BIRKETT DAVENPORT
           DAVID WILLIAMSON, GEO: T. TOD,
           THOMAS ALLEN,   JOHN LATANE

 At a Court of Hustings held for the Corporation of Fredg., the 24th day of June 1797;
This Indenture from BIRKETT DAVENPORT, Exor. of JAS. HACKLEY, to DAVID HENDERSON
was proved by three witnesses thereto and ordered to be recorded
Examd. & deld. Mr. THOMAS ALLEN JUNR.   Teste JNO: CHEW, C. C. H.

pp.
151-
153

       THIS INDENTURE made this Tenth day of May one thousand seven hundred and
Ninety seven Between RICHARD S. HACKLEY, JAMES CARMICHAEL & AUGUSTINE
BOUGHAN in behalf of themselves & said RICHARD S. HACKLEY for and in behalf
of EDWARD HACKLEY of NORFOLK all of one part and DAVID HENDERSON of Town
of Fredericksburg of other part; Witnesseth that whereas BIRKETT DAVENPORT of the
County of CULPEPER in his capacity as Executor to the Will & Testament of JAMES
HACKLEY, late of Town of Fredericksburg deceased, has this day by his Deed of Conveyance bearing date this day conveyed to DAVID HENDERSON certain part of lott number Twenty nine with houses & improvements thereon opposite ROYSTONs WAREHOUSE
and bounded (same description as in the previous Deed). And whereas BIRKETT DAVENPORT
by his Deed aforesaid has not granted a full & compleat warranty to said DAVID HENDER-
SON against the claims of all persons, and RICHARD S. HACKNEY for himself & in behalf
of EDWD. HACKLEY & the said JAMES CARMICHAEL & AUGUSTINE BOUGHAN for themselves in consideration of their respective shares of the proceeds of the sale of the
property aforesaid as heirs & Legatees under the said Will of JAMES HACKLEY deceased
having agreed to warrant and defend the said Lott to DAVID HENDERSON, Now These
Presents Witnesseth that RICHARD S. HACKNEY, JAMES CARMICHAEL, AUGUSTINE
BOUGHAN & RICHARD S. HACKLEY for and in behalf of EDWARD HACKLEY of NORFOLK
their several Executors & assigns do hereby agree with DAVID HENDERSON that they
will forever warrant & defend the premises aforesaid from all claims mortgages and
any demand whatsoever; In Witness whereof the parties have hereunto set their hands
and seals the day and year first before written

Before these Witnesses signed sealed   (RD. S. HACKLEY for himself, EDWD.
& acknowledged in presence of   (HACKLEY of NORFOLK & the younger
    DAVID WILLIAMSON,   (Children of JAS: HACKLEY deceased
    GEO: T. TOD, THOMAS ALLEN   JAMES CARMICHAEL
    JOHN LATANE   AUGT. BOUGHAN

At a Court of Hustings held for the Corporation of Fredericksburg the 24th of June 1797
This Indenture from RICHARD S. HACKNEY and others to DAVID HENDERSON was proved
by three witnesses thereto and ordered to be recorded
Exd. and deld. Mr. THOS: ALLEN JUNR.   Teste   JNO: CHEW, C. C. H.

pp.   THIS INDENTURE made this T(blank) day of May one thousand seven hundred
153-   and ninety seven Between BIRKETT DAVENPORT of County of CULPEPER & State
155   of Virginia of one part & GEO: MURRAY of Town of Fredericksburg of other part;
    Witnesses that Whereas JAMES HACKLEY late of Town of Fredericksburg de-
ceased (the conditions of appointing BIRKETT DAVENPORT repeated as in the Deed pages 149-151)
Now This Indenture further Witnesseth that BIRKETT DAVENPORT as Executor of JAMES
HACKLEY and by virute of the power and authority to him given by the said Will, and
for sum of Three hundred pounds current money of Virginia by these presents doth
bargain and sell unto the said GEORGE MURRAY his heirs all the right title and interest
in lotts and houses of which JAMES HACKLEY died possessed lying and being in Town of
Fredericksburg opposite ROYSTONs WAREHOUSE and known by the number Twenty nine
and bounded begining on AMELIA STREET at D. HENDERSONs part of said Lott thence
with the line of Lott No. 29 to SOPHIA STREET front ninety four feet, thence binding in
the same to DUNCANSONs part of Lott No. 29 purchased of T. COLSON, thence binding on
the said DUNCANSONs to the Division between DAVID HENDERSON and with this Division
line to the begining; together with all hereditaments & appurtenances belonging; To
have and to hold unto GEORGE MURRAY his heirs and BIRKETT DAVENPORT in the capacity aforesaid will warrant and defend against the claims of all persons; In Witness
whereof he hath hereunto set his hand and seal the day and year first above written
Signed sealed & acknowledged in presence of
    DAVID WILLIAMSON, GEO: T. TOD,   BIRKETT DAVENPORT
    THOMAS ALLEN, JOHN LATANE
At a Court of Hustings held for the Corpo. of Fredg. the 24th day of June 1797
This Indenture from BIRKETT DAVENPORT to GEORGE MURRAY was proved by three
witnesses thereto & ordered to be recorded
Exd. & deld. G. MURRAY   Teste JNO: CHEW C. C. H.

pp.   THIS INDENTURE made this (blank) day of May one thousand seven hundred and
155-   ninety seven Between RICHARD S. HACKLEY, JAMES CARMICHAEL & AUGUSTINE
157   BOUGHAN in behalf of themselves & the said RICHARD S. HACKLEY in behalf of
    EDWARD HACKLEY of NORFOLK all of the one part and GEORGE MURRAY of Town
of Fredericksburg of other part; Witnesseth that Whereas BIRKETT DAVENPORT of
County of CULPEPER in his capacity as Executor to the Will & Testament of JAMES HACK-
LEY late of Town of Fredg., deceased has this day by his Deed of Conveyance conveyed to
GEORGE MURRAY a certain part of lott number Twenty nine with the houses and improvements thereon opposite ROYSTONs WAREHOUSES and bounded (description as in the
foregoing Deed), And Whereas BIRKETT DAVENPORT by his Deed has not granted the full
warranty to GEORGE MURRAY against the claims of all persons & RICHARD S. HACKLEY
for himself & in behalf of EDWARD HACKLEY and JAMES CARMICHAEL & AUGUSTINE
BOUGHAN each for themselves in consideration of their respective share of the proceeds of the sale of the property afsd. as Legatees under the said Will of JAMES HACKLEY

having agreed to warrant and defend the said lott to GEORGE MURRAY, Now This Indenture Witnesseth that RICHARD S. HACKLEY, JAMES CARMICHAEL & AUGUSTINE BOUGHAN and RICHARD S. HACKLEY in behalf of EDWARD HACKLEY of NORFOLK do hereby warrant and defend the premises aforesaid in peaceable & quiet possession of said GEORGE MURRAY; In Witness whereof the parties have hereunto set their hands and seals the day & year first before written

Witness DAVID WILLIAMSON,   (RICHD. S. HACKLEY for himself, EDWD.
       GEORGE T. TOD,   (HACKLEY of NORFOLK and the Younger
       THOMAS ALLEN   (Children of JAS: HACKLEY deced.
       JOHN LATANE   JAMES CARMICHAEL
                                       AUGT. BOUGHAN

At a Court of Hustings held for the Corporation of Fredericksburg the 24th of June 1797 This Indenture from RICHARD S. HACKLEY and others to GEORGE MURRAY was proved by three witnesses thereto and ordered to be recorded
Exd. & deld. G. MURRAY   Teste   JNO: CHEW, C. C. H.

pp.   THIS INDENTURE made and entered into this Twelfth day of May one thousand
157-   seven hundred and ninety seven Between RICHARD S. HACKLEY and ANN his
160   Wife of Town of Fredg., of one part and CHARLES YATES of same place of other
         part; Witnesseth that RICHARD S. HACKLEY and ANN his Wife for sum of Four
hundred pounds lawful money of Virginia to them in hand paid by CHARLES YATES, by these presents do bargain and sell unto CHARLES YATES his heirs a certain parcel of land lying in County of Spotsylvania near the Town of Fredericksburg containing Ten acres be the same more or less and bounded, Begining in the said CHARLES YATES's Yard and thence runing Twenty one pole four feet 3 In. to a Ditch, the dividing line between JERE. MORTON & the said RICHARD S. HACKLEY, thence fifty three poles with the said Ditch to Colo. LEWIS WILLIS's Meadow Fence, thence thirty poles three linkes with said Fence to the corner of ROBERT BROOKE's line and thence seventy four poles seventeen links with said BROOKE's & YATES's line to the begining; together with all rents & profits thereof; To have and to hold the parcel of land unto CHARLES YATES his heirs and RICHARD S. HACKLEY and ANN his Wife and their heirs will and do warrant and forever defend by these presents; In Witness whereof RICHARD S. HACKLEY & ANN his Wife have hereunto set their hands and seals the day & year first above written
Signed sealed & acknowledged in the presence of
         EDWARD HERNDON, WILLIAM PORTER,   RD. S. HACKLEY
         BENJN. PARKE, CHARLES DAVIS,   ANN HACKLEY
         DANIEL GRINNAN JR., BEN: DAY,
         GEO: FRENCH, JNO: CHEW;
         ROBT. L. CHEW, JOHN CHEW JR.
The Commonwealth of Virginia to WILLIAM HARVEY, GEORGE FRENCH, FONTAINE MAURY Magistrates for ye Corpo: of Fredericksburg Gent. Greeting; (the Commission for the privy Examination of ANN, Wife of RICHARD S. HACKLEY) Witness JOHN CLERK, Clerk of our said Court the 13th day of May 1797 and in the 21st year of the Commonwealth
  In Obedience to the within Commission to us directed (the return of the execution of the privy examination of ANN HACKLEY);   WILLIAM HARVEY
                                          GEO: FRENCH

At a Court of Hustings held for the Corpo. of Fredg. the 24th day of June 1797 This Indenture from RICHARD S. HACKLEY to CHARLES YATES was proved by three of the witnesses thereto and together with the Commission annexed and Certificate of execution thereof Indorsed, are ordered to be recorded
Exd. & deld. CH: YATES   Teste JNO: CHEW, C. C. H.

pp.   THIS INDENTURE made the eighteenth day of June in year of our Lord one thou-
160- sand seven hundred & ninety seven Between CHARLES CROUGHTON of Town of
162   Fredericksburg of one part and THOMAS SOUTHCOMB of same Town of other part;
      Witnesseth that whereas CHARLES CROUGHTON did in the month of April Anno
Domini 1791 as an Agent and factor to said SOUTHCOMB purchase of WILLIAM HARVEY a
part of two certain lotts for which lotts said HARVEY executed a Deed to said CROUGHTON
bearing date the 23rd April 1791; And said CROUGHTON being now required to make
legal conveyance of the same to said SOUTHCOMB to whom the said parts of Lotts in
Equity belong, said CHARLES CROUGHTON in consideration of the premises by these presents doth grant and confirm unto THOMAS SOUTHCOMB his heirs the part of the lotts
number thirty three and thirty four situate in Town of Fredericksburg butting & bounding, beginning on CAROLINE STREET at the corner of Lott No. 33 where it joins Lott No.
35; and runing thence sixty five feet two inches more or less along CAROLINE STREET to
the corner of the Store now occupied by JAMES SOMERVILLE, thence at right angles by
a straight line parrallel to WOLFE STREET till it intersects or runs to PRINCESS ANN
STREET, to the Lott No. 36, thence with Lotts No. 36 & 35 to the begining, together with
the Mansion or Dwelling House and all out houses & buildings belonging; To have and
to hold the said Lotts with appurtenances unto THOMAS SOUTHCOMB his heirs against
the lawful title claim & demand of CHARLES CROUGHTON; In Witness whereof CHARLES
CROUGHTON hath hereunto set his hand and seal the day & year first above written
Signed sealed & Delivered in presence of
    JERE: MORTON,   CHARLES CROUGHTON
    THOMAS SEDDON JR., JOHN ENGLISH
  At a Court of Hustings held for the Corporation of Fredg. the 24th day of June 1797
This Indenture from CHARLES CROUGHTON to THOMAS SOUTHCOMB was acknowledged by
said CHARLES CROUGHTON & ordered to be recorded

pp.   THIS INDENTURE made this 16th day of January in year of our Lord one thou-
162- sand seven hundred and ninety seven Between SALLY CARTER, (Widow of ED-
165   WARD CARTER deceased) of one part and LARKIN STANARD of the second part,
      both of Town of Fredericksburg, Whereas EDWARD CARTER deced. did in and by
his last Will and Testament among other things devise unto his Wife, the said BETTY
CARTER, during her Widowhood all his houses and lotts in Town of Fredericksburg, that
at her death of marriage to his Son, WM. CHAMPE CARTER, which Will is duly recorded
in the County Court of Spotsylvania; And Whereas SALLY CARTER for a valuable consideration hath sold LARKIN STANARD his heirs all her right title & claim which she
hath under the Will before mentioned or may hereafter have in four lotts of land; NOW
THIS INDENTURE WITNESSETH that SALLY CARTER for sum of Fifty pounds current
money of Virginia to her truly paid by LARKIN STANARD by these presents doth bargain sell release and forever quit claim unto LARKIN STANARD his heirs all claim
which she said SALLY CARTER hath or may hereafter have in four lotts of ground lying
in Town of Fredg., fronting the Livery Stable known by numbers 129, 130, 131 & 132;
bounded Westwardly by PRINCE EDWARD STREET, Northwardly by AMELIA STREET,
Eastwardly by CHARLES STREET and Southwardly by WILLIAM STREET and being part of
the lotts devised to said SALLAY CARTER as aforesaid; To have and to hold the four lotts
of ground unto LARKIN STANARD his heirs and SALLY CARTER to said LARKIN STANARD
his heirs will warrant and defend by these presents; In Witness whereof SALLY CARTER
hath hereunto set her hand and affixed her seal the day & year within written
Signed Sealed & Delivered in the presence of
    CHAS. CARTER, JOHN C. CARTER,   SALLY CARTER
    MOSES PERRY, BEV. C. STANARD

It is the intention of SALLY CARTER to convey to Mr. LARKIN STANARD four lotts
bounded by the lotts of Mr. GOODWIN & McWILLIAMS on one side & on the other side the
lotts of Messrs. MERCER & WALLACE where the LIVERY STABLE lately stood
    At a Court of Hustings held for the Corporation of Fredg. the 24th day of June 1797
This Indenture from SALLY CARTER to LARKIN STANARD was proved by two of the witnesses thereto and ordered to be certified

pp.   THIS INDENTURE made and entered into this third day of June one thousand
165-   seven hundred and ninety seven Between LARKIN STANARD and ELIZABETH his
169   Wife of Town of Fredericksburg of one part and WILLIAM DRUMMOND of the
            same place of other part. Whereas EDWARD CARTER deceased, late of Fredericks-
burg by his last Will and Testament in writing among other things devised to his Wife,
SALLY CARTER four certain lotts to her untill her marriage or death then to his Son,
WILLIAM CHAMPE CARTER, and his heirs; And Whereas WILLIAM CHAMPE CARTER and
MARIA his Wife by their Deed indented bearing date the 9th day of June one thousand
seven hundred and ninety four and duly recorded in the Corporation Court of
Fredericksburg conveyed all their title and reversionary Interest in said lotts to LAR-
KIN STANARD and his heirs with covenants to make other conveyances and assurances;
And Whereas SALLAY CARTER by her Deed bearing date 16th day of January 1797 hath
conveyed to LARKIN STANARD and his heirs all the title and Interest which she under
the Will of her Husband hath in the four lotts; NOW THIS INDENTURE WITNESSETH that
LARKIN STANARD and ELIZABETH his Wife in consideration of Three hundred and
ninety pounds lawful money of Virginia to them in hand paid by WM. DRUMMOND by
these presents doth bargain & sell unto WILLIAM DRUMMOND and his heirs the square
containing the said four lotts fronting the LIVERY STABLE & the house at present
occupied by JOHN CHEW as an Office numbered 129, 130, 131 & 132; and bounded Westwardly by PRINCE EDWARD STREET, Northwardly by AMELIA STREET, Eastwardly by
CHARLES STREET and Southwardly by WILLIAM STREET, To have and to hold the four
lotts of ground unto WILLIAM DRUMMOND and his heirs and LARKIN STANARD and
ELIZABETH his Wife and their heirs will warrant and forever defend against every
person; In Testimony whereof LARKIN STANARD and ELIZABETH his Wife have here-
unto set their hands and seals the day and year first above written
Signed Sealed & Delivered in presence of
                W. S. STONE,   GEORGE W. B. SPOONER,   LARKIN STANARD
                DAVID C. KER; WM. SMOCK,   ELIZABETH STANARD
                MOSES PERRY
June 21st. Received from WILLIAM DRUMMOND Three hundred and ninety pounds
Virginia Currency being the consideration mentioned in this Deed
Teste THO: GOODWIN,   LARKIN STANARD
                WILLIAM SALE JR.
    The Commonwealth of Virginia to WILLIAM HARVEY, GEORG W. B. SPOONER & WM. S.
STONE Gent., Greeting; (the Commission for the privy Examination of ELIZABETH, the Wife of
LARKIN STANARD); Witness JOHN CHEW, Clerk of our said Court, the 3d day of June 1797 &
in the 21st year of the Commonwealth   JNO: CHEW
    Corporation of Fredericksburg to wit, We the Subscribers, two of the Justices within
mentioned (the return of the Execution of the privy Examination of ELIZABETH STANARD); Given
under our hands and seals this 5th day of June 1797   GEO: W. B. SPOONER
                                                           W. S. STONE
    At a Court of Hustings held for the Corporation of Fredericksburg the 24th day of June
1797   This Indenture from LARKIN STANARD and Wife to WM. DRUMMOND was proved
by three witnesses thereto and together with the Commission annexed and Certificate of

the Execution thereof Indorsed, are ordered to be recorded
Exd. & Deld. WM. DRUMMOND   Teste JNO: CHEW, C. C. H.

pp.   THIS INDENTURE made the twenty first day of June one thousand seven hun-
169-   dred and ninety seven Between THOMAS SOUTHCOMB of Town of Fredericksburg
170   of one part and THOMAS HAYDON of County of Spotsylvania of other part; Witnesseth that THOMAS SOUTHCOMB for Five hundred pounds current money of
Virginia to him in hand paid doth bargin and sell unto THOMAS HAYDON his heirs his
portion or part of lotts number thirty three & thirty four situate in Town of Fredericksburg begining on CAROLINE STREET at the corner of lott number thirty three where it
joins lott No. 35, the Corner of EDWARD HERNDON, and runing thence sixty five feet two
inches more or less down CAROLINE STREET to the corner of the Store now occupied by
JAMES SOMERVILLE and commonly called REIDS STORE, thence at right angles by a
straight line to WOLFE STREET till it intersects PRINCESS ANN STREET, thence with
PRINCESS ANN STREET to the lott number thirty six thence with lott number thirty six
and thirty five to the begining, together with all appurtenances; To have and to hold
lotts number thirty three and thirty four with appurtenances unto THOMAS HAYDON
his heirs and THOMAS SOUTHCOMB and his heirs will warrant and defend against all
persons; In Witness whereof THOMAS SOUTHCOMB hath hereunto subscribed his name
and affixed his seal the day and year above written
Signed Sealed and Delivere din presence of
     CHAS. LEWIS   THO: SOUTHCOMB
  At a Court of Hustings held for the Corporation of Fredericksburg the 24th day of June
1797   This Indenture from THOMAS SOUTHCOMB to THOMAS HAYDON was acknowledged
by the said SOUTHCOMB & ordered to be recorded
Exd. & deld. JESSE HAYDON SENR., Adm. of THOS: HAYDON   Teste JNO: CHEW C. C. H.

pp.   THIS INDENTURE made this 21st day of July in year of our Lord one thousand
171-   seven hundred and ninety seven Between GEORGE FRENCH and ANN BRAYNE his
173   Wife of one part and JOHN TAYLOR of other part; Witnesseth that GEORGE
FRENCH and ANN his Wife for sum of Four hundred pounds specie to them in
hand paid by JOHN TAYLOR, by these presents do bargain and sell unto JOHN TAYLOR his
heirs one half of the lott number 237, Begining at the lower corner upon the Street
called CAROLINE and thence extending up the same one half of the front of said lott,
thence runing a straight course to the back line, thence down the back to the lower
course of the same, thence with the lower line of said lott to the begining, that part of
sd. lott whereon the Dwelling House in which said TAYLOR resides now stands, Together
with all houses woods profits and hereditaments belonging; To have and to hold the
premises unto JOHN TAYLOR his heirs and GEORGE FRENCH and his heirs against all persons will warrant and defend by these presents; In Witness whereof GEORGE & ANN
BRAYNE have hereunto set their hands & affixed their seals the day and year first
above written
Signed Sealed & Delivered in presence of us
     WM. TAYLOR   GEO: FRENCH
                                              ANN BRAYNE FRENCH
  The Commonwealth of Virginia to WM. HARVEY & WM. TAYLOR Gent., Greeting; (the
Commission for the privy Examination of ANN BRAYNE, Wife of GEORGE FRENCH); Witness JOHN
CHEW Clerk of our said Corpo: Court the 22nd. day of July 1797 and in the 22nd year of
the Commonwealth   JNO: CHEW
  Corpo. of Fredericksburg Sct., In obedience to the within Commission to us directed, we
the Subscribers did personally go to the within named ANN BRAINE (the return of the

Execution of the privy Examination of ANN BRAINE FRENCH); Given under our hands & seals
the 22nd day of July 1797   WM. HARVEY
                                                       WM. TAYLOR
   At a Court of Hustings held for the Corporation of Fredericksburg the 22nd day of July
1797   This Indenture from GEORGE FRENCH to JOHN TAYLOR was acknowledged by said
GEORGE FRENCH & together with the Commission annexed and Certificate of the execution therof Indorsed, are ordered to be recorded
Exd. & deld. SAML. CHEWNING   Teste JNO; CHEW, C. C. H.

p.   WHEREAS GEORGE WEEDON, late of Fredericksburg deceased by his last Will and
174   Testament in Writing did require that after the death of his Wife, Mrs. CATHA-
         RINE WEEDON, his Negro man Bob was to be liberated and set free from slavery,
reference being had to said Will recorded in the Corporation Court of Fredericksburg,
And Whereas said Mrs. CATHARINE WEEDON hath since departed this Life, NOW KNOW
ALL MEN by these presents that we ROBERT PATTON and JOHN MERCER of Town aforesaid
Executors of said last Will and Testament of GEORGE WEEDON in consideration of the Will
hereby liberate and set free from slavery the said Negro man Bob and forever discharge him from any farther service whatsoever that might appurtain to him in the
character and capacity of a slave; In Witness whereof we have hereunto set our hand
and seal the 25th day of November in year of our Lord One thousand seven hundred and
ninety seven   ROBERT PATTON
                                               JOHN MERCER
   At a Court of Hustings held for the Town & Corporation of Fredericksburg on Saturday
the 25th day of November 1797   This Deed of Emancipation from ROBERT PATTON
and JOHN MERCER, Executors of GEORGE WEEDON deced., to Negro Bob was acknowledged
by said JOHN MERCER, one of the said Executors, & ordered to be recorded
Exd. & Copy deld. Bob   Teste JNO: CHEW, C. C. H.

pp.   THIS INDENTURE made this 19th day of January Anno Domini One thousand
175-   seven hundred and ninety eight Between GEORGE MURRAY of Town of
176   Fredericksburg, Executor of the Last Will and Testament of ALEXANDER NAIRNE
         deceased, of the first part and RICHARD H. TALIAFERRO of Town aforesaid of the
second part; Whereas said ALEXANDER NAIRNE by his last Will and Testament duly recorded in the Corporation Court of Fredericksburg did authorise and direct his Executors after the payment of his just debts to remit the rest of his Estate to his Brother,
GEORGE NAIRNE of LONDON, to be disposed of as afterwards directed by his said Will; And
the said GEORGE MURRAY having qualified as Executor thereof has among other Estate
of ALEXR. sold at publick auction to said RICHARD the Houses and part of a lott in the
Town aforesaid whereon said ALEXANDER resided; Now This Indenture Witnesseth that
GEORGE MURRAY as Executor aforesaid for five shillings to him in hand paid by said
RICHARD and in consideration of the balance of the purchase money hereafter to be
paid agreeably to the Terms of the Sale, hath bargained and sold to said RICHARD the
said houses and part of the Lot subject to the terms of a Lease of the same made by
SUSANNA and JAMES HEATH to WILLIAM REAT of whom the said ALEXANDER NAIRNE
purchased the said premises, together with the appurtenances thereunto belonging; To
have and to hold the said house and part of a lot in as ample manner as said ALEXANDER
held them of said SUSANNAH and JAMES HEATH, and GEORGE MURRAY doth warrant and
defend the said lot unto RICHARD H. TALIAFERRO his heirs against the claim of all
persons; In Witness whereof GEORGE MURRAY as Executor aforesaid hath hereunto set
his hand and affixed his seal the day and year above written

Signed Sealed and delivered in the presence of
WILL: SALE JR., WILLIAM ROBB,   GEO: MURRAY
RICHD. KENNEY, PETER R. JOHNSON   Executor of ALEXR. NAIRNE deceased
At a Hustings Court held for the Town & Corporation of Fredericksburg the 27th day of
January 1798 This Indenture for a Lott of land from GEORGE MURRAY, Executor of
ALEXANDER NAIRNE deced, to RICHARD H. TALIAFERRO was proved by the oaths of two of
the witnesses thereto; And at a Court held for said Corporation the 23d day of June 1798,
It was acknowledged by said GEORGE MURRAY, Exr. of ALEXANDER NAIRNE deced, &
ordered to be recorded
Exd. & deld. RD. H. TALIAFERRO   Teste JNO: CHEW, C. C. H.

pp.   THIS INDENTURE made this 24th day of February in year of our Lord one thou-
177-   sand seven hundred and ninety eight and in the twenty second year of the
178   Commonwealth between JAMES FERGUSON and JENNY his Wife of Town of
         Fredericksburg of one part and JAMES JONES (Son of WM. JONES) of same Town of
second part; Witnesseth that JAMES FURGUSON & JENNY his Wife for sum of Five
shillings current money to them in hand paid by JAMES JONES, by these presents doth
bargain sell and confirm unto JAMES JONES his heirs one third part of the lott of
ground lying in Town of Fredg., known by No. 211, and which lott JAMES FERGUSON
purchased of PHILIP ROOTES as by Indenture from said ROOTES to said FERGUSON
bearing date the 5th day of December 1791 and duly recorded in the Court of Hustigns
aforesaid will appear; the said third part being the lower part of said lott lying on
PRINCESS AUGUSTA & PRINCESS ELIZABETH STREETs and contains Fifty five feet in front
with all houses buildings profits and appurtenances belonging; To have and to hold the
said one third part of lott hereby conveyed to JAMES JONES his heirs and JAMES FERGU-
SON & JENNY his Wife and their heirs against every person claiming under them will
warrant and forever defend by these presents; In Witness whereof JAMES FERGUSON
and JENNY his Wife have hereunto set their hands and seals the day first afore written
Signed Sealed & Delivered in presence of
JNO: CHEW,   JAMES FERGUSON
JOHN CHEW JR.,   JENNY her mark × FERGUSON
JAMES ALLAN Feby. 24. 1798
At a Court of Hustings held for the Town & Corporation of Fredericksburg February
24th 1798   This Indenture from JAMES FERGUSON & JENNY his Wife to JAMES JONES
was proved by the witnesses thereto as to the execution thereof by said JAMES FERGU-
SON and acknowledged by said JENNY, she being first privately examined as the Law
directs, and ordered to be recorded
Examd. & delivered WM. JONES   Teste JNO: CHEW, C. C. H.

pp.   STATE of SOUTH CAROLINA.
179-   KNOW ALL MEN by these presents that I GUSTAVUS BROWN WALLACE, late of
180   Fredericksburg Virgnia, now of the City of CHARLESTON, SOUTH CAROLINA,
         Gentleman by these presents do appoint my friend GEORGE W. B. SPOONER of
Fredericksburg, Virginia, Merchant, my true and lawful Attorney to convey sell and
dispose of a certain lott of land lying on THE HILL in Town of Fredericksburg whereon
the FREDERICKSBURG LIVERY STABLES were by me erected and now stand either in part
or in the whole, allowing and holding firm all my Attorney shall lawfully do about the
premises; In Witness whereof I have hereunto set my hand and seal dated at CHARLE-
STON the 16th day of January in year of our Lord one thousand seven hundred and
ninety eight and in the Twenty second year of American Independence

Sealed and Delivered in the presence of
    WM. DRUMMOND,   GUSTAVUS B. WALLACE
    CHARLES DRUMMOND
At a Court of Hustings held for Fredericksburg April 28th 1798
This Letter of Attorney from GUSTAVUS B. WALLACE to GEO: W. B. SPOONER was produced
in Court and it appearing to the Court that the subscribing witnesses are not inhabitants of this State, JOHN BENSON, JAMES ALLAN and JOHN CHEW were sworn and severally deposed that they were well acquainted with the hand writing of the said WALLACE
and that they verily believed the signature to said Letter of Attorney was written by
said WALLACE, thereupon it is ordered to be recorded

pp.   THIS INDENTURE made this the 21st day of March Anno Domini one thousand
180-   seven hundred and ninety Six Between the Mayor and Commonalty of the Town
183   of Fredericksburg to wit (this Deed is similar to the one appearing on pages 124-127
         containing the same names of the Common Council and the wording of the Act of the
Legislature to sell the MARKETT HOUSE LOTTS) and said DAVID CORBIN KER became the purchaser. Now This Indenture witnesseth that the Mayor and Commonalty in consideration of the Rents and Covenants herein after mentioned by DAVID CORBIN KER to be
paid and performed by these presents do bargain and sell unto DAVID C. KER his heirs
the Lotts number One and four with all advantages and commodities to the same belonging; To have and to hold the lotts number one and four unto DAVID C. KER his heirs
during the natural lives of CHARLES and DAVID BENSON (Sons of JOHN) and Doctor
DAVID C. KER for lot number one; and WILLIAM and JAMES BENSON, (Sons of JOHN) and
Doctor DAVID C. KER for Lot number four; or the natural life of the survivor of them;
paying for the same on the 21st day of March next ensuing the sum of Eleven pounds
sixteen shilings Virginia Currency and yearly during the term, And said DAVID CORBIN
KER for himself and assigns doth covenant that he will build in a workman like manner two houses eighteen feet front and twenty eight feet deep and keep and deliver up
the same in good repair at the expiration of the Term; In Witness whereof the parties
have hereunto affixed their hands and seals the day and year first mentioned
Signed Sealed and Delivered in presence of
    JNO: CHEW,   WILLIAM HARVEY, Mayor
    ROBT. S. CHEW   FONTAINE MAURY, Recorder
    JAMES ALLAN JUNR.   ELISHA HALL, Alderman
    BEVY. C. STANARD   GEO: W. B. SPOONER
          WILLIAM HERNDON, ZACH. LUCAS, JAMES BROWN,
          JOHN BENSON, RICHARD PEACOCK, WM. PEARSON,
          FIELDING LUCAS, RICHD. S. HACKLEY, DAVID C. KER
At a Court of Hustings held for the Town and Corporation of Fredericksburg the 28th
day of April 1798   This Indenture of Lease from the Mayor and Common Council of
the Corporation of Fredericksburg to DAVID C. KER was proved by the oaths of two of
the witnesses thereto & ordered to be certifyed
Deld. Docr. KER   Teste   JNO: CHEW, C. C. H.

pp.   THIS INDENTURE made and entered into the 28th day of April one thousand
184-   seven hundred and ninety Eight Between FRANCES HARVEY of Town of
185   Fredericksburg of one part and DAVID CORBIN KER, the Son of said FRANCES
         of said place of other part; Witnesseth that said FRANCES as well for the natural
love and affection which she hath and beareth unto said DAVID as also for the further
consideration of One Dollar to said FRANCES in hand paid by said DAVID, by these pre-

sents doth give and confirm unto said DAVID his heirs a certain lott of ground lying in Town of Fredericksburg on the Streets PRINCESS AUGUSTA and FREDORI (?) number Two hundred and nineteen lately the property of WILLIAM HARVEY deceased, and purchased by him of JAMES JAMIESON, together with all houses and appurtenances to said lott belonging; To have and to hold the lott of ground unto said DAVID his heirs and the said FRANCES the said lott of ground against all persons unto said DAVID will warrant and forever defend by these presents; In Witness whereof said FRANCES hath hereunto set her hand and seal the day and year first above written
Signed Sealed and Acknowledged in presence of us
    JACOB KUHN,   FRANCES HARVEY
    JOHN BENSON, CHARLES LEWIS
  At a Court of Hustings held for the Town and Corporation of Fredericksburg the 28th day of April 1798   This Deed of Gift from FRANCES HARVEY to DAVID C. KER was proved by the oaths of JACOB KUHN, JOHN BENSON and CHARLES LEWIS the witnesses thereto and ordered to be recorded
Exd. & deld. D. C. KER   Teste JNO: CHEW, C. C. H.

pp.   THIS INDENTURE Witnesseth that JOHN TAYLOR, Son of ELIZABETH TAYLOR of
186-   County of KING GEORGE by these presents, with the consent of his said Mother,
187   doth of his own free will and accord put himself Apprentice to GEORGE NORWOOD
      of Corporation of Fredericksburg to learn his art trade and mistery after the manner of an Apprentice to serve said GEORGE NORWOOD from the day of the date hereof and during the full term of five years two months and 26 days next ensuing, in all things behave himself as a faithful Apprentice ought to do and the said Master shall use the utmost of his endeavour to teach or cause to be taught and instructed his said Apprentice in the trade and mistery of a Shoe Maker and give him one years Schooling; said Apprentice is to have at the expiration of said term a suit of new cloathes; In Witness whereof the said parties have interchangeably set their hands and seals hereunto dated the Twenty third day of June in year of our Lord one thousand seven hundred and ninety eight, 1798.
Sealed and Delivered in the presence of us   ELIZA: her mark X TAYLOR
    (no witnesses shown)   GEORGE NORWOOD
  At a Court of Hustings held for the Town and Corporation of Fredericksburg the 23rd day of June 1798   This Indenture was acknowledged by the parties and ordered to be recorded

pp.   KNOW ALL MEN by these presents that I ARCHIBALD McAUSLAND, Merchant
188-   in GRENOCK in County of RENFREW North Britain considering that my Brother,
192   HUMPHREY McAUSLAND, Merchant in Fredericksburg, Virginia in the United
      State of America is now dead and that it is requisite I as nearest relation should impower persons of honor and trust in America to take necessary steps for collecting the debts due him and winding up his whole affairs for my behalf of those to whom he may stand indebted, Now Know ye that I by these presents do appoint my trusty and well beloved friends JAMES SOMERVILLE and WILLIAM DRUMMOND of Fredericksburg, Merchants, WALTER COLQUHOUN of FALMOUTH, Merhcant and ADAM DARBY of Fredericksburg, Merchant, to be my true and lawfull Attornies for me and in my name as Brother German and sole Executor of the said HUMPHREY McAUSLAND conform to his Testament in my favor dated the eighteenth day of May Seventeen hundred and eighty years granting to my Attorney controul and direction to administer the Estate of HUMPHREY McAUSLAND; In Witness whereof I have hereunto set my hand and seal at GRENOCK aforesaid this thirtieth day of November in year of our Lord one thousand

seven hundred and Ninety two and of his Majesty George the third King of Great Britain
France & Ireland, defender of the faith, the thirty third year;
Sealed and Delivered in presence of
        ARCHD. CLERK,   ARCHD. McAUSLAND
        JOHN McKINNON
I HUMPHREY McAUSLAND, Cooper in GREENOCK, being at present going abroad in the
prosecution of my lawfull business and known the certainty of death and the uncer-
tainty of the time thereof, am resolved so to settle my worldly affairs in manner under-
written, Therefore and for the love favour and affection which I have and bear to
ARCHIBALD McAUSLAND, my Brother German, do make and appoint my Brother to be
my sole and only Executor; In Witness whereof these presents written on Stampt. paper
by DANIEL LAMONT, Apprentice to WILLIAM PATON, Writer in GRENOCK, are subscribed
by me att GRENOCK the eighteenth day of May one thousand seven hundred and eighty
years before these witnesses, the said WILLIAM PATTON and DANIEL LAMONT
                                        HUMPHREY McAUSLAND
    At a Court of Hustings held for the Town and Corporation of Frederickburg on Saturday
the 28th day of July 1798   This Letter of Attorney from ARCHIBALD McAUSLAND to
JAMES SOMERVILLE, WILLIAM DRUMMOND, WALTER COLQUHOUN and ADAM DARBY together with the affidavit of JOHN McKINNON and a Certificate of GILBERT HAMILTON,
Lord Provost and Chief Magistrate of the City of GLASGOW hereto annexed are on the
motion of said WILLIAM DRUMMOND ordered to be recorded
Exd. & Deld. W. DRUMMOND   Teste JNO: CHEW, C. C. H.

pp.   KNOW ALL MEN by these presents that I FRANCIS GARDEN, Merchant in
192-   GRENOCK, Trustee for the sequestrated Estate of ARCHIBALD McAUSLAND, Mer-
194   chant then in County of RENFREW North Britain by these presents do appoint
        Messrs. JAMES SOMERVILLE, WALTER COLQUHOUN, WILLIAM DRUMMOND and
ADAM DARBY, Merchants in Frederickburg joining and severally to be my true and
lawfull Attornies for me as Trustee for the said Estaste; In Witness whereof I have hereunto set my hand and Seal at GRENOCK the Twenty second day of May in the year of our
Lord One thousand seven hundred and ninety three and of his Majestys reign the thirty
third year
Signed Sealed and delivered being first duly stamped
  in the presence of us WM. CAMPBELL,   F. GARDEN
        JOHN HYND
    At a Court of Hustings held for the Town & Corporation of Fredericksburg on Saturday
the 28th day of July 1798   This Letter of Attorney from FRANCIS GARDEN to JAMES
SOMERVILLE, WILLIAM DRUMMOND, WALTER COLQUHOUN and ADAM DARBY together
with the affidavit of WILLIAM CAMPBELL and a Certificate of JAMES ANDERSON Esqr.
Chief Magistrate of the Burgh of GREENACK hereto annexed are on the motion of WIL-
LIAM DRUMMOND ordered to be recorded
Exd. & Deld. W. DRUMMOND   Teste JNO: CHEW C. C. H.

p.   KNOW ALL MEN by these presents taht I ADAM DARBY of City of Fredericksburg
195   Virginia have taken upon myself the execution of the power confided in me by
        ARCHIBALD McAUSLAND of Town of GREENOCK in the County of RENFREW North
Britain and having also taken upon myself the sole execution of the joint powers
conferred upon JAMES SOMERVILLE, WALTER COLQUHOUN, WILLIAM DRUMMOND and
myself by FRANCIS GARDEN Trustee of ARCHIBALD McAUSLAND by a letter bearing date
2nd day of May 1793, and as one of the Executors of the Estate of HUMPHREY McAUS-
LAND had the sole management and receipt thereof due by virtue of said powers do

release WILLIAM DRUMMOND from all claims that may accrue against him as one of the
Administrators; In Witness whereof I have hereunto set my hand and seal this 28th day
of July 1798
    ANTHY. McDONNELL   ADAM DARBY
  At a Court of Hustings held for the Town & Corporation of Fredericksburg on Saturday
the 28th day of July 1798   This Release from ADAM DARBY to WILLIAM DRUMMOND
was acknowledged by said ADAM DARBY and ordered to be recorded
Exd. & deld. WM. DRUMMOND   Teste JNO: CHEW, C. C. H.

p.   KNOW ALL MEN by these presents that I GODLOVE HEISKILL of Fredericksburg
196   in consideration of the good Conduct of Jack, my Negro man slave, do by these
        presents liberate, emancipate and set free the said Jack from all manner of
slavery and servitude and declare him to be in as perfect a state of Freedom and entitled
to all the priviledges and advantages arising therefrom as he can legally enjoy, In
Testimony whereof I the said GODLOVE HEISKILL have hereunto set my hand and affixed
my seal
Sign'd Sealed and delivered in the presence of
   (no witnesses shown)   G. HEISKILL
  At a Court of Hustings held for the Town & Corporation of Fredericksburg the 27th day
of October 1798   This Deed of Emancipation from GODLOVE HEISKILL to his slave
Jack was acknowledged by the said HEISKILL and ordered to be recorded
Copy deld. Jack.   Teste JNO: CHEW C. C. H.

pp.   TO ALL TO WHOM these presents shall come, I JAMES McDOWALL Esquire, Lord
197-   Provost and Cheif Magistrate of City of GLASGOW in County of LANARK in that
208   part of Great Britain called SCOTLAND hereby certify and make known that upon
      the day of the date hereof came before me JOHN FLEMING of said City, Attorney
at Law, the Deponent named in the annexed affidavit, which Deponent upon the Holy
Evangelists of the Almighty God did solemnly depose and declare to be true the several
maters & things mentioend and contained in the annexed affidavit; Dated this fourteenth day of July one thousand seven hundred and ninety seven
            JAMES McDOWALL
  GLASGOW (Vizt.) JOHN FLEMING of City of GLASGOW in County of LANARK in that part
of Great Britain called SCOTLAND, Attorney at Law maketh Oath and saith that he was
present together with JAMES SHAW of the said City, Gentleman, and did see GEORGE
McCALL, GEORGE THOMSON and WILLIAM FLEMING of said City, Merchants, sign seal and
as their act and deed deliver the Letter of Attorney to have been subscribed by the said
parties upon the twenty second day of this month June, and purporting to be a Letter of
Attorney granted by said GEORGE McCALL and by JOHN TAYLOR of CRAIGS in County of
TOFAR in Scotland as only surviving partners of the concern carrined on under the
firm of GEORGE McCALL and COMPANY and also granted by said GEORGE THOMSON as only
acting Executor and by WILLIAM FLEMING as Trustee therein mentioned to Messrs.
JAMES SOMERVILLE, DAVID BLAIR and JAMES BLAIR of Town of Fredericksburg in
America, Merchants, And further the deponent saith not so help him God
Sworn at City of GLASGOW fourteenth day of July 1797
before me JAMES McDOWALL, Lord Provost   JOHN FLEMING
    (WILLIAM BUCHANAN of said Burgh, Clerk in the Office of the Town Clerk, made Oath that
the things in the affidavit annexed were true, which writing was sworn at the Burgh of MONTROSE
the fourth day of July 1797 before THOS: WEBSTER, Provost and Chief Magistrate); (There follows
several pages of a document that was signed sealed and delivered in presence of JOHN FLEMING,
JAMES SHAW, WM. BUCHANAN & JOHN MILNE, signed by GEORGE McCALL, JOHN TAYLOR and

GEORGE THOMSON, only acting Executor of the late ANDREW THOMSON; followed by a Power of Attorney made by ANDREW THOMSON Merchant in Glasgow appointing his four Eldest Sons, GEORGE THOMSON, JOHN THOMSON, ANDREW THOMSON and JAMES THOMSON or survivor sole executors; written by WILLIAM LINDSAY, Writer in Glasgow the Thirteenth day of October Seventeen hundred and Eighty six years before the witnesses JAMES BURNSIDE, Merchant in Glasgow and said WILLIAM LINDSAY. all of which is followed by lengthy documents concerning the trade and debts of various merchants in Glasgow made by JOHN FLEMING, Notary Public).

At a Court of Hustings held for the Town and Corpora;tion of Fredericksburg on Saturday the 26th day of January 1799   This Letter of Attorney from GEORGE McCALL, JOHN TAYLOR, GEORGE THOMSON only Acting Executor of the late ANDREW THOMSON, and WILLIAM FLEMING, Trustee for the Creditors of McCALL, SMELLIE & COMPANY and GEORGE McCALL as an Individual partner of said Company to JAMES SOMERVILLE, DAVID BLAIR and JAMES BLAIR, together with the affidavit of JOHN FLEMING and Certificate of JAMES McDOWALL Esqr. Lord Provost and Chief Magistrate of the City of GLASGOW, and the affidavit of WILLIAM BUCHANAN and Certificate of THOMAS WEBSTER, Provost and Chief Magistrate of the Burgh of MONTROSE and also the Certificate of JOHN FLEMING, Notary Public of the City of Glasgow hereto annexed are on the motion of the said DAVID & JAMES BLAIR ordered to be recorded
Exd. & deld. Mr. DANL. GRINNAN JR.   Teste JNO: CHEW, C. C. H.

(Pages 209-216, contain several affidavits and certificates as explained in the recording,)
At a Court of Hustings held for the Town and Corporation of Fredericksburg on Saturday the 26th day of January 1799   This Letter of Attorney from JOHN LODGE, DEVEREUX HUSTLER, JOSEPH HOLMES, JOHN RANSON and EDWARD OGLE to DANIEL GRINNAN, together with the affidavit of HENRY EVATT and RICHARD CURSON BERRY and Certificates of WILLIAM NEWTON, Notary Public of the City of LONDON, and the right Honble. WILLIAM ANDERSON, Lord Mayor of the City of LONDON, hereto annexed are on the motion of said DAVID GRINNAN ordered to be recorded
Examd. and delivered Mr. DANL. GRINNAN   Teste JNO: CHEW, C. C. H.

(Pages 217-224, also contain several more affidavits and certificates part of which from page 218 is as follows). Whereas prior to the peace concluded between Great Britain and the United State of America there were due and owing by sundry persons, citizens or inhabitants of the said United States, unto McCALL, SMELLIE & COMPANY, of the City of GLASGOW, in the County of LANARK, in that part of Great Britain called SCOTLAND, Merchants, several debts to a considerable amount and which said debts still remain owing and unpaid; And Whereas by the Sixth Article of the Treaty of Amity Commerce and Navigation between his Britannic Majesty and the aforesaid United States, signed at LONDON on the nineteenth day of November one thousand sevenhundred and ninety four and since ratified by the said United States, it is declared that by the operation of various lawful impediments since the peace not only the full recovery of such Debts (as those above mentioned) has been delayed but also the value and security thereof have been in several instances impaired and lessened; so that by the ordinary course of judicial proceedings the British Creditors cannot now obtain and actually have and receive full and adequate compensation for the losses and damages which they have thereby sustained . . . .

At a Court of Hustings held for the Town and Corporation of Fredericksburg on Saturday the 26th day of January 1799   This Letter of Attorney from GEORGE McCALL, RICHARD SMELLIE & WILLIAM FLEMING, Trustees for the Creditors of McCALL, SMELLIE and Company and the individual partners of said Company to JAMES SOMERVILLE,

DAVID BLAIR and JAMES BLAIR together with the affidavit of JOHN FLEMING and Certificate of JAMES McDOWALL Esqr. Lord Provost and Chief Magistrate of the City of GLASGOW, JOHN FLEMING, Notary Publick of the City of GLASGOW re on the motion of the said DAVID & JAMES BLAIR, ordered to be recorded
Exd. and deld. Mr. DANL. GRINNAN JR.   Teste JNO: CHEW, C. C. H.

p.   THIS INDENTURE made this second day of January one thousand seven hundred
225   and ninety nine Between CHARLES MORTIMER SENIOR and WILLIAM GLASSELL,
         both of Town of Fredericksburg, Witnesseth that said CHARLES MORTIMER for
the sum of One hundred pounds to him in hand paid by WILLIAM GLASSELL, by these
presents doth bargain & sell unto WILLIAM GLASSELL his heirs all that lot or Tenement begining at the lower side of WILLIAM GLASSELL's WHARF, thence down the bank
of the River one hundred feet, thence up the rising ground a South West course one
hundred and fifty feet until it is in a line with the South Corner of WILLIAM GLASSELLs
WAREHOUSE, thence across to the said one hundred feet, thence down the River to the
begining; To have and to hold said parcel of land unto WILLIAM GLASSELL his heirs
and CHARLES MORTIMER and his heirs the said premises unto WILLIAM GLASELL his
heirs will warrant and forever defend by these presents; In Witness whereof he hath
hereunto set his hand and seal the day and year first above written
Signed sealed & Deliver'd in presence of
      J. HARRIS JR.,   CHS. MORTIMER
      FRANCIS J. WIATT, THOMAS P. BASYE
At a Court of Hustings held for the Town & Corporation of Fredericksburg on Saturday
the 26th day of January 1799   This Indenture was proved by the oaths of JONATHAN HARRIS JR., FRANCIS J. WIATT and THOMAS P. BASYE, the three witnesses thereto,
and ordered to be recorded
Exd. & deld. ANTHY. BUCK   Teste JNO: CHEW, C. C. H.

p.   THIS INDENTURE made this 20th day of November one thousand seven hundred
226   and ninety eight Between WILLIAM GLASSELL and THOMAS P. BASYE, both of the
         Town of Fredericksburg, Witnesseth that WILLIAM GLASSELL for sum of Five
shillings to him in hand paid by THOMAS P. BASYE, by these presents doth bargain and
sell unto THOMAS P. BASYE and heirs all that lott in Town of Fredericksburg adjoining
to lot at present occupied by ANN RIDLEY, alias ANN CROSBY, and lying Beginning at
the line which divides the said lotts and extending in front Ninety nine feet on CAROLINE STREET, thence two hundred and sixty four feet on WOLF STREET, thence ninety
nine feet on PRINCESS ANN STREET and thence two hundred and sixty four feet to the
begining; To have and to hold the parcell of land unto THOMAS P. BASYE his heirs and
WILLIAM GLASSELL and his heirs the land unto THOMAS P. BASYE his heirs will warrant and forever defend by these presents; In Witness whereof he hath hereto set his
hand and seal the day and year first above written
Signed sealed and Delivered in presence of
      GEO: FRENCH, .   WM. GLASSELL
      TH: POSEY, FRANCIS J. WIATT
At a Court of Hustings held for the Town & Corporation of Fredericksburg on Saturday
the 26th day of January 1799   This Indenture was acknowledged by the within
mentioned WM. GLASSELL and ordered to be recorded
Exd. & deld. Mr. WALKER   Teste JNO: CHEW, C. C. H.

pp.   KNOW ALL MEN by these presents that we JAMES JAMISON and JOHN BUCHANAN
227-   of City of GLASGOW in that part of Great Britain called SCOTLAND, Merchants,
229   the only surviving Partners of the Company known by the firm of BOGLE,
         SOMERVELL and COMPANY, thereafter BOGLE, JAMISON & COMPANY, Merchants
in GLASGOW with the consent and concurrence of JOHN ROBERTSON and CUNNINGHAM
CORBETT of GLASGOW, Merchants, Surviving Trustees to whom the Debts and effects and
Estate owing & belonging to the said Company in the State of Virginia and elsewhere in
North America, have been conveyed for the behoof of these Creditors, for certain good
causes and consideration by these presents do make and constitute WILLIAM LAWSON of
the State of Virginia in North America our true and lawfull Factor and Attorney
granting unto WM. LAWSON full power and absolute authority for us and in the name of
said Company to sell and dispose of all lands and hereditaments to the Company of every
kind belonging; And in general to manage, negotiate and transact the affairs of the
said Companys allowing and confirming whatsoever acts and things our said Attorney
shall lawfully do or cause to be done in the premises, In Witness whereof we have hereunto set our respective hands and seals this thirtieth day of April in year of our Lord
one thousand seven hundred and ninety eight
Sealed and Delivered being first duly stampt. in
     presence of JOHN MILLER EWING,   JAMES JAMISON
                   JOHN HALL   JOHN BUCHANAN JUNR.
                                                   JOHN ROBERTSON
                                                   CUNNINGM: CORBETT
     At a Court of Hustings held for the Town & Corporation of Fredericksburg on Saturday
the 23d. day of March 1799   This Letter of Attorney from JAMES JAMISON and JOHN
BUCHANAN JUNR, JOHN ROBERTSON and CUNNINGHAM CORBETT to WILLIAM LAWSON,
together with the affidavit of JOHN HALL and Certificate of JAMES McDOWALL Esqr.,
Lord Provost & Chief Magistrate of the City of GLASGOW hereto annexed, are on the
motion of the said WILLIAM LAWSON ordered to be recorded
Exd. & send G. LAWSON p. order filed   Teste   JNO: CHEW C. C. H.

pp.   THIS INDENTURE made the Twenty first day of December in year of our Lord
230-   one thousand seven hundred and ninety eight Between ADAM DARBY of Town of
232   Fredericksburg & CATHARINE his Wife of one part and JAMES WILSON, JONAH
         THOMPSON & (blank) VEITCH, all of Town of ALEXANDRIA, of other part; Witnes-
seth that whereas ADAM DARBY and CATHARINE his Wife for sum of Eight hundred
pounds current money of Virginia to them in hand paid, by these presents bargain and
sell unto JAMES WILSON, JONAH THOMPSON and (blank) VEITCH, and their heirs that part
of the lott lying on PRINCESS ANN & WOLF STREETs in Town of Fredericksburg numbered 53 containing by estimation two thousand four hudnred & 55 5/9th square yards
be the same more or less and is bounded, Begining at the lower part of said lott, corner
of PRINCE ANN & WOLF STREETs, from thence runing up said PRINCESS ANN STREET one
hundred feet to the boundary line of that part of said lott at present the property of
DAVID BLAIR of said Town, from thence at right angles along said side boundary line
two hundred & 21 feet to the boundary line of that part of said lott now the property of
the Estate of a Free Negro now deceased named REUBEN DIXON, from thence at right
angles along said boundary line one hundred feet to said WOLF STREET and from thence
at right angles along said WOLF STREET to the begining; with all houses gardens & Improvements belonging; the said ADAM DARBY & CATHARINE his Wife their heirs by
these presents do warrant and defend; In Witness whereof ADAM DARBY & CATHARINE
his Wife have hereunto set their hands and seals the day and year first above written

Signed sealed & delivered in presence of
      ROGR: COLTART,   ADAM DARBY
      JAMES D. LANE, JOHN SMITH,   CATHARINE DARBY
      THOS: R. ROOTES, JOHN CHEW JR.

The Commonwealth of Virginia to REUBEN BURNLEY & BELFIELD CAVE, Gentlemen, Justices of our County Court of ORANGE Greeting; Whereas (the Commission for the privy Examination of CATHARINE, the Wife of ADAM DARBY); Witness JOHN CHEW Clerk of our said Court this 21st day of December 1798 and in the 23rd year of the Commonwealth

    Pursuant to the annexed Commission to us directed (the return of the Execution of the privy Examination of CATHARINE DARBY); Certified under our hands and seals this twenty eighth day of January 1799   REUBEN BURNLEY
                                          BELFIELD CAVE

    At a Court of Hustings held for the Town and Corporation of Fredericksburg on Saturday the 27th day of April 1799   This Indenture was proved by the oaths of ROGER COLTART, JOHN SMITH and THOMAS R. ROOTES three of the witnesses thereto and together with the receipt thereon indorsed and the Commission annexed and Certificate of the Execution thereof by the said CATHARINE Indorsed, are ordered to be recorded
Exd. & Deld. JAS. BLAIR JR.   Teste   JNO: CHEW, C. C. H.

p.   The Commonwealth of Virginia to JOHN MERCER and DAVID C, KER Gentleman
233   Greeting, Whereas ROBERT MERCER and MILDRED his Wife by their certain Indenture of bargain and sale bearing date the 27th day of January 1797 have sold and conveyed unto CHARLES CROUGHTON the fee simple estate of one lott of ground lying in the Town of Fredericksburg number 127; And whereas the said MILDRED cannot conveniently tracvel of our Court of Hustings; (the Commission for the privy Examination of MILDRED, the Wife of JOHN MERCER   , Witness JOHN CHEW Clerk of our said Hustings Court the 7th day of December 1797 and inthe 22nd year of the Commonwealth

  Corporation of Fredericksburg, In Obedience to the within Commission, We the Subscribers two of the Justices therein named did personally go to the within named MILDRED MERCER (the return of the Execution of the privy Examination of MILDRED MERCER); Given under our hands and seals this 11th day of October 1797
                                JOHN MERCER
                                DAVID C. KER
          Truly recorded Teste JNO: CHEW, C. C. H.
Examd. & deld. C. CROUGHTON with the Deed

pp.   THIS INDENTURE made this ninth day of December in the year of our Lord one
234-   thousand seven hundred and ninety eight Between THOMAS SYDNOR of County
235   of RICHMOND in State of Virginia of the first part and JOHN SKRYIN of City of
         PHILADELPHIA and State of PENSYLVANIA of the other part; Witnesseth that THOMAS SYDNOR for sum of Five shillings to him in hand paid by JOHN SKRYIN and for the better security the sum of money herein after mentioned justly due to said JOHN SKRYIN, said THOMAS SYDNOR by these presents doth bargain & sell unto JOHN SKRYIN a certain lott of ground in Town of Fredericksburg on CAROLINE STREET between the Lotts of WALTER GREGORY & DOCTOR ELISHA HALL, bounded, begining att the lower corner of lott No. twenty eight on CAROLINE STREET, thence up and along said Street thirty feet; thence at right angles with said Street one hundred feet Eastward, thence paralel with CAROLINE STREET thirty feet to the lower end of said Lott and from thence along said lower line to the begining, together with all houses buildings & appurtenances belonging; Also the upper moiety of a Lott No. Five bounded by WILLIAM STREET on the North West, by SOPHIA STREET on the South West, Lott No. 3 being opposite the

same and on the South East by one other of said lott No. Five and on the North East by
the RIVER RAPPAHANNOCK, containing one quarter of an acre be the same more or
less, together with all its appurtenances; To have and to hold the said lotts unto JOHN
SKRYIN his heirs, PROVIDED nevertheless that if said THOMAS his heirs pay or cause to
be paid unto JOHN SKRYIN his heirs the just and full sum of Fifteen hundred Spanish
mill'd Dollars with legal Interest from the date hereof to be paid on the first day of
November next ensuing, then these presents shall be void and THOMAS SYDNOR his
heirs at all times hereafter warrant and defend the herein granted premises to JOHN
SKRYIN his heirs against the claims of all persons; In Witness whereof THOMAS SYD-
NOR hath hereunto set his hand and seal the day and year first above written
Signed Sealed and Delivered in the presence of
     JNO: ROSS,   THOMAS SYDNOR
     PHILIP GLOVER,   JAMES ROSS,
     RICHARD JOHNSTON JR.,   JAMES ALLAN
  At a Court of Hustings held for the Town and Corporation of Fredericksburg on Satur-
day the 22nd day of June 1799   This Mortgage was proved by the oaths of JOHN
ROSS, PHILIP GLOVER and JAMES ALLEN, three of the witnesses thereto and ordered to
be recorded

pp.   THIS INDENTURE made the twenty fourth day of May Anno Domini one thou-
236-   sand seven hundred and ninety nine Between JOHN T. BROOKE and ANNE his
238   Wife of one part and WILLIAM WILSON of the Town of Fredericksburg o other
     part; Witnesseth that JOHN T. BROOKE & ANNE his Wife in consideration of the
Rents and Covenants hereinafter mentioned and by WILLIAM WILSON to be paid and
performed, by these presents do bargain and sell unto WILLIAM WILSON his heirs the
following piece of ground in Town of Fredericksburg; Begining at a point one hundred
feet & a half from the South side of LEWIS STREET, down the Western side of CAROLINE
STREET, thence at right angles with said side of CAROLINE STREET to a Stone Wall and
Ally between the property owned by WILLIAM S. STONE and the said JOHN T. BROOKE,
thence down with the said Wall and Alley twenty five feet at right angles with the said
Wall & Alley to the said CAROLINE STREET, thence up CAROLINE STREET twenty five feet
to the begining, together with all advantages and commodities belonging; To have and
to hold unto WILLIAM WILSON his heirs paying for the same on the twenty fourth day
of May next ensuing the date of these presents the sum of one hundred Dollars or
Thirty pounds Virginia money and every year as an annual Rent to JOHN T. BROOKE his
heirs and JOHN T. BROOKE and ANNE his Wife their heirs do covenant (subject to the
Rents and Covenants herein contained) to warrant and defend agaisnt them and their
heirs; In Witness whereof the parties have hereunto affixed their hands and seals the
day and year first above written
Teste FONTAINE MAURY,   JOHN T. BROOKE
     WM. DRUMMOND, JNO: TALIAFERRO,   ANNA M. BROOKE
     BETSY MAURY, THOS: MILLER   WM. WILSON
  Memorandum: The said JOHN T. BROOKE and ANNE his Wife their heirs do grant
WILLIAM WILSON his heirs that piece of ground of five feet and extending back to said
Wall lying immediately below and adjoining the said piece hereby granted to said WIL-
LIAM WILSON shall be reserved as an Alley between said WILLIAM WILSON and JOHN T.
BROOKE and ANNA his Wife
Teste FONTAINE MAURY,   JOHN T. BROOKE
     JNO: TALIAFERRO, BETSY MAURY,   ANNA M. BROOKE
     WM. DRUMMOND, THOS: MILLER   WM. WILSON

At a Court held for the Town & Corporation of Fredericksburg on Saturday the 27th day of July 1799   This Indenture of Lease was acknowledged by the parties and ordered to be recorded
Examined and delivered WM. WILSON with Comm:
(Comm: recorded folio 241)   Teste   JNO: CHEW, C. C. H.

pp.   THIS INDENTURE made the twenty second day of February in year of our Lord
238-   one thousand seven hundred and ninety nine Between JOHN LEGG of the Town of
239   Fredericksburg of one part and WILLIAM LOVELL and COLLIN & JAMES ROSS of
          the Town aforesaid of other part; Witnesseth that JOHN LEGG for sum of Eighty
pounds current money of Virginia by WILLIAM LOVELL and COLLIN and JAMES ROSS to
JAMES LEGG in hand paid, by these presents doth bargain sell and confirm unto WIL-
LIAM LOVELL and COLLIN & JAMES ROSS their heirs two lotts of ground in Town aforesaid and numbered One hundred and fifteen and one hundred and Sixteen; bounded on
the South by HAWKE STREET, on the West by PRINCE EDWARD STREET, on the East by
CHARLES STREET and on the North by lotts 117 & 118; the property of said JOHN
LEGG,with the appurtenances to the same belonging; To have and to hold the said lotts
of ground with the appurtenances unto WILLIAM LOVELL and COLLIN & JAMES ROSS
their heirs and JOHN LEGG and his heirs agree to warrant and forever defend the lotts
unto WILLIAM LOVELL and COLLIN & JAMES ROSS their heirs against the claims of all
persons; In Witness whereof JOHN LEGG hath hereunto set his hand and seal the day
and year first above written
Sealed and Delivered in the presence of
     GEORGE ROTHROCK,   JNO: LEGG
     SAMUEL CHEWNING, CHARLES BENSON
At a Court of Hustings held for the Town & Corporation of Fredericksburg on Saturday
the 27th of July 1799   This Indenture was proved by the oath of GEORGE ROTHROCK and
SAMUEL CHEWNING two of the witnesses thereto; And at a Court held for said Corpora-
tion the 28th day of September 1799, this Indenture was fully proved by the oath of
CHARLES BENSON another witness thereto and ordered to be recorded
Examd. and Deld. JAMES ROSS   Teste JNO: CHEW. C. C. H.

pp.   THIS INDENTUREmade the third day of July in year of our Lord one thousand
240-   seven hundred and ninety nine Between THOMAS HAYDON of County of Spotsyl-
241   vania of one part and BELA BADGER of Town of Fredericksburg of other part;
          Witnesseth that THOMAS HAYDON for sum of Four hundred and thirty pounds
current money of Virginia to him in hand paid, by these presents doth bargain and sell
unto BELA BADGER his heirs one half of the lotts number thirty three and thirty four
situate in Town of Fredericksburg being the lower part of the lotts purchased by THO-
MAS HAYDON of THOMAS SOUTHCOMB as will appear by Indenture bearing date the 21st
day of June 1797 and recorded in the Court of Hustings of Fredericksburg which one
half of the lotts hereby conveyed is bounded, Begining on CAROLINE STREET at the
corner of the STORE formerly occupied by JAMES SOMERVILLE deced., and commonly
known by the name of REIDS STORE and at present in the occupation of Mrs. (blank)
RIDLEY, thence up CAROLINE STREET about thirty two feet seven inches, thence at right
angles by a straight line parallel to WOLFE STREET till it intersects or runs to PRINCESS
ANN STREET, thence down PRINCESS ANN STREET about thirty two feet seven inches to
the lott number thirty six, thence with the lotts number thirty six and thirty five to
CAROLINE STREET at the begining; together with all houses stables gardens and appurtenances to that part of Lotts No. 33 & 34 belonging; To have and to hold the said part of
lotts No. 33 & 34 to said BELA BADGER his heirs and THOMAS HAYDON his heirs against all

persons whatsoever shall warrant and forever defend by these presents; In Witness whereof said THOMAS HAYDON hath hereunto set his hand and affixed his seal the day and year first above written

Sealed and Delivered in the presence of

WM. HERNDON,   THOS: HAYDON
STEPHEN McFARLANE,   JOHN METCALFE

At a Court of Hustings held for the Town and Corporation of Fredericksburg on Saturday the 27th day of July 1799   This Indenture was proved by the oaths of WILLIAM HERNDON, STEPHEN McFARLANE and JOHN METCALFE, the three witnesses thereto, and ordered to be recorded

Exd. & deld. BELA BADGER   Teste   JNO: CHEW, C. C. H.

pp.   The Commonwealth of Virginia to THOMAS MOUNTJOY, TRAVERS DANIEL JUNR.,
241-   and HENRY VOWLES Gentlemen Greeting: Whereas (The Commission for the privy
242   examination of ANNA M. Wife of JOHN T. BROOKE, for deed dated the 24th of May 1799 unto
          WILLIAM WILSON); Witness JOHN CHEW, Clerk of our said Hustings Court the 8th
day of October 1799 and in the 24th year of the Commonwealth   JNO: CHEW

In Obedience of the within Commission, we have (the return of the Execution of the privy Examination of ANNA. M. BROOKE); Cerified under our hands & seals the 17th day of October
1799   THOS: MOUNTJOY
                                                      H. VOWLES

Deld. W. WILSON   Truly recorded Teste JNO: CHEW C. C. H.

pp.   THIS INDENTUREmade and entered into this twenty first day of August in year
242-   of our Lord one thosuand seven hundred and ninety nine Between RICHARD S.
245   HACKLEY and ANNE his Wife of Town of Fredericksburg of one part and TIMO-
          THY McNAMARA of Town aforesaid of other part; Witnesseth that the said
RICHARD & ANNE his Wife for sum of Three hundred pounds lawfull money of Virginia in hand paid by said TIMOTHY by these presents do bargain and sell unto said TIMOTHY his heirs all that remaining part of a Lott of land in Town of Fredericksburg number Fifteen Fifteen 15.15. now under an unexpired Lease to ELISHA DICKENSON (deceased) and bounded on the East by CAROLINE or Main Street, on South by lott number Sixteen Sixteen or 16.16; on the West by lott number Thirteen Thirteen or 13.13 sold to JOHN LAMBETH, and onthe North by the line of JAMES NEWBY containing Fifty four feet nine inches on CAROLINE or Main Street by one hundred and thirty two feet deep be the same more or less, likewise that part of lott number sixteen sixteen or 16.16 upon which a part of the BLACKSMITHs SHOP stands erected by said ELISHA DICKENSON deceased, containing two feet on CAROLINE or Main Street by one hundred and thirty two feet deep to DOCTOR GEORGE FRENCHs Lott, together with all profits commodities and appurtenances to said lotts belonging; To have and to hold the said parcels of ground with the appurtenances unto TIMOTHY McNAMARA his heirs and the said RICHARD S. and ANN and their heirs against all persons whatsoever to said TIMOTHY his heirs will warrant and forever defend by these presents; In Witness whereof said RICHARD S. and ANN his Wife have hereunto set their hands and seals the day and year first above written

Signed Sealed and Delivered in presence of

ELLIOT HACKLEY, JAMES NEWBY,   RICHD. S. HACKLEY
THOS: SIMPSON, JNO: LAMBETH,   ANN HACKLEY
RICHARD PEACOCK

The Commonwealth of Virginia to GEORGE FRENCH, FONTAINE MAURY and WILLIAM DRUMMOND, Gentlemen, Greeting, Whereas (the Commission for the privy Examination of ANN the Wife of RICHARD S. HACKLEY); Witness JOHN CHEW, Clerk of our said Corporation Court

the 14th day of September 1799 and in the 24th year of the Commonwealth
In Obedience to the within Commission to us directed (the return of the execution of the
privy Examination of ANN HACKLEY) Given under our hands and seals this 28th Septr. 1799
                                        GEO: FRENCH
                                        WILLM. DRUMMOND
At a Court of Hustings held for the Town & Corporation of Fredericksburg September
the 28th 1799   This Indenture was acknowledged by the said RICHARD S. HACKLEY and
together with the Commission annexed and the Certificate of Execution thereof by the
said ANN Indorsed, are ordered to be recorded
Examined & deld. T. McNAMARA   Teste JNO: CHEW, C. C. H.

pp.   THIS INDENTURE made this 28th day of September in year of our Lord one thou-
245-   sand seven hundred and ninety nine and in the 24th year of American Inde-
247   pendence Between JOHN BENSON of Town of Fredericksburg of one part and
       JAMES BAGGOTT and GEORGE BAGGOTT of the Town aforesaid of other part; Wit-
nesseth that JOHN BENSON for sum of Six hundred and Sixty six Dollars sixty seven Cents
to him in hand paid by JAMES & GEORGE BAGGOTT by these presents do bargain and sell
unto JAMES BAGGOTT and GEORGE BAGGOTT their heirs one undivided fourth part (a
share) of one and a half lott of ground lying in Town aforesaid, it being a fourth part of
half of the Lott No. 39 & of lott No. 40; formerly purchased by the late JOHN BAGGOTT
deced. of JOHN THORNTON, by him the said JOHN BAGGOTT deceased (after the death of his
Wife) to his four Sons, JOHN, JAMES, THOMAS and GEORGE, and the same fourth part sold
by said JOHN BAGGOTT the Younger to said JOHN BENSON as by Indenture from MARGA-
RET BAGGOTT and said JOHN BAGGOT and his Wife to said JOHN BENSON bearing date 25th
day of January 1792; and duly recorded in the Court of Hustigns of Fredericksburg will
more fully appear; together with all houses gardens priviledges and appurtenances
belonging; To have and to hold the said undivided fourth part of said one & a half lott of
ground with appurtenances unto JAMES & GEORGE BAGGOTT their heirs and JOHN BEN-
SON his heirs the undivided fourth part of said one and a half lott of ground against
every person unto JAMES and GEORGE BAGGOTT their heirs will and by these presents
warrant and forever defend; In Witness whereof JOHN BENSON hath hereunto set his
hand and affixed his seal the day month and year first above written
Signed Sealed and Delivered in presence of
       JOHN CHEW JR.   JOHN BENSON
At a Court of Hustigns held for the Town and Corpo: of Fredericksburg the 28th day of
September 1799   This Indenture was acknowledged by said JOHN BENSON and
ordered to be recorded

p.   KNOW ALL MEN by these presents that I RICHARD S. HACKLEY of Fredericks-
248   burg in the County of Spotsylvania in consideration of the good conduct of my
       Negro Woman slave named Betty do by these presents liberate emancipate and
set free the said Negro Woman and do hereby discharge her from all manner of slavery
and servitude whatsoever and declare to be in as perfect a state of Freedom as to all the
priviledges and advantages arising therefrom as she can enjoy; In Witness whereof I
have hereunto set my hand and affixed my seal this 28th day of March one thousand
seven hundred and ninety nine
Signed Sealed & Delivered in presence of
       GEO: FRENCH   RICHD. S. HACKLEY

At a Court of Hustings held for the Town and Corporation of Fredericksburg the 28 day of September 1799   This Indenture of Emancipation from RICHARD S. HACKLEY to his slave Betty was acknowledged by the said RICHARD S. HACKLEY and ordered to be recorded
Exd. & Deld. Betty   Teste JNO: CHEW, C.C.H.

pp.   THIS INDENTURE made the fifteenth day of September in year of our Lord one
248-   thousand seven hundred and ninety seven Between JEREH: MORTON and
250   MILDRED GARNETT his Wife of one part and JAMES GAVAN od County of KING
        WILLIAM of other part; Witnesseth that JERE: MORTON and MILDRED his Wife in consideration of the sum of Five shillings to them in hand paid by JAMES GAVAN by these presents do bargain and sell unto JAMES GAVAN his heirs Two lotts in the Town of Fredericksburg and on the Main Street occupied by JAMES BROWN; the other on SOPHIA STREET occupied by AUGUSTINE BOUGHAN together with all houses advantages and appurtenances belonging; To have and to hold the houses and lotts with every their rights members and appurtenances unto JAMES GAVEN his heirs, Provided Always and upon condition that if JERE: MORTON and his heirs shall guarantee and warrant to JAMES GAVAN his heirs quiet and peaceable possession and title to a certain tract of land in County of KING WILLIAM and by said MORTON and Wife and a certain RICHARD S. HACKLEY and Wife to said JAMES GAVAN for sum of Five hundred pounds Sterling as shall cause to be made by WILLIAM BROCK his heirs a perfect and legall title to such part of said land as belongs to said WILLIAM BROCK or may belong to his heirs, Then and in such case the above obligation shall be void or else to remain in full force
Signed Sealed and Delivered in presence of
        WM. DRUMMOND,   JERE: MORTON
        A. PARKES. ROG. COLTART   MILDRED G. MORTON
    At a Court of Hustings held for the Town and Corporation of Fredericksburg the 28th day of September 1799   This Indenture of Mortgage from JERE: MORTON to JAMES GAVAN was proved by the oaths of two witnesses thereto and ordered to be certified

pp.   THIS INDENTURE made this 25th day of September in year of our Lord one thou-
250-   sand seven hundred and ninety nine and in the 24th year of American Inde-
252   pendence Between JOHN BENSON of Town of Fredericksburg of one part and
        JAMES FERGUSON of the Town aforesaid of other part; Witnesseth that JOHN BENSON for sum of Two hundred and Fifty Dollars to him in hand paid by JAMES FERGUSON by these presents do bargain and sell unto JAMES FERGUSON his heirs a certain parcel of ground lying in Town of Fredericksburg fronting on PRINCESS ANN STREET forty four feet, bounded on one side by HENRY CHILES, one hundred and thirty two feet and on the other side by WALTER PAYNE, it being part of Lott No. 11.11, which the said BENSON purchased of ADAM HUNTER & MARY SULLIVAN; as by their seperate Indentures made to said BENSON and duly recorded in the Court of Hustings will more fully appear; Together with all houses gardens and appurtenances belonging; To have and to hold the parcel of ground unto JAMES FERGUSON his heirs and JOHN BENSON the parcel of ground and his heirs against the claims of every person unto JAMES FERGUSON his heirs will and do by these presents warrant & forever defend; In Witness whereof JOHN BENSON hath hereunto set his hand and affixed his seal the day & year within written
Signed Sealed and Delivered in the presence of
        JOHN FARISH,   JOHN BENSON
        THOMAS WARE, DAVID WILLIAMSON

At a Court of Hustings held for the Town and Corporation of Fredericksburg the 28th day of September 1799   This Indenture was acknowledged by JOHN BENSON and ordered to be recorded
Examd. & deld. JAS. FERGUSON   Teste JNO: CHEW, C.C.H.

pp.   THIS INDENTURE made this 29th day of December in year of our Lord one thou-
253-   sand seven hundred and ninety eight Between Doctor GEORGE FRENCH and ANN
255   B. his Wife of one part and CHARLES CLARKE of other part. Witnesseth that said
GEORGE FRENCH and ANN B. his Wife for sum of Three hundred and twenty pounds to them in hand paid by said CLARKE, by these presents do bargain and sell unto said CLARKE his heirs that part of a lott in the Town of Fredericksburg whereon a Dwelling House now stands, being the lower part of the Lott No. 62 upon PRINCESS ANN STREET and bounded; Beginning at the lower end of the Lott where it corner with Lott No. 132 on PRINCESS ANN STREET which lott is the property of JOHN BAYLOR, thence runing up said Street seventy one and a half feet, thence at right angles with the said Street a straight line across the Lott No. 62 to the back line of Lott No. 62 thence down the back line seventy one and a half feet to another corner of BAYLORs Lott No. 132, thence along the line of BAYLORs lott to the beginning, together with all houses out houses tenements and hereditaments to said lott belonging; To have and to hold the. premises with the appurtenances unto said CLARKE his heirs and the said GEORGE and ANN B., his Wife, and their heirs the parcel of a lott against the claims of every person unto said CLARKE his heirs will warrant and forever defend by these presents; In Witness whereof the said parties have hereunto affixed their hands and seals the day and year first above written
Signed Sealed and Delivered in presence of us
THOMAS LEGG,   GEO: FRENCH
LA; MACKINTOSH, THOS: HIESKELL   ANN FRENCH
The Commonwealth of Virginia to DAVID C. KER, FONTAINE MAURY and WILLIAM DRUMMOND, Gent., of the Corporation of Fredericksburg, Greeting, Whereas (the Commission for the privy Examination of ANN B. the Wife of GEORGE FRENCH); Witness JOHN CHEW Clerk of our said Corpo: Court the 20th day of April 1799 and in the 23rd year of the Commonwealth   JNO: CHEW
Corporation of Fredg. Sct., Pursuant to the within Commission to us directed we waited on Mrs. ANN B. FRENCH (the return of the execution of the privy Examination of ANN B. FRENCH) Given under our hands and seals this 20th day of April 1799
FONTAINE MAURY
WM. DRUMMOND
At a Court of Hustings held for the Town and Corporation of Fredericksburg the 28th day of October 1799   This Indenture was acknowledged by GEORGE FRENCH and together with the Commission annexed and Certificate of Execution thereof Indorsed are ordered to be recorded
Examd. & Deld. THOMAS ALLEN   Teste JNO: CHEW, C.C.H.

pp.   THIS INDENTURE made this second day of November in year of our Lord one
256-   thousand seven hundred and ninety nine Between JAMES LEWIS and JANE his
257   Wife of Town of Fredericksburg of one part and JOHN MINOR JUNR. of the same
place; Witnesseth that JAMES LEWIS and JANE his wife for sum of Two hundred and sixty seven pounds, fourteen shillings and three pence of lawful money of Virginia to them in hand paid by these presents do bargain and sell unto JOHN MINOR his heirs an undivided moiety of a Lott in Fredericksburg adjoining Mr. WALKER's property being the Lott whereon the said LEWIS now lives, also the moiety of Six acres of land

and one quarter lying adjoining Mr. HENDERSONs in Spotsylvania County near the Town of Fredericksburg, also the moiety of two lotts of ground in the Town of NORFOLK, late the property of WM. LEWIS, deced., Father of said JAMES, which descended to said JAMES and WILLIAM his Brother; To have and to hold all the abovementioned property unto JOHN MINOR his heirs, Provided always that if JAMES LEWIS his heirs shall pay or cause to be paid unto JOHN MINOR or his heirs the sum of One hundred and thirty three pounds seventeen shillings and one penny half penny on or before the first day of May next and the like sum on or before the first day of Novr. next with Interest thereon from the date of these presents everything therein shall be utterly void; In Witness whereof the parties to these presents have hereunto set their hands and seals the day and year first above written

Signed sealed and delivered in the presence of

THO: L. LOMAX,   JA: LEWIS JR.
BENJN. PARKE, HENRY MINOR

At a Court of Hustings held for the Town and Corporation of Fredericksburg January 25th 1800   This Indenture of Mortgage was proved by the oath of THOMAS L. LOMAX, BENJAMIN PARKE & HENRY MINOR, the witnesses thereto, and ordered to be recorded
Exd. & deld. J. MINOR   Teste   JNO: CHEW, C. C. H.

p.   KNOW ALL MEN by these presents that I JOHN FENTON MERCER of Town of
257   Fredericksburg have appointed WILLIAM HERNDON of said Town my true and
        lawful Attorney to sell and convey in my name and for my proper use one un-
divided third part of a certain tract of land lying in County of Spotsylvania which tract contains by estimation 320 acres & is held in equal parts by the aforesaid JOHN FENTON MERCER, MARY PEYTON & CHARLES C. TALIAFERRO and is commonly known by the name of DICKS QUARTER, I likewise authorise WILLIAM HERNDON to consent with aforesaid MARY PEYTON & CHARLES C. TALIAFERRO to any Devision he may deem proper & so to act & to do in the premises as I my self might do were I personally present; In Witness whereof I have hereunto set my hand and seal this 29th day of July 1799
Witness WILL: HERNDON JUNR.,   JOHN FENTON MERCER
ROBERT GOODLOE, STEPHEN McFARLINE
At a Court of Hustings held for the Town and Corporation of Fredericksburg January 25th 1800   This Power of Attorney was proved by the oath of WILLIAM HERNDON JUNR., ROBERT GOODLOE and STEPHEN McFARLINE, three witnesses thereto, and ordered to be recorded
Examd. & Deld. CHS. HOLLOWAY   Teste   JNO: CHEW, C. C. H.

pp.   THIS INDENTURE made this sixteenth day of December one thousand seven hun-
258-   dred and ninety nine Between JOHN STEWARD and LUCY his Wife of one part and
260   JOHN DARE of the other part; Witnesseth that JOHN STEWARD and LUCY his Wife
        for sum of Four hundred and fifty pounds to them in hand paid, by these pre-
sents do bargain and sell unto JOHN DARE a certain Lott of ground in Town of Fredericksburg being one half of the two lotts in said Town known by the numbers Eighty nine and Ninety formerly the property of CHARLES LEWIS Esquire, and is bounded Begining at the corner of CAROLINE and HAWKE STREETs and running thence eighty two and one half feet down CAROLINE STREET, thence runing by a line parrallel with HAWKE STREET to PRINCESS ANN STREET, thence up PRINCESS ANN STREET to HAWKE STREET & thence with HAWKE STREET to the begining; To have and to hold the lott of ground to JOHN DARE his heirs and JOHN STEWARD his heirs to JOHN DARE his heirs against the claim of every person will warrant and forever defend by these pre-sents; In Witness whereof JOHN STEWARD & LUCY his Wife have hereunto set their

hands and seals the day and year first above written
Signed sealed and Delivered in presence of
     THOMAS TOWLES,   JOHN STEWARD
     FRANCIS STEWART, GEORGE PENN JUNR.   LUCY STEWARD
     JOS; CHEW

The Commonwealth of Virginia to THOMAS TOWLES, JOSEPH CHEW & JOHN M. HERNDON
Gentlemen Greeting; Whereas (the Commission for the privy Examination of LUCY, the Wife of
JOHN STEWARD); Witness JOHN CHEW, Clerk of our said Court the 18th day of December
1799 and in the 24th year of the Commonwealth   JNO: CHEW
   In Obedience to the within Commission to us directed, we personally went to the within
named LUCY, Wife of said JOHN STEWARD; (the return of the execution of the privy examination
of LUCY STEWARD); as witness our hands and seals this 18th day of December 1799
                          THOMAS TOWLES
                          JOS: CHEW
   At a Court of Hustings held for the Town and Corporation of Fredericksburg January
25th 1800   This Indenture was acknowledged by the said STEWARD and together
with the Commission annexed and Certificate of Execution thereof by the said LUCY indorsed, are ordered to be recorded
Examd. & Deld. THO: R. ROOTES JR.   Teste JNO: CHEW, C. C. H.

pp.   This Indenture made this Seventeenth day of December in year of our Lord one
260-   thousand seven hundred and ninety nine Between JOHN DARE & ANN his Wife of
262   one part and JOHN STEWARD of the other part; Witnesseth that JOHN DARE &
       ANN his Wife for sum of Four hundred and Fifty pounds to them in hand paid, by
these presents do bargain and sell unto JOHN STEWARD a certain lott or half acre of
ground in Town of Fredericksburg being one half of two lotts in said Town knwon by
the numbers Eighty nine and Ninety and bounded (the same description as in the previous
Deed); To have and to hold the parcell of ground to JOHN STEWARD his heirs and JOHN
DARE his heirs will warrant & forever defend by these presents; Provided Always that
if JOHN DARE pay or cause to be paid unto JOHN STEWARD his heirs the just sum of Four
hundred and fifty pounds Virginia Currency on or before the first day of July one
thousand Eight hundred then these presents shall be utterly void; In Witness whereof
we have hereunto set our hands and seals the day & year first before written
Witness THOMAS SIMPSON, JOHN PATTERSON,   JOHN DARE
     F. H. ELLIOTT STURMAN, WILL: WELCH,   ANN M. DARE
     HEZH: ELLIS, ELISHA THATCHER
The Commonwealth of Virginia to DAVID C. KER & GEORGE MURRAY, Gentlemen,
Greeting, Whereas (the Commission for the privy Examination of ANN M. Wife of JOHN DARE)
Witness JOHN CHEW Clerk of our said Hustings Court the 24th day of Janry. 1800 and in
the 24th year of the Commonwealth   JNO: CHEW,
   In Obedience to the within Commission to us directed we went personally to the within
named ANN M. DARE (the return of the execution of the privy Examination of ANN M. DARE)
Given under our hands and seals this 24th day of January Eighteen hundred
                          DAVID C. KER
                          GEO: MURRAY
   At a Court of Hustings held for the Town and Corporation of Fredericksburg January
25th 1800   This Indenture was acknowledged by the said JOHN DARE and together
with the Commission annexed and Certificate of the Execution thereof by the said ANN
M., indorsed are ordered to be recorded
Exd. & deld. JOHN STEWARD   Teste JNO: CHEW, C. C. H.

pp.   THIS INDENTURE made and entered into this first day of October one thousand
263-   seven hundred and ninety nine Between RICHARD S. HACKLEY and ANN his Wife
264   and ROBERT PATTON and ANN G. his Wife of Town of Fredericksburg of one part,
         and COLIN and JAMES ROSS of the same place of other part; Witnesseth that
RICHARD S. HACKLEY and Ann his Wife and ROBERT PATTON & ANN G. his Wife for sum
of Two hundred and sixty pounds current money of Virginia to them in hand paid by
COLIN & JAMES ROSS, by these presents do each of them bargain & sell unto COLIN &
JAMES ROSS their heirs all that parcell of land lying in Town of Fredericksburg and
being part of lott number Fourteen; Beginning at JAMES ADAMS line and running on
CAROLINE STREET twenty three feet nine inches to the partition Wall of RICHARD S.
HACKLEY including half the said Wall, thence running through to SOPHIA STREET two
hundred and sixty five feet deep, thence parrellel with SOPHIA STREET twenty three
feet nine inches to said JAMES ADAMS line, thence with ADAMS line to the begining;
And also all rents profits and appurtenances belonging; To have and to hold the part of
a lott with the appurtenances unto COLIN and JAMES ROSS their heirs, and RICHARD S.
HACKLEY and ANN his Wife and ROBERT PATTON and ANN G. his Wife and their heirs
against all other persons to said COLIN and JAMES ROSS their heirs will warrant and
defend forever by these presents; In Witness whereof said RICHARD and ANN and
ROBERT and ANN G. have hereunto set their hands and seals the day and year first
above written
Signed sealed and Acknowledged in the presence of
        BENJN. PARKE,   RICHD. S. HACKLEY
        WILLIAM PORTER   ANN HACKLEY
        THOMAS WARE,   ROBT. PATTON
        FRANCIS GAINS   ANN G. PATTON
    At a Court of Hustings held for the Town and Corporation of Fredericksburg January
25th 1800   This Indenture was acknowledged by the said RICHARD S. HACKLEY and
ordered to be recorded as to him   Teste JNO: CHEW, C. C. H.
    At a Court of Hustings held for the Town & Corporation of Fredericksburg January 23rd
1802   This Indenture was acknowledged by the said ROBERT PATTON & together with
the Commission annexed and Certificate of execution thererof by said ANN HACKLEY
and ANN G. PATTON Indorsed are ordered to be recorded
Exd. & Deld. JAS. ROSS. (Comm: recorded 281)   Teste JNO: CHEW C. C. H.

pp.   THIS INDENTURE made and entered into this first day of October one thousand
265-   seven hundred and ninety nine Between RICHARD S. HACKLEY and ANN his Wife
266   and ROBERT PATTON and ANN G. his Wife of Town of Fredericksburg of one part
         and JAMES BROWN of the same place of other part; Witnesseth that said
RICHARD and ANN his Wife and ROBERT PATTON and ANN G. his Wife for sum of Two
hundred and Fifty pounds current money of Virginia to them in hand paid by JAMES
BROWN, by these presents do each of them bargain and sell unto JAMES BROWN his
heirs all that parcell of land lying in Town of Fredericksburg being part of a Lott number Fourteen, Begining at RICHARD S. HACKLEYs line and running twenty three feet six
inches front on CAROLINE STREET to the partition Wall of ROBERT PATTON, including
half the said Partition Wall, thence along PATTONs line two hundred and forty four feet
to a Warehouse seventeen feet six inches; thence twenty feet on SOPHIA STREET, thence
parrellel with SOPHIA STREET six feet to said HACKLEYs line, thence along HACKLEYs
line to the begining, and all rents profits & appurtenances to said premises belonging;
To have and to hold the part of a lott with the appurtenances unto JAMES BROWN his
heirs and the said RICHARD and ANN and ROBERT and ANN G. and their heirs against
every person to JAMES BROWN his heirs will warrant and defend by these presents; In

Witness whereof said RICHARD and ANN and ROBERT & ANN G. have hereunto set their
hands and seals the day and year first above written
Signed Sealed and Acknowledged in the presence of
     BENJN: PARKE,   RICHD. S. HACKLEY
     WILLIAM PORTER,   ANN HACKLEY
     THOMAS WARE,   ROBT. PATTON
     FRANCIS GAINES   ANN G. PATTON
   At a Court of Hustings held for the Town and Corporation of Fredg. January 25th 1800
This Indenture was acknowledged by RICHARD S. HACKLEY and ordered to be recorded
   At a Court of Hustings held for the Town and Corporation of Fredericksburg January
23rd. 1802   This Indenture was acknowledged by the sd. ROBERT PATTON and toge-
ther with the Commission annexed and Certificate of execution thereof by said ANN
HACKLEY and ANN G. PATTON, indorsed are ordered to be recorded
Exd. & deld. JAS. BROWN. (Commission recorded 280)   Teste JNO: CHEW C.C.H.

pp.   THIS INDENTURE made and entered into this seventeenth day of December one
267-   thousand seven hundred and ninety nine Between ROBERT PATTON and ANN G.
268   his Wife and RICHARD S. HACKLEY and ANN his Wife all of Town of Fredericks-
      burg of one part and JAMES BAGGOTT of same place of other part; Witnesseth
that ROBERT PATTON and ANN G. and RICHARD S. HACKLEY and ANN for sum of Two
hundred and fifty pounds lawful money of Virginia to them in hand paid by JAMES
BAGGOTT by these presents do bargin and sell unto JAMES BAGGOTT his heirs a lott of
ground lying in Town of Fredericksburg and marked number Fourteen, Begining at
COLIN & JAMES ROSS's line andruning Twenty four feet two inches front on CAROLINE
STREET to the Partition Wall of JAMES BROWNs including half the said Partition Wall,
thence along JAMES BROWNs line two hundred and sixty four feet to SOPHIA STREET,
thence parrellel with SOPHIA STREET twenty four feet two inches to COLIN and JAMES
ROSS's line, thence along said ROSS's line to the begining; and all rents profits and appurtenances belonging; To have and to hold the lott of ground unto JAMES BAGGOTT his
heirs and ROBERT PATTON and ANN G. his Wife, RICHARD S. HACKLEY and ANN his Wife
their heirs will warrant and forever defend by these presents; In Witness whereof the
said ROBERT and ANN G. and RICHARD S. and ANN have hereunto set their hands and
seals the day and year first above written
Signed sealed & acknowledged in presence of
     DAVID WILLIAMSON as to R. P.   ROBT. PATTON
     THOMAS WARE   ANN G. PATTON
     P. F. ARMISTEAD   RICHD. S. HACKLEY
                                ANN HACKLEY
   At a Court of Hustings held for the Town and Corporation of Fredericksburg January
25th 1800   This Indenture was acknowledged by the said RICHARD S. HACKLEY and
ordered to be recorded as to him
   At a Court of Hustings held for the Town & Corporation of Fredericksburg January the
23rd. 1800   This Indenture was acknowledged by said ROBERT PATTON and together
with the Commission annexed and Certificate of Execution thereof by said ANN HACK-
LEY and ANN G. PATTON Indorsed, are ordered to be recorded
Exd. & deld. GEO: BAGGOTT   (Commission Recorded 279) Teste JNO: CHEW C.C.H.

pp.   THIS IDNENTURE made and entered into this second day of November one thou-
269-   sand seven hundred and ninety nine Between RICHARD S. HACKLEY and ANN
270   his Wife of Town of Fredericksburg of one part and SAMUEL LUCAS of same
      place of other part; Witnesseth that RICHARD S. HACKLEY and ANN his Wife for

sum of one hundred and five pounds current money of Virginia to them in hand paid
by SAMUEL LUCAS, by these presents do bargain and sell unto SAMUEL LUCAS his heirs
all that parcell of land lying in Town of Fredericksburg and being part of a lott in said
Town marked number Sixteen Sixteen, Begining at REUBIN DANIEL's Corner (a part of
lott number sixteen sixteen) and runing thirty feet front on CAROLINE STREET, thence
through said lott (number sixteen sixteen) one hundred and thirty two feet to GEORGE
FRENCHes Lott number fourteen fourteen, thence with said FRENCHes line thirty feet to
said REUBIN DANIEL's Corner, thence with DANIEL's line to the begining, and all rents
profits and appurtenances belonging; To have and to hold the said aprt of a lott unto
SAMUEL LUCAS his heirs and the said RICHARD and ANN his Wife and their heirs to said
SAMUEL LUCAS his heirs will warrant and defend forever by these presents; In
Witness whereof the said RICHARD and ANN have hereunto set their hands and seals
the day and year first above written
Signed sealed and acknowledged in the presence of
        P. F. ARMISTEAD, WILLIAM PORTER,   RICHD. S. HACKLEY
        ELLIOT HACKLEY, CHAS. LEWIS,   ANN HACKLEY
        GEORGE ROTHROCK, DANIEL GRINNAN JR. to RSH
        TINSLEY CHEWNING, JOSEPH CHRISTY
  At a Court of Hustings held for the Town and Corporation of Fredericksburg January
25th 1800   This Indenture was acknowledged by said RICHARD S. HACKLEY and
ordered to be recorded
Exd. & Deld. SAML. LUCAS (Commission recorded 277)   Teste JNO: CHEW C.C.H.

pp.   THIS INDENTURE made and entered into thirteenth day of December one thou-
270-   sand seven hundred and ninety nine Between RICHARD S. HACKLEY and ANN his
272   Wife of Town of Fredericksburg of one part and GEORGE CHAPMAN of same place
       of other part; Witnesseth that RICHARD S. HACKLEY and ANNE his Wife for sum
of Thirty six pounds Fifteen shillings current money of Virginia to them in hand paid
by GEORGE CHAPMAN, by these presents do bargain and sell unto said CHAPMAN his
heirs a certain part of a lott of ground lying in Town of Fredericksburg number sixteen
sixteen or 16.16, and beginning at SAMUEL LUCAS's line runing thence ten and a half
feet on CAROLINE STREET to TIMOTHY McNAMARA's line, thence with McNAMARA's line
through to GEORGE FRENCHes lott number fourteen fourteen or 14.14; thence with
FRENCHes line to SAMUEL LUCAS's upper corner, thence with LUCAS's line to the begining; and all rents profits and appurtenances belonging; To have and to hold said
part of a lott unto GEORGE CHAPMAN his heirs and RICHARD S. HACKLEY and ANN his
Wife and their heirs the said premises shall warrant and forever defend by these presents; In Witness whereof the said parties have hereunto set their hands and seals the
day and year first above written
Acknowledged in presence of
        ANTHY: BUCK, WILLIAM JONES   RICHD. S. HACKLEY
        WILLIAM PORTER, ELISHA THATCHER   ANN HACKLEY
  At a Court of Hustings held for the Town and Corporation of Fredericksburg January
25th 1800   This Indenture was acknowledged by the said RICHARD S. HACKLEY and
ordered to be recorded
Delivered DAVID COYLE (Comm. recorded 276)   Teste JNO: CHEW, C.C.H.

pp.   THIS INDENTURE made and entered into this Twenty ninth day of September
272-   one thousand seven hundred and ninety nine Between RICHARD S. HACKLEY
274   and ANN his Wife of County of Spotsylvania and Town aforesaid of one part and
           DAVID COYLE of said County and Town of other part; Witnesseth that RICHARD S.
HACKLEY and ANN his Wife for sum of Twenty nine pounds fifteen shillings to them in
hand paid by said DAVID, by these presents doth bargain and sell unto DAVID COYLE his
heirs part of a lott of ground lying in Town of Fredericksburg described by the number
sixteen sixteen or 16.16; Beginning at the North end of the sixteen feet of ground (a part
of said lott & at the lower corner thereof) before sold to said COYLE as by Deed made to
him the Twenty sixth Instant hereof and recorded in the District Court of Fredericksburg and at the distance of nineteen feet six inches from the North corner of the
Dwelling House of said COYLE, and runing thence ten feet six inches on CAROLINE or
Mane Street, thence through said lott number sixteen sixteen or 16.16, to GEORGE
FRENCHes Lott number Fourteen Fourteen or 14.14; being one hundred and fifty two
feet, thence with said FRENCHes line ten feet six inches to the back corner of the sixteen feet before mentioned as sold to said DAVID COYLE and thence with the line to the
begining; or front on CAROLINE STREET; To have and to hold the parcell of ground unto
said COYLE his heirs and RICHARD S. HACKLEY and ANN his Wife their heirs do by these
presents warrant and forever defend against the claim of every person; Nevertheless it
is understood between RICHARD S. HACKLEY and ANN his Wife and DAVID COYLE that
whereas in laying off & runing the lines of the lott sixteen sixteen or 16.16, the said lott
does not interfere and take from the lott upon which said COYLE at present resides (and
which said COYLE purchased of ROGER DIXON as by Deed bearing date the seventh day of
March 1789 and recorded in the Court of Hustings of ye Corporation) Four feet six
inches of said lott is is understood that said RICHARD S. HACKLEY now conveyes to said
COYLE the right and title in fee simple of said Four feet six inches and that the same is
included in the above ten feet six inches; In Witness whereof said RICHARD S. and ANN
his Wife have hereunto set their hands and seals the day and year first above written
Signed Sealed & Acknowledged in presence of
        ANTHY. BUCK,   WILLIAM JONES,   RICHD. S. HACKLEY
        WILLIAM PORTER, ELISHA THATCHER   ANN HACKLEY
  At a Court of Hustings held for the Town and Corporation of Fredericksburg January
25th 1800   This Indenture was acknowledged by the said RICHARD S. HACKLEY and
ordered to be recorded
(Commission recorded 278)

pp.   THIS INDENTURE made this first day of September Anno Domini one thousand
274-   seven hundred and ninety nine Between SUSANNAH HEATH and JAMES HEATH of
276   one part and JAMES CARMICHAEL of the second part; Witnesseth that SUSANNAH
           HEATH and JAMES HEATH in consideration of the Covenants Rents & agreements
hereafter expressed by these presents do bargain and sell unto JAMES CARMICHAEL or
assigns a lott of ground lying in Town of Fredericksburg, begining at THOMAS BARWISE
Corner on the Main Street, thence with his House back eighteen feet, thence across
parallel with the Main Street nine feet to SUSANNA HEATH's Compting Room, thence
Eighteen feet parallel with THOMAS BARWISE's House to the said Main Street, thence
nine feet parallel with the back line on the Main Street to the begining; To have and to
hold the part of above lott with all its appurtenances unto JAMES CARMICHAEL or
assigns during the full term of Twenty one years next ensuing the date of these presents paying unto said SUSANNA and JAMES HEATH or assigns the sum of Four pounds 19
shillings on the first day of September 1800 and the same sum each succeeding year
and JAMES CARMICHAEL doth covenant that he will pay Taxes & Publick incumbrances

which may accrue; In Testimony whereof the parties have hereunto set their hands
and seals the day & year aforesaid
Signed sealed & delivered in presence of

PHILIP HENSHAW,	SUSANNA HEATH
JOSA: INGHAM,	JAMES HEATH
WILLIAM HERNDON JUNR.	JAMES CARMICHAEL

At a Court of Hustings held for the Town and Corporation of Fredericksburg January
25th 1800   This Indenture was proved by the oath of PHILIP HENSHAW, JOSHUA
INGHAM and WILLIAM HERNDON JUNR. the witnesses thereto and ordered to be recorded
Examd. & Delivered JAS: CARMICHAEL   Teste   JNO: CHEW, C. C. H.

pp.   The Commonwealth of Virginia to GEORGE FRENCH, DAVID C. KER & GEO: MUR-
276-   RAY Gentlemen Greeting, Whereas (the Commission for the privy Examination of
277   ANN, the Wife of RICHARD S. HACKLEY for Indenture of Bargain and Sale unto GEORGE
        CHAPMAN bearing date 13th day of December 1799); Witness JOHN CHEW, Clerk of our
said Hustings Court the 19th day of December 1799 and in the 24th year of the Commonwealth   JNO: CHEW
  Corporation of Fredg. to wit: Pursuant to the within Commission, we the Subscribers
(the return of the execution of the privy examination of ANN HACKLEY); Given under our hands
and seals this (blank)   GEO: FRENCH
                                              DAVID C. KER

pp.   The Commonwealth of Virginia to GEORGE FRENCH, DAVID C. KER and GEORGE
277-   MURRAY Gentlemen, Greeting, Whereas (the Commission for the privy Examination of
278   ANN, the Wife of RICHARD S. HACKLEY, for Indenture of Bargain and Sale bearing date the
        2nd day of November 1799 to SAMUEL LUCAS); Witness JOHN CHEW, Clerk of our said
Court the 6th day of December 1799 and in the 24th year of the Commonwealth
  Corporation of Fredg. to wit: Pursuant to the within Commission, we the subscribers
(the return of the execution of the examination of ANN HACKLEY); Given under our hands and
seals this 20th day of December 1799   GEO: FRENCH
Truly Recorded Teste JNO. CHEW, C. C. H.   DAVID C. KER
Exd. & Deld. SAML. LUCAS

pp.   The Commonwealth of Virginia to GEORGE FRENCH, DAVID C. KER and GEORGE
278-   MURRAY Gentlemen, Greeting: Whereas (the Commission for the privy Examination
279   of ANN, the Wife of RICHARD S. HACKLEY, for Indenture of Bargain and Sale bearing date
        the 29th day of September 1799 to DAVID COYLE); Witness JOHN CHEW, Clerk of our
said Hustings Court the 18th day of December 1799 and in the 24th year of the Commonwealth   JNO: CHEW
  Corporation of Fredg., to wit; Pursuant to the within Commission, we the Subscribers
(the return of the execution of the examination of ANN HACKLEY); Given under our hands and
seals this 20th day of Decr. 1799   GEO: FRENCH
                                             DAVID C. KER

pp.   The Commonwealth of Virginia to GEORGE FRENCH, DAVID C. KER and GEORGE
279-   MURRAY Gentlemen, Greeting: Whereas (the Commission for the privy Examination of
280   ANN, the Wife of RICHARD S. HACKLEY, for Indenture of Bargain and Sale bearing date the
        17th day of December 1799 to JAMES BAGGOTT); Witness JOHN CHEW, Clerk of our said
Court the 18th day of December 1799 and in the 24th year of the Commonwealth
  Corporation of Fredg., to wit: Pursuant to the within Commission, we the Subscribers
(the return of the execution of the privy examination of ANN HACKLEY);

                                                        GEO: FRENCH
Truly Recorded Teste JNO: CHEW, C. C. H.   DAVID C. KER
Exd. & deld. J. BAGGOTT

pp.   The Commonwealth of Virginia to GEORGE FRENCH, DAVID C. KER and GEORGE
280-   MURRAY Gentlemen, Greeting, Whereas (the Commission for the privy Examinations
281   of ANN, the Wife of RICHARD S. HACKLEY and of ANN G., the Wife of ROBERT PATTON for
           an Indenture of Bargain and Sale bearing date the first day of October 1799 unto JAMES
BROWN); Witness JOHN CHEW Clerk of our said Court the 18th day of Decr. 1799 and in the
24th year of the Commonwealth   JNO: CHEW
  Corporation of Fredg.,to wit: Pursuant to the within Commission, we the Subscribers
did on the 20th day of December 1799 examine the within named ANN HACKLEY and on
the 14th day of March 1800 did examine the within named ANN GORDON PATTON (the
return of the execution of the privy examinations of ANN HACKLEY and ANN GORDON PATTON);
Given under our hands and seals this 14th day of March 1800
Truly recorded Test J. CHEW C. C. H.   GEO: FRENCH
Exd. & Deld. JAS. BROWN   DAVID C. KERR

pp.   The Commonwealth of Virginia to GEORGE FRENCH, DAVID C. KERR and GEORGE
281-   MURRAY Gentlemen, Greeting, Whereas (the Commission for the privy Examinations
282   of ANN the Wife of RICHARD S. HACKLEY and ANN G., the Wife of ROBERT PATTON for an
           Indenture bearing date the first day of October 1799 unto COLIN & JAMES ROSS) ; Wit-
           ness JOHN CHEW Clerk of our said Court the 18th day of December 1799 and in the
24th year of the Commonwealth   JNO: CHEW
  Corpo. of Fredg. to wit; Pursuant to the within Commission, we the Subscribers did on
the 20th day of December 1799 examine the within named ANN HACKLEY and on the
14th day of March 1800 did examined the within named ANN GORDON PATTON; the return
of the executions of the privy examinations of ANN HACKLEY and ANN GORDON PATTON); Given
under our hands and seals this 14th day of March 1800
Truly recorded Teste   J. CHEW. C. C. H.   GEO: FRENCH
Exd. & Deld. JS. ROSS   DAVID C. KER

pp.   THIS INDENTURE made this 25th day of July one thousand seven hundred and
283-   ninety nine Between JOSEPH NORWOOD of Town of Fredericksburg of one part
284   and SAMUEL LUCAS of the Town aforesaid of other part; Witnesseth that where-
           as JOSEPH NORWOOD is now greatly indebted unto SAMUEL LUCAS in the just sum
of One hundred and forty pounds Virginia currency which money will become due the
fifthteenth day of October next ensuing the date hereof, and being willing to secure the
payment of said money to SAMUEL LUCAS as far as in his power lies; does hereby make
over and convey unto SAMUEL LUCAS his heirs two Negro Women, one by the name of
Delphia and the other by the name of Cate, To have and to hold the said slaves unto said
LUCAS in Trust that in case the said money is not paid when it becomes due and after
the space of ninety days thereafter, then it shall be lawful for SAML. LUCAS (after
giving ten days publick notice) for ready money to pay himself the aforesaid sum of
money with any interest that may accrue on the same, also the costs of sale, and the
residue, if any, to go to said JOSEPH NORWOOD his heirs, and in case the said sale should
take place the said NORWOOD hereby agrees to convey the said slaves unto the Purchaser or Purchasers clear of any claim from him or his heirs. In Witness whereof the
said parties ahve hereunto set their hands & seals
Witness: WILL: WELCH   JOSEPH NORWOOD

(The memorandum to pay any amount not covered by the sale is witnessed by JAMES SLATER.)
At a Court of Hustings held for the Town & Corporation of Fredericksburg March 22nd 1800.   This Indenture of Mortgage for slaves from JOSEPH NORWOOD of the one part and SAMUEL LUCAS of the other part; was proved by the oath of WILLIAM WELCH a witness thereto and together with the writing thereon indorsed which was proved by the oath of JAMES SLATER, a Witness thereto are ordered to be recorded

pp.   THIS INDENTURE made and entered into this 10th day of April in the year one
284-   thousand Eight hundred Between DAVID C. KER and MARGARET his Wife of Town
286   of Frederickburg of one part and JOHN W. BAYLOR of County of CAROLINE of
          other part; Witnesseth that DAVID C. KER and MARGARET his Wife for the sum of
One Dollar to them in hand paid by JOHN W. BAYLOR by these presents do bargain and sell unto JOHN W. BAYLOR his heirs a certain lott of ground being in Town of Fredericksburg on the Streets PRINCESS AUGUSTA and FEDORIC and known by number Two hundred and nineteen, together with all houses and appurtenances belonging; To have and to hold said lott of ground unto JOHN W. BAYLOR his heirs and DAVID C. KER and MARGARET his Wife and their heirs the lott of ground against all persons to said JOHN W. BAYLOR his heirs will warrant and forever defend by these presents; In Witness whereof the said DAVID C. KER and MARGARET his Wife have hereunto set their hands and seals the day and year first above written
Signed Sealed and Acknowledged in presence of us
          JOHN BENSON, ROBT. CASEY,   DAVID C. KER
          CHARLES BENSON   MARGARET KER
    At a Court of Hustings held for the Town & Corporation of Frederickburg the 26th day of April 1800   This Indenture was acknowledged by the said DAVID S. KER and ordered to be recorded

pp.   THIS INDENTURE made and entered into this nineteenth day of February in
286-   year of our Lord one thousand Eight hundred Between ROBERT PATTON & ANN G.
289   his Wife and ROBERT S. HACKLEY and ANN his Wife of Town of Fredericksburg
          of one part and RICHARD JOHNSTON of same place of other part; Witnesseth that
ROBERT & ANN G. and RICHARD S. & ANN in consideration of the sum of Three hundred and two pounds lawfull money of Virginia to them in hand paid by RICHARD JOHNSTON by these presents bargain and sell unto RICHARD JOHNSTON his heirs all that parcel of ground lying in Town of Fredericksburg and is part of a lot in said Town number Fourteen; Begining at the lower corner of GEORGE FRENCH's Lott number Sixteen upon which stands a STONE HOUSE lately occupied by GEORGE NORWOOD), and runing on CAROLINE STREET twenty three feet nine inches to the Partition Wall of said JOHNSONs tenement number Two, including half the Wall, thence runing through to SOPHIA STREET two hundred and sixty four feet, thence parrellel with SOPHIA STREET twenty three feet nine inches to GEO: FRENCH's Lot number Fifteen, thence with said FRENCH's line to the begining; and all the rents issues profits and appurtenances belonging; To have and to hold the part of a lot with the appurtenances unto RICHARD JOHNSON his heirs and ROBERT & ANN and RICHARD S. and ANN and their heirs the said premises against all persons to said JOHNSON his heirs will warrant and forever defend by these presents; In Witness whereof said ROBERT & ANN G. and RICHARD S. & ANN have hereunto set their hands and seals the day and year first above written
Signed sealed and acknowledged in the presence of
          THOMAS WARE,   ROBT. PATTON
          DAVID WILLIAMSON,   ANN G. PATTON

<table>
<tr><td>FRANCIS GAINES,   WM. BARBER,</td><td>RICHD. S. HACKLEY</td></tr>
<tr><td>JAMES DONOHOE,   BARTHO: BLUNT</td><td>ANN HACKLEY</td></tr>
</table>

The Commonwealth of Virginia to GEORGE FRENCH and GEORGE MURRAY Gentlemen, Greeting, Whereas (the Commission for the privy Examination of ANN G., the Wife of ROBERT PATTON); Witness JOHN CHEW, Clerk of our said Hustings Court the 1st day of March 1800 and in the 24th year of the Commonwealth

Corporation of Fredericksburg, Sct. In Obedience to the within Commission to us directed, we this day (the return of the execution of the privy Examination of ANN G. PATTON) Given under our hands and seals this first day of March 1800

GEO: FRENCH
GEO: MURRAY

The Commonwealth of Virginia to WILLIAM WINCHESTER, WILLIAM RUSSELL of the County of BALTIMORE in the State of MARYLAND Gentlemen, Greeting; (the Commission for the privy Examination of ANN, the Wife of RICHARD S. HACKLEY); Witness JOHN CHEW, Clerk of our said Hustings Court the 1st day of March 1800 and in the 24th year of our Commonwealth   JNO: CHEW

CITY of BALTIMORE, to wit; On the 29th day of March in the year 1800 before us the Subscribers, Justices of BALTIMORE County, personally appeared ANN HACKLEY, the Wife of RICHARD S. HACKLEY (the return of the execution of the privy Examination of ANN HACKLEY); Witness our hands and seals the day and year above written

W. WINCHESTER
WM. RUSSELL

At a Court of Hustings held for the Town and Corporaltion of Fredericksburg April 26th 1800   This Indenture was proved by the oath of WILLIAM BARBER, JAMES DONOHOE & BARTHO: BLUNT three of the witnesses thereto and together with the Commission annexed and Certificates of the acknowledgment thereof by the said ANN G. PATTON and ANN HACKLEY indorsed, are ordered to be recorded
Exd. & deld. RICHD. JOHNSTON   Teste JNO: CHEW C. C. H.

pp.   THIS INDENTURE made and entered into this 1st day of October One thousand
291-   seven hundred and ninety nine Between RICHARD S. HACKLEY and ANN his Wife
293   and ROBERT PATTON and ANN G. his Wife of Town of Fredericksburg of one part
             and RICHARD JOHNSTON of same place of other part; Witnesseth that said
RICHARD and ANN his Wife and ROBERT and ANN G. his Wife for sum of Two hundred and fifty four pounds current money of Virginia to them in hand paid by RICHARD JOHNSON, by these presents do bargainand sell unto RICHARD JOHNSTON his heirs all that parcell of land lying in Town of Fredericksburg and being a part of a lott in said Town marked as number Fourteen, begining at HASLEWOOD FARISHes line and runing twenty three feet front on CAROLINE STREET to the Partition Wall of JAMES ADAM including half of said Partition Wall, thence through to SOPHIA STREET two hundred & sixty four feet deep, thence parrallel with SOPHIA STREET twenty three feet to HASLE-WOOD FARISHes line, thence with said FARISHes line to the begining; And also all rents issue profits and appurtenances belonging; To have and to hold the said aprt of a lot with appurtenances unto RICHARD JOHNSTON his heirs, and the said RICHARD and ANN and ROBERT and ANN G. their heirs against all persons to RICHARD JOHNSTON his heirs shall warrant and defend forever by these presents; In Witness whereof the said RICHARD and ANN and ROBERT and ANN G. have hereunto set their hands and seals the day and year first above written
Signed Sealed and Acknowledged in the presence of

<table>
<tr><td>BENJN. PARKE as to RSH</td><td>RICHD. S. HACKLEY</td></tr>
<tr><td>WILLIAM PORTER do.</td><td>ANN HACKLEY</td></tr>
</table>

THOMAS WARE ass to H & P   ROBT. PATTON
FRANCIS GAINES   ANN G. PATTON

At a Court of Hustings held for the Town and Corporation of Fredericksburg April 26th 1800 This Indenture was proved by the oath of WILLIAM PORTER, BENJAMIN PARKE and THOMAS WARE as to the execution thereof by RICHARD S. HACKLEY and by the oath of said WARE as to the execution thereof by the said ROBERT PATTON and ordered to be recorded as to RICHARD S. HACKLEY; And at a Court of Hustings held for the Town & Corporation of Freds:burg January 23rd 1802, This Indenture was acknowledged by the said ROBERT PATTON & ordered to be recorded as to him
Exd. & Delivered RICHARD JOHNSTON with Comm.
Deed returned & Comm. recorded folio 393.   Teste JNO: CHEW, C. C. H.

pp.   THIS INDENTURE made this eleventh day of November in year of our Lord one
293- thousand seven hundred and ninety nine Between WALKER RANDOLPH CARTER
297   and SALLY CHAMPE his Wife of the Corporation of Fredericksburg of one part
and STEPHEN WINCHESTER of the Corporation aforesaid of other part; Witnesseth that WALKER R. CARTER and SALLY C. his Wife for sum of Two hundred & seventy five dollars to them in hand paid by STEPHEN WINCHESTER by these presents do bargain and sell unto STEPHEN WINCHESTER his heirs two lotts of ground lying in Town of Fredericksburg known by the numbers 69 & 70; and bounded on the North by PITT STREET, on the East by the RIVER RAPPAHANNOCK, on the South by HAWKE STREET and on the West by SOPHIA STREET; which Lotts WALKER R. CARTER of JOHN FERNEYHOUGH and MARGARET his Wife as by an Indenture of Bargain & Sale from said FERNEYHOUGH & Wife to said CARTER bearing date the 29th day of August 1796 and duly recorded in the District Court of Fredericksburg will appear; together with all houses gardens ways advantages & appurtenances to said lotts belonging; To have and to hold the said two lotts of ground with the appurtenances unto STEPHEN WINCHESTER his heirs and WAL-KER R. CARTER and SALLY C. his Wife andtheir heirs the two lotts of ground with all appurtenances against the calim of all persons unto said STEPHEN WINCHESTER his heirs shall and do by these presents warrant and forever defend; In Witness whereof WALKER R. CARTER and SALLY CHAMPE his Wife have hereunto set their hands and affixed their seals the day month and year first above written
Signed sealed and Delivered in the presence of   W. R. CARTER
      (no witnesses shown)   SALLY CHAMPE CARTER
The Commonwealth of Virginia to GEORGE MURRAY, DAVID C. KER and WILLIAM DRUMMOND Gentlemen, Greeting; Whereas (the Commission for the privy Examination of SALLY CHAMP, Wife of WALKER RANDOLPH CARTER); Witness JOHN CHEW Clerk of our said Court the 12th day of November 1799 and in the 23rd year of the Commonwealth
In Obedience to the within Commission to us directed (the return of the execution of the privy Examination of SALLY CHAMPE CARTER); Given under our hands and seals this twelfth day of November 1799   DAVID C. KER
                              W. DRUMMOND
At a Court of Hustings held for the Town & Corporation of Fredericksburg April 26th 1800 This Indenture was acknowledged by the said WALKER R. CARTER and together with the Commission annexed and Certificate of the Execution thereof by the said SALLY CHAMPE CARTER indorsed, are ordered to be recorded
Exd. & deld. S. WINCHESTER's Clerk   Teste JNO: CHEW, C. C. H.

pp.   THIS INDENTURE made the fifteenth day of April Anno Domini Eighteen hun-
297-   dred Between WALKER R. CARTER of Town of Fredericksburg of one part and
298   RICHARD WINCHESTER of other part; Witnesseth that WALKER R. CARTER in
         order to secure the payment money which he now owes as well as that which he
may at any time hereafter owe to a certain STEPHEN WINCHESTER by Bond Note or
Account and in consideration of One dollar to him in hand paid by said RICHARD
WINCHESTER by these presents doth bargain and sell unto RICHARD WINCHESTER the
lots No. Sixty eight situate lying and being in Town of Fredericksburg together with the
houses thereon now in the occupancy of said WALKER R. CARTER; To have and to hold
the said Lotts and Houses unto RICHARD WINCHESTER his heirs upon Trust nevertheless
that said RICHARD WINCHESTER shall as soon as convenient he can (after having advertised the time and place of the sale of the property in some public Newspaper
nearest to the residence of said WALKER R. CARTER) proceed to sell the same to the
highest bidder for the best price that can be obtained and out of the monies arising
from the sale in the first place to pay and satisfy all reasonable charges attending such
sale and then the debts above mentioned and residue of the monies arising from such
sale to the use of WALKER R. CARTER, In Witness whereof WALKER R. CARTER hath
hereunto set his hand and seal the day and year first above written
Signed Sealed and Delivered in the presence of
         (no witnesses shown)   W. R. CARTER
  At a Court of Hustings held for the Town and Corporation of Fredericksburg April 26th
1800 This Indenture was acknowledged by the said WALKER R. CARTER and ordered to
be recorded
Exd. & Deld. WM. BROOKE for RICHD. WINCHESTER   Teste   JNO: CHEW, C. C. H.

pp.   THIS INDENTURE made and entered into this 25th day of April in the year one
299-   thousand Eight hundred Between JOHN BENSON of Town of Fredericksburg of one
300   part and DAVID C. KER of Town aforesaid of other part; Witnesseth that JOHN
         BENSON for sum of One Dollar to him in hand paid by DAVID C. KER by these
presents doth bargain and sell unto DAVID C. KER his heirs a certain parcel or part of a
lot of ground No. 17 lying in Town of Fredericksburg on CAROLINE STREET begining at
the lot in the possession of the WIDOW ROSS running eighteen feet up CAROLINE STREET
thence back the lot occupied by MARY SULLIVAN and thence along said SULLIVANs
line WIDOW ROSS's dividing line and thence to the begining, together with all the
houses priviledges and appurtenances to said lott of ground belonging; To have and to
hold the said lot of ground with all appurtenances unto DAVID C. KER his heirs and
JOHN BENSON his heirs the lot of ground against all persons to said DAVID C. KER his
heirs will warrant and forever defend by these presents; In Witness whereof JOHN
BENSON hath hereunto set his hand and seal the day and year first above written
Signed sealed and acknowledged in the presence of
    JOHN B. BENSON,   JOHN BENSON
    NIMROD CHISHOLME, WM. TODD
  At a Court of Hustings held for the Town and Corporation of Fredericksburg April 26th
1800   This Indenture was acknowledged by the said JOHN BENSON and ordered to be
recorded   Teste JNO: CHEW, C. C. H.

pp.   THIS INDENTURE made the seventeenth day of May in the year one thousand
300-   Eight hundred Between JOSEPH JONES of County of LOUDOUN of one part and
301   JOHN LEWIS of Town of Fredericksburg of other part; Witnesseth that said
         JOSEPH for the sum of Seven hundred and fifty pounds to him in hand paid by

the said JOHN, by these presents doth bargain and sell unto said JOHN his heirs a certain lott of ground lying in Town of Fredericksburg on the RIVER RAPPAHANNOCK known by the name of the BREWERY LOTT No. 272; (which said moiety was formerly purchased by PRESOR BOWDEN of the Town of NORFOLK of GEORGE THORNTON Esqr. deceased and sold by said BOWDEN to said JOSEPH and afterwards conveyed to said JOSEPH by GEORGE THORNTON, Son and heir of GEORGE THORNTON deceased as will appear by a Deed from said GEORGE to said JOSEPH on Record in the District Court of Fredericksburg and is bounded, Begining on the said River at the lower end of a lott of ground owned by DAVID and JAMES BLAIR and runing with their line to WATER STREET, thence down and with WATER STREET to a Lott of Doctr. CHARLES MORTIMER, thence with his line to the River, thence up and along the River to the begining, together with all the buildings profits emoluments and appurtenances to the said Lott belonging; To have and to hold the described Lott of Ground unto the said JOHN his heirs and the said JOSEPH and his heirs the said Lott of Ground free from the claim of every person will and do warrant and forever defend by these presents In Witness whereof the said JOSEPH hath here-unto set his hand and seal the day and year first above written
Signed sealed and delivered in the presence of us
      WM. PEARSON   JOS: JONES
      GEORGE ROTHROCK, JOSA: INGHAM
  At a Court of Hustings held for the Town and Corporation of Fredericksburg on Satur-day the 28th of June 1800   This Indenture from JOSEPH JONES to JOHN LEWIS was proved by the oaths of WILLIAM PEARSON, GEORGE ROTHROCK and JOSHUA INGHAM the three witnesses thereto and ordered to be recorded
Exd. & deld. Mr. ROBT. LEWIS   Teste JNO: CHEW, C. C. H.

pp.   THIS INDENTURE made this 31st day of November in year of our Lord one
301-   thousand seven hundred and ninety nine Between GEORGE W. B. SPOONER of
303   Town of Fredericksburg of one part and JACOB KUHN of Town aforesaid of other
             part; Witnesseth that GEORGE W. B. SPOONER in order to secure the payment of
the sum of Seven hundred Dollars due on account to JOAQUIN MOUTEIRE of the City of NEW YORK for MADEIRA WINES and in consideration of the sum of one Dollar to him in hand paid by said JACOB KUHN said GEORGE W. B. SPOONER doth bargain and sell unto JACOB KUHN three feather beds with bedsteads and furniture compleat, one mattress and Cot, one Crib with furniture, one Chest of Drawers, one Book Case, three Writing Desks, four Walnut Tables, one small ditto; two large Pine ditto, three pier glasses, one Dressing ditto, one large walnut armed chair, eighteen windsor and six flag chairs, one case Bottle and Stand, two carpetts, one water and tea Equipage, one hundred pieces Crockery ware consisting of plates dishes &c., one large painted chest, one large copper kettle, six pots, two ovens, one frying pan, two skillets, four pewter dishes, one doz. pewter plates, four water ditto, one set large scales and wates, twleve pictures in frames, six candle sticks, one thosuand bushell of Ashes at the Manufactury, ten barrells of Rossin, two large Iron Kettles, nine stands of pewter Moulds, two frames for diping candles with a shaft and table, two thousand weight of hard soap, Five hundred weight dips and mould candles, one thousand weight of hard Soap, Five hundred weight of Tallow and eight emty hhds. or tubs; To have and to hold the said property herein mentioned Upon Trust nevertheless that the said JACOB KUHN as soon as conveniently he can (after advertizing the time and place of the sale of the property aforementioned in some publick newspaper) proceed to sell the same to the highest bidder for the best price that can be obtained and out of the monies arising from the sale in the first place to pay and satisfy all reasonable charges attending such sale and then the Debt afore-

mentioned; and the residue of the monies arising from such sale to the use of GEORGE W. B. SPOONER his heirs or to such person he shall by writing under his hand appoint; In Witness whereof have set hand and affixed seal the day and year first written Signed sealed and Delivered in the presence of

WILLIAM VASS;   GEO: W. B. SPOONER
DAVID ESPEY, GEO: D. ASHTON   JACOB KUHN

At a Court of Hustings held for the Town and Corporation of Fredericksburg on Saturday the 16th day of July 1800   This Indenture of Trust was acknowledged by the parties thereto and ordered to be recorded

p.   KNOW ALL MEN by these presents and it is witnessed by this Indenture that I
303   FRANCIS BROOKE, an Attorney in fact for JOHN BROOKE, do by these presents
          emancipate and set free from slavery and all further service, a Negroe slave called Hester for and during the remainder of her life. In Witness whereof I have hereunto set my hand and seal this 27th day of May 1797

                                        FRANCIS BROOKE
                               Attorney in Fact for JOHN BROOKE

At a Court of Hustings held for the Town and Corporation of Fredericksburg on Saturday the 27th day of May 1797   This Letter of Emancipation from FRANCIS T. BROOKE, Attorney in fact for JOHN T. BROOKE to his slave, Hester, was acknowledged by the said FRANCIS T. BROOKE and ordered to be recorded

pp.   KNOW ALL MEN by these presents that I WILLIAM A. DAINGERFIELD, Student of
304-   Medicine in the City of LONDON, and formerly of the County of Spotsylvania in
306   the State of Virginia (hereby first solemnly revoking all former power or
          powers by me made to any person or persons whatsoever to act in my behalf touching the premises) by these presents ordain and appoint DAVID HENDERSON of the Town of Fredericksburg in State of Virginia, Merchant, to be my true and lawful Attorney, First to bargain sell and dispose of for my use the following Negroe slaves in the said County being my property, Vizt., Benjamin a Negro man, Sarah a Negro woman and her two Sons, Isaac and Abraham, and to the purchaser or purchasers of said Negro slaves true and lawful Title or Titles to make and the money arising from such sale or sales to receive and hold subject to my will and disposal and for the above purposes to exercise all the right power and authority that I the said WILLIAM A. DAINGERFIELD then rightful owner could do if present; Secondly, for me and in my name to demand and receive all debts owing unto me and I do ratify and confirm all my Attorney shall legally do touching the premises; In Witness whereof I have hereunto set my hand and seal the Fifteenth day of July in year of our Lord one thousand Eight hundred
Sealed & Delivered in the presence of
          W. PAINE, R. JOHNSTON   WM. A. DAINGERFIELD

At a Court of Hustings held for the Town and Corporation of Fredericksburg the 24th day of January 1801   This Letter of Attorney from WILLIAM DAINGERFIELD to DAVID HENDERSON together with the Certificate of WILLIAM GIBSON, Notary Publick Dwelling in LONDON and of JOHN HAWKINS and WILLIAM DUFF, Notary Publicks, (also of LONDON); are on the motion of the said DAVID HENDERSON ordered to be recorded

pp.   THIS INDENTURE made this Twentieth day of June Anno Dom: one thousand
307-   eight hundred between PATRICK HOME, Exr. and Devisee of JAMES HUNTER
309   deced., of STAFFORD County of one part and MARY SULLIVAN of other part of

the Town of Fredericksburg, Witnesseth t. ..t PATRICK HOME, Exr. & devisee of JAMES
HUNTER deced. for sum of Three hundred and fifty pounds to him in hand paid by said
MARY SULLIVAN by these presents do bargain and sell unto MARY SULLIVAN her heirs
all that parcell of land lying in Town of Fredericksburg and bounded, Begining at the
corner House of RICHARD PEACOCK on PRUSSIA STREET, thence with said Street North
sixty two East eight pole to WATER STREET, thence up WATER STREET North twenty eight
West fourteen poles five feet six inches, thence with the line of the lott belonging to
the Estate of JAMES HUNTER JR. deceased, South seventy five West seven poles thirteen
feet, South three East eight feet six inches, thence North seventy one and a half East
five feet six inches to the Corner of the BRICK HOUSE, thence with the end of said House
South eighteen and half East twenty five feet and from thence South twenty seven East
fourteen poles twelve inches to the begining; containing One hundred and nineteen
and a half square poles, Together with all profits and appurtenances to said parcel of
land belonging; To have and to hod the parcel of land and all the premises unto MARY
SULLIVAN her heirs and PATRICK HOME, Exr. and Devisee of JAMES HUNTER deced., his
heirs the parcel of land unto MARY SULLIVAN her heirs shall warrant and forever
defend by these presents; In Witness whereof PATRICK HOME hath set his hand and
affixed his seal the day and year above written
Signed Sealed & Delivered in the presence of
   JOS: ENNEVER,   PAT: HOME
   C. HOLLOWAY, JOHN BENSON, Exor. & Devisee of JAS. HUNTER deced
   JAMES SMOCK, JAMES ADAM,
   JOSEPH CHRISTY
 At a Court of Hustings held for the Town and Corporation of Fredericksburg January
24th 1801 This Indenture was proved by the Oath of JAMES SMOCK, JAMES ADAM
and JOSEPH CHRISTY three of the witnesses thereto and ordered to be recorded
Exd. & Deld. BURWELL LEAVELL,
   Owner of the property   Teste JNO: CHEW, C. C. H.

p. KNOW ALL MEN by these presents that I MARGARET JULIAN of Town of
309 Fredericksburg in consideration of the natural love and affection which I bear
   unto MILDRED ABBOTT as well as for the further consideration of One Dollar to
me in hand paid by these presents do give and grant unto MILDRED ABBOTT and assigns
the following slaves, Vizt., a Negroe Woman slave named Anne, her Child named Fanny
and a Negroe girl named Pol, together with all and every the future increase of them
the said slaves; To have and to hold the said slaves with their increase unto MILDRED
ABBOTT and assigns; In Witness whereof I have hereunto fixed my hand and seal this
(blank) in year of our Lord one thousand seven hundred and ninety nine
Sealed & Delivered in presence of
   ROBERT MERCER,   MARGT. JULIAN
   THOMAS DANIELL   Acknowledged 24th January 1801
   W. R. CARTER   THOS: COCHRAN
            JAMES LILLY
 At a Court of Hustigns held for the Town and Corporation of Fredericksburg January
24th 1801 This Deed of Gift was proved by the oath of THOS: COCHRAN and JAMES
LILLY two of the witnesses thereto and ordered to be recorded

p. KNOW ALL MEN by these presents that I MARGARET JULIAN of Town of
310 Fredericksburg in consideration of the natural love and affection which I bear
   to JOHN JULIAN ABBOTT as well as for the further consideration of One Dollar

in hand paid by these presents do give and grant unto JOHN JULIAN ABBOTT and assigns the following slaves, Vizt., Negro Woman Rose with all her future offspring, also a Negro Boy named Daniel, the said slave now being in possession of said MARGARET JULIAN; To have and to hold said slaves unto JOHN JULIAN ABBOTT and assigns, But in case JOHN JULIAN ABBOTT should die before his arrival at the age of Twenty one years or intermarriage I then give unto my Daughter, MILDRED ABBOTT, Mother of said JOHN JULIAN ABBOTT (or in case of her death before that of the said JOHN) to her legal representative in consideratin of the natural love and affection I bear her and a farther consideration of One Dollar the aforesaid slaves to be disposed in such manner as she may ordain by her last Will and Testament; In Witness whereof I have hereunto affixed my hand and seal this (blank) in the year of our Lord one thousand seven hundred and ninety nine

Sealed & Delivered in presence of
    ROBERT MERCER.   MARGT. JULIAN
    THOMAS DANIELL, THOS: COCHRAN
    W R. CARTER,   JAMES LILLY   Acknowledged on 24 Jany. 1801.

At a Court of Hustings held for the Town and Corporation of Fredericksburg January 24th 1801   This Deed of Gift was proved by the oath of THOMAS COCHRAN & JAMES LILLY, two of the witnesses thereto and ordered to be recorded

p.   KNOW ALL MEN by these presents that I MARGARET JULIAN of the Town of
311   Fredg. in consideratin of the natural love and affection which I bear to my
       Daughter, LUCY DUNN, as well as for the further sum of One Dollar to me in hand paid, by these presents do give and grant unto LUCY DUNN for her natural life the following slaves, a Negro woman named Clary with her Son, Richmond, and a Negroe girl named Voilet with all the future increase of them the said slaves; To have and to hold the said slaves during her life and after her death the abovenamed with their increase to be equally divided between her Children; In Witness whereof I have hereunto affixed my hand and seal this 18th day of April in year of our Lord one thousand Eight hundred

Sealed & Delivered in the presence of
    THOS: L. JOHNSTON,   MARGT. JULIAN
    BENJN: PARKE
Acknowledged 24th Janry. 1801   THOS: COCHRAN
                             JAMES LILLY

At a Court of Hustings held for the Town and Corporation of Fredericksburg January 24th 1801   This Deed of Gift was proved by the oath of THOMAS COCHRAN and JAMES LILLY two of the witnesses thereto and ordered to be recorded

pp   THIS INDENTURE made the twenty sixth day of August in year of our Lord one
312-   thousand eight hundred and in the twenty fifth year of the Independence of the
315   United States of America, Between WILLIAM REAT and CATHERINE, both of Town
      of Fredericksburg of one part and JOHN NEWTON, Merchant, in Town of
Fredericksburg of other part; Witnesseth that WILLIAM REAT and CATHERINE for sum of Five pounds current money of Virginia to WILLIAM REAT and CATHERINE his Wife in hand paid by JOHN NEWTON, by these presents do bargain sell and confirm unto JOHN NEWTON his heirs all that parcell of land in Town of Fredericksburg lying on CAROLINE STREET twenty four feet eight inches to the lower corner of WILLIAM JACKSONs Lease from ROGER DIXON, thence runing a straight line at right angles with CAROLINE STREET the whole debth of the Lot one hundred and thirty two feet, from thence another

straight line towards PRUSSIA STREET from thence to the begining; together with all
the houses out houses and improvements thereon to the same belonging; To have and to
hold the parcel of land unto JOHN NEWTON his heirs, And WILLIAM REAT and CATHE-
RINE his Wife and their heirs the parcel of land being part of Lot No. 248, against all
persons to said JOHN NEWTON his heirs will warrant and forever defend by these presents; In Witness whereof the said parties have to these presents interchangeably set
their hands and seals the day and year first above written
Sealed & Delivered in presence of

THOMAS SACRAE,   JACOB GROTZ,   WILLIAM REAT
CHARLES WARDELL,   ROB: DYKES,   CATHERINE REAT
JOHN CRUMP, AUGUSTINE NEWTON

The Commonwealth of Virginia to GEORGE FRENCH, FONTAINE MAURY and JOHN LEWIS
Gentlemen, Greeting, Whereas (the Commission for the privy Examination of CATHERINE, the
Wife of WILLIAM REAT); Witness JOHN CHEW, Clerk of our said Hustings Court the 10th day
of September 1800 and in the 25th year of the Commonwealth

Town of Fredericksburg, to wit: Agreeable to the within Commission to us directed we
have this day (the return of the execution of the privy examination of CATHERINE REAT); Given
under our hands and seals this Tenth day of September 1800

FONTAINE MAURY
JOHN LEWIS

At a Court of Hustings held for the Town and Corporation of Fredericksburg January
24th 1801.   This Indenture was proved by the oath of THOMAS SACRAE, CHARLES
WARDELL and AUGUSTINE NEWTON, three of the witnesses thereto and together with the
Commission annexed & Certificate of the execution thereof by the said CATHERINE
Indorsed, are ordered to be recorded

pp.   KNOW ALL MEN by these presents that I JAMES MAURY of LIVERPOOL in the
315-   County of LANCASTER and Kingdom of Great Britain, Merchant, and Consul of
318   the United States of America at LIVERPOOL for divers good causes and considera-
        tions me hereunto moving by these presents do make and appoint CHRISTOPHER
JOHNSTON of BALTIMORE in the United States my true and lawful Attorney and Agent for
me and in my name to ask demand sue for recover and receive of and from FONTAINE
MAURY of Fredericksburg all such sums of money as are now due to me on Mortgage of
my Estate. slaves lands or hereditaments in North America, And for me and in my behalf to prosecute any action or suits in any Court of the United States of North America
for the foreclosure of all right and equity of redemption whatsoever of said FONTAINE
MAURY of in or to the said Estate, slaves, lands, building and premises mortgaged by
said FONTAINE MAURY to me and generally I do authorise and empower my said Attorney to all such such other acts and deeds as shall be necessary for obtaining possession
and for the sale and disposal of said mortgaged premises and for conveying the same to
the respective purchasers thereof in as ample manner as I might or could do myself in
my own proper person ratifying and confirming all my said Attorney shall lawfully do
or cause to be done by virtue hereof; In Witness whereof I the said JAMES MAURY have
hereunto set my hand and seal this twenty second day of August one thousand eight
hundred
Sealed & Delivered in the presence of

JAMES SAMPSON,   JAMES MAURY
WILLM. MARTIN

BALTIMORE County to wit. On the 17th day of November 1800 personally appeared
before me the Subscriber one of the Justices of the Peace for said County, JAMES SAMP-
SON one of the Subscribing witnesses to the foregoing Power of Attorney and made oath

that he saw JAMES MAURY seal and deliver the same as his act and deed in his presence and also saw WM. MARTIN, the other witness, sign his name as such at the request of said JAMES MAURY, Consul of the United States of America at LIVERPOOL,

Sworn before JOSHUA LEMMON

State of MARYLAND BALTIMORE County Sct.

I hereby certify to all whom it doth concern that JOSHUA LEMMON Gentlemen is a Justice of the Peace for the County aforesaid and duly commissioned; In Testimony whereof I have hereunto set my hand and affixed the Seal of my Office the Sixth day of January Eighteen hundred and one   WM. GIBSON, Clk., Balto: County

At a Court of Hustings held for the Town and Corporation of Fredericksburg January 24th 1801   This Letter of Attorney from JAMES MAURY to CHRISTOPHER JOHNSTON together with the affidavit of JAMES SAMPSON and the Certificate of WILLIAM GIBSON, Clerk of BALTIMORE County are on the motion of said CHRISTOPHER JOHNSTON ordered to be recorded

Exd. & Deld. THOS: GOODWIN 22nd April 1808   Teste JNO: CHEW, C. C. H.

pp.   THIS INDENTURE made this 24th day of October Anno Domini eighteen hundred
318-   Between GEORGE W. B. SPOONER, Attorney in fact for GUSTAVUS B. WALLACE of
319   one part and MARGARET WEST of the other part; Witnesseth that GEORGE W. B.
        SPOONER Attorney as aforesaid for sum of Five shillings to him in hand paid by these presents does bargain and sell unto MARGARET WEST her heirs a certain parcel of ground, part of Lot No. 128, in Town of Fredericksburg begining at the corner of the aforesaid Lot adjoining Mr. CROUGHTON's KITCHEN, (formerly Mr. MERCERs) and extending twenty feet parallel to the said CROUGHTONs lot to the back line being the part of Lot No. 128 excepted in the Deed from said GEORGE W. B. SPOONER to a certain THOMAS W. WEST bearing date the eighteenth day of February Seventeen hundred and ninety seven which said Deed is recorded in the District Court Office of Fredericksburg, together with all houses gardens profits and advantages thereunto belonging; To have and to hold the piece of ground and premises with the appurtenances unto MARGARET WEST her heirs, In Witness whereof GEORGE W. B. SPOONER has hereunto set his hand and seal the day and year first above written

Signed Sealed and Delivered in presence of

JAMES STEVENSON JR.,   GEO: W. B. SPOONER
T. W. GREEN, WM. BROOKE,
WILLIAM VASS

At a Court of Hustings held for the Town and Corporation of Fredericksburg January 25th 1801   This Indenture was proved by the oaths of WILLIAM BROOKE and WILLIAM VASS two of the witnesses thereto

Teste   JNO: CHEW, C. C. H.

pp.   THIS INDENTURE made this 24th day of October in the year Eighteen hundred
320-   Between GEORGE W. B. SPOONER, Attorney in fact for GUSTAVUS B. WALLACE, of
321   one part and MARGARET WEST, Executrix of THOMAS W. WEST deceased, of the
        other part; Whereas THOMAS W. WEST deceased in his life time by Deed bearing date the eighteenth day of February one thousand seven hundred and ninety seven and of record in the District Court Office of Fredericksburg did mortgage unto GEORGE W. B. SPOONER, Attorney as aforesaid, all that lot of ground lying in Town of Fredericksburg known by No. 128 (a small part excepted) being the same lot of ground whereon the THEATRE now stands; and which was conveyed by GEORGE W. B. SPOONER, Attorney as aforesaid, to said THOMAS W. WEST for the purpose of securing the payment of sundry

sums of money more particularly mentioned in the before recited Deed And Whereas
said several sums of money have been fully paid; This Indenture Witnesseth that
GEORGE W. B. SPOONER, Attorney as aforesaid, in consideration of the premises and Five
shillings to him in hand paid by said MARGARET WEST by these presents do bargain sell
release and confirm unto MARGARET WEST all the said GEORGE W. B. SPOONER, Attorney
as aforesaid, title interest and demand of in and to lot No. 128; the small part excepted;
and GEORGE W. SPOONER doth covenant with MARGARET WEST her heirs against the
claims or any person whatsoever from by or under the mortgage aforesaid; In Witness
whereof GEORGE W. B. SPOONER, Attorney as aforesaid, has hereunto set his hand and
affixed his seal the day and year first above mentioned
Signed sealed & Delivered in presnece of
    JAMES STEVENSON JR.,   GEO: W. B. SPOONER
    T. W. GREEN, WILLIAM VASS,
    WM. BROOKE
  At a Court of Hustings held for the Town and Corporation of Fredericksburg January
24th 1801   This Indenture was proved by the oath of WILLIAM BROOKE and
WILLIAM VASS two of the witnesses thereto
                        Teste JNO: CHEW C. C. H.

pp.   KNOW ALL MEN by these presents me Ensign WILLIAM SUTHERLAND of the late
322-   Ninety Fifth Regiment of Foot then Commanded by Colonel BURTON and Brother
324   German of the deceased Doctor JOHN SUTHERLAND of Fredericksburg in Virginia
       do hereby make and appoint Messrs. DAVID BLAIR, JAMES BLAIR & DANIEL
GRINNAN of Fredg. in Virginia jointly or any one of them seperately my true and lawful Attornies for me to sell and transfer a tract of Land or Plantation (commonly called
FONTAIN BLEAU) formerly belonging to said Doctor JOHN SUTHERLAND, my Brother
German, situated on the FALL HILL Spotsylvania County in Virginia to any person they
shall think fit and convenient; and for me to execute and deliver such Deeds, Convey-
ances Bargains and Sales for the absolute sail & disposal thereof, ratifying and appro-
ving whatever matters my said Attornies shall lawfully do concerning the premises; In
Witness whereof I have hereunto set my hand and seal at KIRKWALL in County of
ORKNEY North Britain the tenth day of July in the thirty ninth year of the Reign of our
sovereign Lord George the Third by the grace of God of Great Britain France & Ireland
Defend of the faith &c., and in the year of our Lord one thousand seven hundred and
ninety nine
Signed sealed and delivered being first duly stamped
  agreeable to the Laws in this County in presence of
      JOHN HEDDLE. N. P.   WILL: SUTHERLAND
      PTK. FOTHERINGHAME, RO: HEDDLE
The within named JOHN HEDDLE, Notary Publick, PATRICK FOTHERINGHAME and
ROBERT HEDDLE, Subscribing Witnesses to the execution of the within written Letter of
Power of Attorney by WILLIAM SUTHERLAND within designed being solemnly sworn
and examined make oath and say that they were present and did see WILLIAM SUTHER-
LAND sign seal and of his own proper act and deed deliver the said Letter or Power of
Attorney; Sworn before me this Tenth day of July one thousand seven hunered and
ninety nine years   THOS: TRAILL, Provost   JOHN HEDDLE
                                           PATK. FOTHERINGHAME
                                           RO: HEDDLE
  At a Court of Hustings held for the Town and Corporation of Fredericksburg February
28th 1801;   This Letter of Attorney from WILLIAM SUTHERLAND to DAVID BLAIR,

JAMES BLAIR & DANIEL GRINNAN together with the affidavit of JOHN HEDDLE, PATRICK FOTHERINGHAME & ROBERT HEDDLE and the Certificate of THOMAS TRAILL Esquire, Lord Provost & Chief Magistrate of the City of KIRKWALL in the County of ORKNEY in that part of Great Britain called Scotland thereto annexed are on the motion of the said DANIEL GRINNAN ordered to be recorded
Exd. & Deld. D. GRINNAN   Teste JNO: CHEW, C. C. H.

pp.   KNOW ALL MEN by these presents that me Ensign WILLIAM SUTHERLAND late
325-   of the Ninety Fifth Regiment of Foot then Commanded by Colonel BURTON,
328   Whereas the right honourable LORD DUNMORE late Governor of the Province of
            Virginia in North American by his Warrant dated the twenty fourth day of
February one thousand seven hundred and seventy four years directed the Surveyor of
FINCASTLE County to Survey and locate the number of Two thousand acres of land for
me on some of the Western Waters in that Province, And Whereas there was one tract of
One thousand acres on the OHIO RIVER in JEFFERSON County joining to WILLIAM
PEACHEY's One thousand acre Tract which lies on the OHIO about seven miles above the
FALLS and another tract of one thousand acres also on the OHIO about thirty miles
below SCIOTO RIVER now in the State of KENTUCKY, located and set apart for me and to
which I have right by the foresaid Warrant and Report of the Surveyor in consequence
thereof and other Deeds respecting the same; NOW KNOW YE, that I WILLIAM SUTHER-
LAND do by these presents make and appoint Messrs. DAVID BLAIR, JAMES BLAIR &
DANIEL GRINNAN of Fredericksburg in Virginia jointly or any one of them seperately
my true and lawful Attornies for me to sell & transfer the said two Tracts or Two thousand acres of land to any person or persons they shall think fit, And also for me and in
my name to make & deliver all such Deeds & Conveyances for the absolute sale and disposal thereof with such clauses covenants and agreements therein to be contained as
the said DAVID BLAIR, JAMES BLAIR and DANIEL GRINNAN or any one of them shall
think fit and expedient; In Witness whereof I have hereunto set my hand & seal at
KIRKWALL in the County of ORKNEY North Britain the Eleventh day of August in the
Thirty eighth year of the reign of our Sovereign Lord George the Third by the Grace of
God, King of Great Britain France and Ireland, Defender of the faith &c., and in the year
of our Lord one thousand seven hundred & ninety eight
Signed Sealed & Delivered being first duly stamped
  agreeable to the Laws of this County in the
  presence of JOHN HEDDLE, N. P.   `   WILL: SUTHERLAND
           PATK. FOTHERINGHAME, RO: HEDDLE
(This Letter of Attorney is followed on page 327), by the Certificates as cited above following the previosu Letter of Attorney of WILLIAM SUTHERLAND):
  At a Court of Hustings held for the Town and Corporation of Fredericksburg February
28th 1801   This Letter of Attorney from WILLIAM SUTHERLAND to DAVID BLAIR,
JAMES BLAIR and DANIEL GRINNAN, together with the affidavit of JOHN HEDDLE,
PATRICK FOTHERINGHAME and ROBERT HEDDLE, and the Certificate of THOMAS TRAILL,
Esqr., Lord Provost and Chief Magistrate of the City of KIRKWALL in the County of ORK-
NEY in that part of Great Britain called Scotland thereto annexed are on the motion of
the said DANIEL GRINNAN ordered to be recorded
Exd. & deld. D. GRINNAN   Teste JNO: CHEW C. C. H.

pp.   THIS INDENTURE made this fifth day of December in year of our Lord one thou-
328-   sand Eight hundred Between ROBERT PATTON of Town of Fredericksburg, Mer-
332   chant of one part and the President, Directors & Company of the Bank of
            ALEXANDRIA of the other part; Whereas it has been represented to the Presi-

dent, Directors & Company of ALEXANDRIA that the following Notes issued by the Bank of ALEXANDRIA Viz., one note No. 4320 for One thousand Dollars payable to WILLIAM TAYLOR or order ten days after date and dated the 10th day of December 1798; one other note No. 4511 for Five hundred Dollars issued on the 10th day of December 1798 payable to JOHN P. PLEASANTE or Order six days after date and dated the 10th of December 1798 were accidently lost by WILLSON & SWAN of Fredericksburg on or about the twenty seventh day of August one thousand seven hundred ninety nine and the said President Directors and Company of the Bank of ALEXANDRIA having agreed to pay said ROBERT PATTON & GEORGE MURRAY to whom the said WILSON and SWANN have transferred their right to the said Notes supposed to be lost the sum of Fifteen hundred Dollars; NOW THIS INDENTURE WITNESSETH that ROBERT PATTON & ANN GORDON his Wife as well in consideration of the premises as of the sum of One Dollar to said ROBERT PATTON in hand paid by said President, Directors & Company of the Bank of ALEXANDRIA by these presents bargain and sell unto the President, Directors & Company of the Bank of ALEXANDRIA & to their Successors, a certain lott of ground lying in Town of Fredericksburg and bounded, Beginning on the North side of a Gate on the Main Street called CAROLINE STREET seventy one feet from the South corner that is formed by an intersection on the Cross Street called LEWIS STREET, & the said Main Street, from this beginning extending up the Main Street Fifty eight feet, from thence at right angles to the Main Street to extend across the whole of Lotts No. 71 & 72 to the Back Street called SOPHIA STREET, from thence to the Corner of Messrs. COLIN & JAMES ROSS's Lott fifty eight feet & from thence to the beginning on Main Street and all houses buildings and Improvements to said lott of land belonging; To have and to hold the said Lott or parcel of Ground with all appurtenances thereunto belonging unto the said President, Directors & Company of the Bank of ALEXANDRIA & their Successors; and ROBERT PATTON & his heirs the lott of ground shall warrant & forever defend by these presents; In Witness whereof ROBERT PATTON & ANN GORDON his Wife have hereunto set their hands & affixed their seals the day & year first before written
Sealed & Delivered in the presence of

THOMAS WARE,	FRANCIS GAINES,	ROBT. PATTON
REUBEN THORN,	DAVID WILLIAMSON,	ANN G. PATTON
JNO: NEWTON,	WM. TALBOTT,	
AUGUSTINE NEWTON		

The Commonwealth of Virginia to DAVID C. KER, HUGH MERCER & WILLIAM S. STONE Gentlemen, Greeting, Whereas (the Commission for the privy Examination of ANN GORDON, Wife of ROBERT PATTON); Witness JOHN CHEW, Clerk of our said Court the 11th day of December 1800 and in the 25th year of the Commonwealth
Corporation of Fredg. to wit. In Conformity to the within Comm: we this day have examined (the return of the execution of the privy Examination of ANN GORDON PATTON); Given under our hands this 11th December 1800 HUGH MERCER
W. S. STONE
At a Court of Hustings held for the Town & Corporation of Fredericksburg the 25th day of April 1801 This Indenture was acknowledged by the said ROBERT PATTON and together with the Commission annexed and the Certificate of the execution thereof by the said ANN GORDON Indorsed are ordered to be recorded

pp. 332-335   THIS INDENTURE made the fourth day of February in the year of our Lord one thousand Eight hundred and one Between WILLIAM S. STONE and MILDRED his Wife of the Town of Fredsburg of one part and CHARLES BROWN of the Town aforesaid of other part; Witnesseth that WILLIAM S. STONE and MILDRED his Wife

for sum of Two hundred pounds to WILLIAM S. STONE in hand paid by CHARLES BROWN
by these presents do bargain and sell unto CHARLES BROWN his heirs one certain
parcel of ground lying in Town of Freds:burg and is that part of Lott (blank) which said
CHARLES BROWN now occupies and which said STONE purchased of THOMAS SOUTHCOMB,
Attorney in fact for JOHN CALLENDER, as by Deed from said SOUTHCOMB to said STONE
bearing date the 15th day of December 1797 and duly recorde din the District Court of
Freds:burg; together with all houses gardens priviledges & appurtenances to said parcell of ground belonging; To have and to hold the parcell of ground with the appurtenances unto CHARLES BROWN his heirs, And WILLIAM S. STONE and MILDRED his Wife
and their heirs the parcell of ground against the claim of every person unto CHARLES
BROWN his heirs will and by these presents do warrant and forever defend; In Witness
whereof WILLIAM S. STONE and MILDRED his Wife have hereunto set their hands and
affixed their seals the day and year first within written
Signed Sealed & Delivered in presence of   W.S.STONE
          (No witnesses shown)   MILLY STONE
    The Commonwealth of Virginia to GEORGE FRENCH, THOMAS GOODWIN & DAVID C. KER
Gentlemen, Greeting, Whereas (the Commission for the privy Examination of MILDRED, the
Wife of WILLIAM S. STONE); Witness JOHN CHEW, Clerk of our said Court, the 5th day of
Feby. 1801 and in the 25th year of the Commonwealth   JNO: CHEW
    Fredg. to wit; Agreeable to the within Comm: to us directed, we have this day examined
(the return of the execution of the privy Examination of MILDRED STONE); Given under our
hands and seals this 25th day of March 1801   GEO: FRENCH
                                                     THO: GOODWIN

    At a Court of Hustings held for the Town and Corporation of Fredericksburg on Satur-
day the 25th day of April 1801   This Indenture was acknowledged by the said
WILLIAM S. STONE and together with the Commission annexed and Certificate for the
execution thereof by the said MILLY indorsed, are ordered to be recorded
Examd. & Delivered CHARLES BROWN   Teste JNO: CHEW, C.C.H.

pp   THE STATE of SOUTH CAROLINA
336-   KNOW ALL MEN by these presents that I GUSTAVUS BROWN WALLACE of the City
338   of CHARLESTON in the State aforesaid in consideration of the sum of Three thou-
         sand Dollars by JOHN WALLACE of County of STAFFORD & of the further sum of
One Thousand Dollars by THOMAS WALLACE of the County of CULPEPER in the State of
Virginia to me in hand paid by these presents do bargain sell and release unto JOHN
WALLACE & THOMAS WALLACE (the said JOHN WALLACE to hold three fourths & the said
THOMAS WALLACE to hold one fourth thereof) all those two lotts of Land situate on
CAROLINE STREET in Town of Fredericksburg occupied by MARY FISHER & reserving to
myself for the term of my natural life so much of the annual Rents and Profits thereof
as may remain due and payable after discharging a Debt due to ROBERT PATTON of
Fredericksburg for the payment of which the said two lots stand mortgaged, and keep
the houses &c. in repair (the profits arising first from the said Lots to be applied to the
extinguishment of the afsd. Debt & Mortgage); and to the repair of the buildings, together with all the rights members and appurtenances to the said premises belonging; To
have and to hold the premises before mentioned unto JOHN WALLACE & THOMAS
WALLACE (in the proportion afsd.) their heirs; Witness my hand & seal this twentieth
day of April in the year of our Lord one thousand Eight hundred & one and in the
Twenty fifth year of the Independence of the United States of America
Sealed & Delivered in the presence of
    ANDREW NORRIS,   GUSTAVUS B. WALLACE
    BENJAMIN JAMES, JAMES ONEAL

STATE of SOUTH CAROLINA. Personally appeared Mr. BENJAMIN JAMES, who being duly sworn and made oath that he was present & saw GUSTAVUS BROWN WALLACE sign seal and by his act and deed deliver the within Instrument of Writing to and for the purposes therein set forth, And this Deponent with JAMES ONEAL & ANDREW NORRIS signed their names as witnesses thereto
Sworn to the 23d day of April 1801 before
        STEPHEN RAVENEL
STATE of SOUTH CAROLINA: Register of Mesne Conveyance Office for CHARLESTON District recorded in Book B, No. 7, page 460 this 23d day of April 1801 & examined by
                        STEPHEN RAVENEL
STATE of SOUTH CAROLINA: By his Excellency JOHN DRAYTON, Governor & Commander in Chief in and over the State aforesaid, To all to whom these presents shall come, Know ye that STEPHEN RAVENEL Esquire, whose signature appearing to the Instrument of Writing hereunto annexed is Register of Mesne Conveyances for the District of CHARLESTON in the said State and one of the Justices of the Quorum for said State; Therefor all due faith credit and authority is and ought to be hand & given to his proceedings and certificates as such, In Testimony whereof I have hereunto set my hand & caused to be affixed the Seal of the State in the City of CHARLESTON this ninth day of May in year of our Lord one thousand eight hundred & one, and in the Twenty fifth year of the Independence of the United States of America
                        By the Governor,
                        ISAAC MOTTE DARK Secretary of State
    At a Court of Hustigns held for the Town & Corporation of Fredericksburg July the 25th 1801   This Deed from GUSTAVUS BROWN WALLACE of the one part and JOHN WALLACE and THOMAS WALLACE of the other part together with the affidavit of BENJAMIN JAMES and the Certificate of his Excellencey JOHN DRAYTON, Governor of the State of SOUTH CAROLINA under the Seal of the State are on the motion of the said JOHN & THOMAS WALLACE ordered to be recorded
Exd. & Deld. to CHS: WITHERS for JNO: WALLACE   Teste JNO: CHEW, C.C.H.

pp.   THIS INDENTURE made this twenty fifth day of July Anno Domini Eighteen
338-   hundred and one Between GEO: W. B. SPOONER & ELIZABETH his Wife of Town of
340   Fredericksburg of one part and ROBERT PATTON of the same place of other part;
        Witnesseth that in consideration of the uses herein after declared and the sum of One Dollar in hand paid to GEO: W. B. SPOONER and ELIZABETH his Wife by ROBERT PATTON, by these presents do bargain andsell unto ROBERT PATTON and his heirs one half acre lott of land lying in Town of Fredg., late the property of GUSTAVUS B. WALLACE and conveyed by him to said GEO: W. B. SPOONER by a certain Instrument of Writing bearing date the seventeenth day of December AD Seventeen hundred and ninety three situated on THE HILL and bouned on the South by WILLIAM STREET, on the West by BARTONs, formerly LEWIS's Field, on the East by GOODWINs formerly EVANS's lot and known by number One hundred & forty two, together with all appurtenances thereunto belonging; To have and to hold the said Lot unto ROBERT PATTON and his heirs, that is to say, to the use of RICAHRD KENNY and MILLY his Wife of Town of Freds:burg for their lives and life of the survivor of them; and after the determination of that Estate to the use of the Children of RICHARD KENNY and his Wife, MILLY, or the survivor of them at the time of the death of said RICHARD KENNY and MILLY his Wife, to be equally divided amongst them the said Children; And GEO: W. B. SPOONER & ELIZABETH his Wife and their heirs unto ROBERT PATTON his heirs free from the claim of every person shall and do warrant & forever defend by these presents; In Witness whereof GEO: W. B. SPOONER

and ELIZABETH his Wife have hereunto affixed their hands & seals the day and year
above written
Signed sealed & acknowledged in the presence of
    JOHN JOHNSTON,   GEO: W. B. SPOONER
    WILLIAM VASS, WM. SMITH   ELIZABETH SPOONER
  At a Court of Hustings held for the Town & Corporation of Fredericksburg July 25th
1801   This Indenture was acknowledged by the said GEORGE W. B. SPOONER & ordered to
be recorded   Teste JNO: CHEW, C. C. H.

pp.   THIS INDENTURE made this 25th day of July Anno Domini one thousand Eight
340-   hundred and one Between GEORGE W. B. SPOONER of the one part and DAVID
341   WILLIAMSON, both of Town of Fredericksburg of the other part; Whereas said
       GEORGE W. B. SPOONER is indebted to ROBERT PATTON in the sum of 525$ with
Interest untill paid for that sum paid for premium on Insurance of the *HANNAH and
NANCY* and to WILLIAM TAYLOR of the City of BALTIMORE 1000$ without Interest; to
WILLIAM S. STONE 290$; to JACOB KUHN 100$., to ARCHIBALD McCALL 43 81/100$, to
JAMES STEWART 65 25/100$; to ROBERT PATTON & CO. 82$, to JO. S. HAZY 100$ and to
BENJAMIN DAY 78$. and is desirous to secure the payment thereof to ROBERT PATTON
and WILLIAM TAYLOR in full and the rest of the claims herein named in proportion to
their several claims aforesaid. NOW THIS INDENTURE WITNESSETH that for the consider-
ation aforesaid and consideration of One Dollar paid by DAVID WILLIAMSON, said
GEORGE W. B. SPOONER have assigned over to DAVID WILLIAMSON all his right title and
Interest in and to a Policy of Insurance upon the *HANNAH and NANCY* entered into by
BETHUNE and SMITH of the City of NEW YORK amounting to the sum of 2100$. on account
of ROBERT PATTON for said GEORGE W. B. SPOONER in Trust for the purposes herein
mentioned and for no other, to wit, after deducting all expences of Collection either by
suit or otherwise to pay to the said ROBERT PATTON and to WILLIAM TAYLOR their claims
in full and the small claims of WM. S. STONE, JACOB KUHN, ARCHIBALD McCALL, JAMES
STEWART, ROBERT PATTON & CO:, JOHN S. HAZY & BENJAMIN DAY, in proportion their
several and respective amounts; In Witness whereof GEORGE W. B. SPOONER hath hereunto set his hand & seal the day and year first written
In presence of JOHN JOHNSTON,   GEO: W. B. SPOONER
    WILLM: VASS, WM. SMITH
  At a Court of Hustings held for the Town & Corporation of Fredericksburg July 25th
1801   This Indenture was acknowledged by the said GEORGE W. B. SPOONER and ordered
to be recorded
Exd. & deld. D. WILLIAMSON p Order filed   Teste JNO: CHEW, C. C. H.

pp.   To all whom it may concern, Know ye that for the services heretofore rendered
341-   by my Negroe Woman, Hannah, I do hereby Emancipate & set free the said
342   Negroe Woman, Hannah, who is now about Forty five years of age; Given under
       my hand and seal this fifth day of June one thousand eight hundred and one
Signed Sealed and Acknowledged in the presence of
    JOSEPH CHRISTY,   EDWARD HERNDON
    BENJN: PARKE
  At a Court of Hustings held for the Town & Corporation of Freds:burg July 25, 1801
This Letter of Emancipation was proved by the Oaths of JOSEPH CHRISTY & BENJN.
PARKE the witnesses thereto & ordered to be recorded
Exd. & Delivered   Teste JNO: CHEW, C. C. H.

pp.   THIS INDENTURE made and entered into this twenty seventh day of December
342-   in the year of our Lord one thousand eight hundred Between RICHARD PEACOCK
344   and HANNAH his Wife of the Town of Fredericksburg of one part and JOHN K.
        HILL of the same place of the other part; Witnesseth that RICHARD PEACOCK and
HANNAH his Wife for sum of Three hundred and sixty pounds current money of Virginia to them in hand paid by JOHN K. HILL, by these presents do bargain & sell unto
JOHN K. HILL his heirs one half of the lott in the said Town and numbered Eleven
Eleven and contains in front on PRINCESS ANN STREET eighty two and a half feet; and
runs back the full depth of the said Lott on PRUSSA STREET together with all appurtenances belonging; and the Rents issue and profits thereof; To have and to hold the said
half of a Lott of ground unto JOHN K. HILL his heirs and RICHARD PEACOCK and HAN-
NAH his Wife and their heirs doth covenant that they will warrant and forever defend
the said lott of ground unto JOHN K. HILL against the claim of every person claiming
under them or either of them; And it is further agreed by the parties to these presents
that MARY GIBBS, who at present occupies the House & Garden on the premises herein
shall possess and enjoy the said House and Garden without molestation during her
natural life and for which she shall not pay any Rent; In Witness whereof RICHARD
PEACOCK and HANNAH his Wife have hereunto set their hands and seals the day & year
first above written
Sealed Signed and acknowledged in the presence of
        JAMES NEWBY,   RICHARD PEACOCK
        JOHN LAMBETH,   BENJN; PARKE   HANNAH PEACOCK
  The Commonwealth of Virginia to GEORGE FRENCH & HUGH MERCER, DAVID C. KER
Gent., Greeting; Whereas (the Commission for the privy Examination of HANNAH, the Wife of
RICHARD PEACOCK); Witness JOHN CHEW, Clerk of our said Hustings Court the 23rd day of
April 1801 and in the 25th year of the Commonwealth   JNO: CHEW
  Corporation of Fredericksburg, to wit: We the within named GEORGE FRENCH & HUGH
MERCER have personally waited on the within named HANNAH PEACOCK (the return of the
execution of the privy Examination of HANNAH PEACOCK); Given under our hands this 23rd
April 1801   GEO: FRENCH
                                               HUGH MERCER
  At a Court of Hustings held for the Town & Corporation of Freds:burg July 25th 1801
This Indenture was acknowledged by the said RICHARD PEACOCK and together with the
Commission annexed & Certificate of the execution thereof by the said HANNAH
indorsed are ordered to be recorded
Exd. and Delivered J. K. HILL   Teste JNO: CHEW, C. C. H.

p.   KNOW ALL MEN by these presents that I DAVID HENDERSON of the Town of
345   Frederickburg and County of Spotsylvania in conformity with Instructions sent
        me by Mr. WILLIAM A. DAINGERFIELD of the City of LONDON Great Britain ac-
companyed by an Instrument of Writing under his hand and seal dated and tested in the
City of LONDON the fifteenth day of July Anno Domini one thousand eight hundred and
appointing me his true and lawful Attorney, in consideration of the sum of One hundred & Fifty five pounds current money of Virginia to me in hand paid by these presents do bargain and sell unto ALEXANDER DUNCAN of Town of Fredg., in behalf of said
WILLIAM A. DAINGERFIELD, one Negroe woman named Sarah and her two Sons, the
Eldest named Isaac and the youngest named Abraham, To have and to hold the said
slaves and their increase forever. In Witness whereof I have hereunto set my hand
and seal dated in Fredg. this Twentieth day of November 1800.

Signed sealed and delivered in the presence of
    DAVID HENDERSON JR.,   DAVID HENDERSON
    JAMES DIXON   Attorney in Fact for WILLIAM A. DAINGERFIELD
At a Court of Hustigns held for the Town & Corporation of Freds:burg July 25th 1801
This Bill of Sale for slaves was proved by the oath of DAVID HENDERSON JR., & JAMES
DIXON the witnesses thereto & ordered to be recorded

pp.   THIS INDENTURE made this first day of October in year of our Lord one thou-
346- sand Eight hundred Between DAVID BLAIR of one part & DANIEL GRINNAN of
347   other part; Witnesseth that DAVID BLAIR in consideration of the love and af-
fection which he bears to his Wife, SARAH BLAIR, and to his two Sons, JAMES &
DAVID BLAIR, and for the further consideration of five Shillings to him in hand paid
by DANIEL GRINNAN by these presents doth bargain sell and confirm unto said DANIEL
GRINNAN his heirs the following lott of ground lying in Town of Freds:burg number
Fifty three & bounded beginning on PRINCESS ANN STREET at the upper Corner of said
Lott, thence runing down said Street sixty five feet, thence parallel with WOLF STREET
Westerly runing through Lot number Sixty six, thence Northerly parallel with PRIN-
CESS ANN STREET sixty five feet and from thence to the beginning; together with all its
appurtenances; To have and to hold the said lott of land unto DANIEL GRINNAN his
heirs, also the following Negroe slaves, Betty and Dianne, with their future increase
and also the Plate, Household & Kitchen furniture now belonging to and in the possession of said DAVID BLAIR; To have and to hold the premises unto DANIEL GRINNAN his
heirs upon this special Trust and Confidence, that DANIEL GRINNAN shall and will
receive all the rents issues and profits of the said lott and the hire of the said Negroes
and will apply the same, together with the Plate, Household & Kitchen furniture to the
use of said SARAH BLAIR, JAMES BLAIR and DAVID BLAIR (Sons of said DAVID) during
the life of said SARAH and at her decease will sell the same & divide the amount
received therefor between said JAMES & DAVID BLAIR their heirs; and DANIEL GRIN-
NAN covenants to and with said DAVID BLAIR that he will justly perform the Trust in
this Deed specified and declared; In Witness whereof the parties have hereunto affixed
their hands & seals the day and year first afore written
Signed Sealed & Delivered in presence of
    JAMES BLAIR,   DAVID BLAIR
    JNO: METCALFE, JOHN M. SHEPHERD   DANIEL GRINNAN
At a Court of Hustings held for the Town & Corporation of Freds:bug July 25th 1801
This Indenture was proved by the Oath of JOHN METCALFE, one of the witnesses thereto,
as to the execution of DAVID BLAIR and acknowledged by DANIEL GRINNAN & ordered to
be recorded as to him.

p.   TO ALL TO WHOM these presents shall come, Whereas WILLIAM GLASSELL now
348   deceased did by Deed bearing date the 3rd day of May 1799, convey unto me his
man slave named PRIMUS GIBBS in Trust for the purpose of liberating him at
the expiration of seven years or at the death of the said WM. GLASSELL whichever
should first happen; and the said WILLIAM GLASSELL hath lately departed this life, Now
Know ye that I the said JOHN MINOR in pursuance of the said Trust and consideration of
the sum of five shillings in hand paid have manumitted emancipated and forever set
freen the said slave PRIMUS GIBBS from all slavery or servitude whatsoever and he is
by these presents declared to be forever freed from all slavery & servitude; In Witness
whereof I have hereto set my hand and seal this 26th day of September 1801.
                              JOHN MINOR

At a Court of Hustings held for the Town & Corporation of Fredericksburg the 26th day
of September 1801   This Letter of Emancipation from JOHN MINOR to his slave, PRI-
MUS GIBBS, was acknowledged by the said JOHN MINOR & ordered to be recorded
Exd. & Deld. PRIMUS GIBBS   Test JNO: CHEW, C. C. H.

pp.   THIS INDENTURE made this twenty seventh dy of May Anno Dom: one thousand
349-   Eight hundred and one Between MARY SULLIVAN of Town of Fredericksburg
350   of one part and JOHN T. WALKER of the same Town of the other; Witnesseth that
        MARY SULLIVAN for sum of One hundred & thirty pounds specie to her in hand
paid by JOHN T. WALKER, by these presents doth bargain and sell unto JOHN T. WALKER
his heirs a parcel of land lying in Town of Fredericksburg being bounded, Beginning
at the Intersection of the corner of WATER & PRUSIA STREETs runing North sixty two
degrees East on PRUSIA STREET to Low Water Mark, thence from the beginning North
twenty eight degrees West on WATER STREET until it meets the intersection of the adjoining square lying to the Northwd. of it; thence by such square & runing tothe Low
Water Mark, the aforesd. square being the whole of it sold to sd. WALKER as described
and numbered Three hundred and four; together with all Profits and appurtenances to
said parcel of land belonging; To have and to hold with the appurtenances unto JOHN T.
WALKER his heirs and MARY SULLIVAN her heirs doth warrant and defend the parcel
of land unto JOHN T. WALKER his heirs against the claim of every person whatsoever;
In Witness whereof MARY SULLIVAN hath hereunto set her hand and affixed her seal
the day & date above written
Signed sealed & Delivered in the presence of
        C. HOLLOWAY,   MARY SULLIVAN
        JAMES HOLLADAY; BENJA: ALSOP,
        WILLIAM JONES
At a Court of Hustings held for the Town & Corporation of Fredericksburg the 26th day
of September 1801   This Indenture was proved by the oath of WILLIAM JONES &
BENJAMIN ALSOP two of the witnesses thereto
                Test   JNO: CHEW, C. C. H.
At a Court of Hustings held for the said Town & Corpo: the 11th day of June 1807
This Indenture was fully proved by the oath of JAMES HOLLADAY another witness
thereto and ordered to be recorded
                Test R. S. CHEW, C. C. H.

pp.   THIS INDENTURE made the fifteenth day of June in year of our Lord Eighteen
351-   hundred and one Between DAVID C. KER & MARGARET his Wife of Town of
352   Fredericksburg of one part and JOHN LEWIS of said Town of other part; Witnes-
        seth that DAVID C. KER and MARGARET his Wife for sum of Sixty pounds Virginia
Currency to them in hand paid by said LEWIS, by these presents do bargain & sell unto
said LEWIS a certain piece of ground lying within the Town of Fredericksburg and is
part of Lott number Two hundred & sixty eight, lying on RAPPAHANNOCK RIVER and
formerly the property of WILLIAM HARVEY, deced., and is bounded, Beginning on the
RIVER RAPPAHANNOCK adjoining the upper side of the Wharf call'd the MERCHANTS
WHARF which stands on part of said Lott No. 268 and running thence in a line paralel
with the Cross Streets of Freds:burg to WATER STREET, thence up and along WATER
STREET one hundred and twenty five feet to Lott Two hundred & sixty nine, thence with
said lott to the RIVER RAPPAHANNOCK, thence down and with the meanders of said
River to the beginning, Together with all the appurtenances thereunto belonging; To
have and to hold the lott of ground unto JOHN LEWIS his heirs and DAVID C. KER and

MARGARET his Wife and their heirs the said lott of ground unto JOHN LEWIS his heirs free from the claim of them or of their heirs shall & do warrant & forever defend by these presents; In Witness whereof DAVID C. KER and MARGARET his Wife have hereunto set their hands & seals the day & year first above written

Signed Sealed & Delivered in presence of   DAVID C. KER
        (no witnesses shown)   MARGARET KER

At a Court of Hustings held for the Town & Corporation of Frederickburg the 26th day of September 1801   This Indenture was acknowledged by the said DAVID C. KER and ordered to be recorded

Exd. & Deld. WARNER LEWIS with Commission   Teste JNO: CHEW, C. C. H.

pp.   THIS INDENTURE made this third day of December in the year 1801 Between
352-   JOHN LEWIS of Town of Fredericksburg of one part and JOSEPH CHRISTY of said
353   Town of other part; Witnesseth that JOHN LEWIS in consideration of the sum of
          Seventy pounds lawful money of this Commonwealth to him in hand paid by said
JOSEPH CHRISTY by these presents do bargain and sell unto said JOSEPH his heirs three half acre lotts of ground in Town of Fredericksburg and designated by numbers 162, 163 and 164; and are bounded; Lott No. 162 is bounded on the South by PITT STREET, on the West by the land of SETH BARTON, on the North by Lott No. 164, and on the East by Lott No. 1651; (note Lott No. 161 is the property of JOHN MINOR, a Free Negroe); Lott No. 163 is bounded on the East by PRINCE EDWARD STREET, on the South by Lott No. 161, and on the West by Lott 164. Lot No. 164 is bounded on the West by the land of SETH BARTON, on the South by Lott No. 162, and on the East by Lott No. 163; Together with all advantages whatsoever to said lotts belonging; To have and to hold the said three lotts of land, And JOHN LEWIS and his heirs the three half acre lotts of land with all appurtenances thereunto belonging unto said JOSEPH his heirs free from the claims of every person will and do warrant and forever defend by these presents; In Witness whereof JOHN LEWIS hath hereunto set his hand and seal the day and year first above mentioned

Sealed & Delivered in presence of
        PHILIP HENSHAW,   JOHN LEWIS
        WILLIAM VASS, TINSLEY CHEWNING,
        THOMAS WALLACE, SAML. CHEWNING

At a Court of Hustigns held for the Town & Corporation of Freds:burg the 23rd January 1802   This Indenture was proved by the oaths of PHILIP HENSHAW, TINSLEY CHEWNING and SAMUEL CHEWNING three of the witnesses thereto and ordered to be recorded

Exd. & deld. JOS: CHRISTY   Teste   JNO: CHEW, C.C.H.

pp.   THIS INDENTURE made the ninth day of June in year one thousand eight hun-
354-   dred and one Between CHARLES A. LEWIS and CATHARINE his Wife of County of
356   CAROLINE of one part and JOHN LEWIS of Town of Fredericksburg of second part,
          Witnesseth that CHARLES A LEWIS & CATHARINE his Wife for sum of Seven hun-
dred and fifty pounds to them in hand paid by JOHN LEWIS by these presents doth bargain and sell unto JOHN LEWIS his heirs one moiety of a certain lott of ground in Town of Fredericksburg on the RIVER RAPPAHANNOCK known by the name of the BREWERY LOTT; No. 273; (which said moiety was formerly purchased by PRESON BOWDEN of Town of NORFOLK of GEORGE THORNTON Esquire deced., and sold by said PRESON BOWDEN to JOSEPH JONES Esquire and afterwards conveyed to said JOSEPH JONES by GEORGE THORN-TON, Son and Heir of GEORGE THORNTON deced., as will appear by a Deed from said GEORGE THORNTON to JOSEPH JONES of record in the District Court of Fredericksburg), afterwards by said JOSEPH JONES to CHARLES A. LEWIS and is bounded Beginning on said

River at the lower end of a Lott of ground own'd by DAVID and JAMES BLAIR and running with their line to WATER STREET thence down & along WATER STREET to a lott of
JOHN MORTIMER's, thence with his line to the aforesaid River, thence up and along the
said River to the beginning; together with all buildings profits advantages and appurtenances belonging; To have and to hold the lott of ground unto JOHN LEWIS his heirs,
And CHARLES A. LEWIS and CATHARINE his Wife and their heirs shall and do warrant
and forever defend by these presents; In Witness whereof CHARLES A. LEWIS and
CATHARINE his Wife hath hereunto sett their hands & seals the day & year first written
Signed sealed & delivered in the presence of us

THO: GOODWIN as to C. L.	CHS. A. LEWIS
THO: L. LOMAX as to C. L..	CATHARINE LEWIS
WM. HERNDON,	
ELISHA THATCHER as to C. L.	

The Commonwealth of Virginia to DANIEL COLEMAN and RICHARD HAWES Gentlemen
Greeting, Whereas (the Commission for the privy Examination of CATHARINE the Wife of
CHARLES A. LEWIS); Witness JOHN CHEW, Clerk of our said Corporation Court the 10th day
of June 1801 and in the 25th year of the Commonwealth   JNO: CHEW
    CAROLINE County Sct. Agreeable to the within Commission to us directed, (the return of
the execution of the privy examination of CATHARIANE LEWIS); Given under our hands and
seals this 10th day of June 1801   DANL. COLEMAN
                                                            RICHARD HAWES

    At a Court of Hustings held for the Town & Corporation of Fredericksburg the 23rd day
of January 1802   This Indenture was proved by the oaths of THOMAS GOODWIN,
THOMAS L. LOMAX and ELISHA THATCHER, three of the witnesses thereto and together
with the Commission annexed & Certificate of execution thereof by the said CATHARINE
indorsed, are ordered to be recorded
Exd. & deld. WARNER LEWIS   Teste JNO: CHEW, C.C.H.

pp.   THIS INDENTURE made this ninth day of July in the year Eighteen hundred and
357-   one Between BARTHOLOMEW BLUNT of Fredericksburg and WILLIAM HERNDON,
358   THOMAS L. LOMAX of same place, Witnesseth that BARTHOLOMEW BLUNT for se-
        curing the payment of Two hundred and Ten Dollars & Fifty one Cents to ELISHA
THATCHER and COMPANY with Interest, by these presents doth bargain and sell unto
WILLIAM HERNDON and THOMAS L. LOMAX the following goods & chattles, viz., Four feather beads and furniture, one square walnut table, two small square pine tables; one
writing desk, (painted Mohogany colour), one Cupboard (corner glazed and painted
red), one half gallon China Bowl, two dozen green & blue edged plates, six blue or green
edged Dishes, one and an half dozen flag bottom chairs, (painted red and black), three
Iron bound ten gallon Stands (painted blue), two iron Potts, two Dutch ovens, three
pairs shovels & Tongs with sundry other articles including the whole of my household
furniture; To have and to hold the goods and chattles to them and their heirs upon
Trust, neverthesless, that if BARTHOLOMEW BLUNT shall pay ELISHA THATCHER and
COMPANY the said sum of Two hundred Ten Dollars & 51 Cents on or before the first day
of November in the present year with legal interest that then these presents and every
thing therein contained shall be void and of no effect; But should the said money be not
paid that then WILLIAM HERNDON and THOMAS L. LOMAX shall after advertising the said
property in one of the Freds:burg Newspapers proceed to sell the same and the profits
arising from the same and the proceeds thereof, to be applied to the discharge the said
sum and the interest thereon, and the residue of the monies arising from the sale (if
there be any after paying the Debt and Interest and the expense of advertising the said

goods and chattles) shall go to said BARTHOLOMEW BLUNT his heirs; In Witness whereof
the parties to these presents have hereunto set their hands & seals the day & year first
above written
Signed sealed and delivered in presence of d
     EDWD. HYDE,   BARTHO: BLUNT
     F. M. E. STURMAN, D. CASTERBROOK
  At a Court of Hustings held for the Town & Corporation of Fredericksburg the 23rd
January 1802 This Indenture of Trust was acknowledged by the said BARTHOLOMEW
BLUNT & ordered to be recorded
Exd. & Deld. E. THATCHER   Teste JNO: CHEW, C. C. H.

pp.   THIS INDENTURE made this first day of August in the year one thousand Eight
358-   hundred and one Between WILLIAM BURNETT of one part of the Town of
360   Fredericksburg & COLIN & JAMES ROSS of said Town of other part; Witnesseth
       that WILLIAM BURNETT for the sum of Two hundred and fifty Dollars to said W.
BURNETT in hand paid, by these presents do bargain sell and confirm unto COLIN &
JAMES ROSS their heirs one Negro Woman named Prue, one grey Horse, two feather
Beds, one Desk and book Case, six Windsor Chairs and two Mahogany tables, To have and
to hold all the above property unto COLIN & JAMES ROSS their heirs, Provided always
and upon condition that if said W. BURNETT his heirs shall pay or cause to be paid to sd.
C. & J. ROSS or their certain Attorney the full sum of Two hundred and fifty Dollars on
or before the first day of December in the year one thousand eight hundred & two, with
lawful Interest thereon from the date then these presents shall cease and be void; And
for the more effectual carrying these presents into execution according to the true intent and meaning thereof, the sd. W. BURNET has made & appointed sd. COLIN & JAMES
ROSS their heirs the true & lawful Attorney of said WILLIAM BURNETT and if the said
sum shall not be paid full power to sell the property aforesaid; Provided always that
untill such sale shall take place sd. W. BURNET shall have the undisturbed possession &
use; In Witness whereof WILLIAM BURNET hath hereunto set his hand & affixed his seal
the day & year above written
Sign'd Seal'd & Deliver'd in presence of
     JOHN STEWART JUNR.   WILLIAM BURNETT
     HENRY RICE
  At a Court of Hustings held for the Town and Corporation of Freds:burg February the
27th 1802   This Indenture of Mortgage was acknowledged by the said WILLIAM
BURNETT & ordered to be recorded

pp.   THIS INDENTURE of Mortgage made this twenty seventh day of August in year
360-   year of our Lord one thousand eight hundred and one Between THOMAS L.
362   JOHNSTON of Town of Fredericksburg of one part and RICHARD JOHNSTON of the
       Town aforesaid of other part; Whereas THOMAS L. JOHNSTON hath this day pur-
chased of RICHARD JOHNSTON and ANN his Wife one moiety of a certain tract of land
with its appurtenances lying in the County of Spotsylvania adjoining the Town of
Fredericksburg (which tract contains ten and one half acres) for the price of One
thousand one hundred & forty Dollars, to be paid on or before the expiration of Twenty
years from the twentyeth day of Feby. last past with an annual Interest thereon at six
per centum to be paid annually the first payment of Interest to be on the twentyeth day
of February next ensuing the date hereof; and on the Twentyeth day of February in
each succeeding year hereafter; This Indenture Witnesseth that THOMAS L. JOHNSTON
in consideration of the premises and for the sum of One Dollar to him in hand paid by

RICHARD JOHNSTON by these presents do bargain and sell unto RICHARD JOHNSTON his
heirs that moiety of ten and one half acres of land be the same more or less together
with its rights members and appurtenances; To have and to hold the parcel of land with
its appurtenances to said RICHARD JOHNSTON his heirs, Provided nevertheless that if
THOMAS L. JOHNSTON his heirs shall pay or cause to be paid to RICHARD JOHNSTON his
heirs (or to the Trustees of the CHARITY SCHOOL of the Town of Freds:burg), the
aforesaid sum before the end of twenty years then this Indenture of Mortgage and
every thing therein contained shall be void and of none effect; In Testimony whereof
THOMAS L. JOHNSTON doth hereunto set his hand & seal the day & year first written
Signed Sealed and Delivered in the presence of
   JAMES ADAM, WILLIAM PORTER,   THOMAS L. JOHNSTON
   JOHN ALCOCK, WALKER JOHNSTON
 At a Court of Hustings held for the Town & Corporation of Freds:burg February the
27th 1802 This Indenture of Mortgage was acknowledged by the said THOMAS L.
JOHNSTON & ordered to be recorded
Exd. & deld. RD. JOHNSTON   Teste JNO: CHEW, C.C. H.

pp. THIS INDENTURE made this 27th day of August in year of our Lord one thousand
363- Eight hundred & one Between RICHARD JOHNSTON of Town of Freds:burg and
366 ANN his Wife of one part and THOMAS L. JOHNSTON of Town aforesaid of other
   part; Witnesseth that RICHARD JOHNSTON and ANN his Wife for sum of one thousand, one hundred and forty Dollars to them in hand paid by THOMAS L. JOHNSTON by
these presents do each of them bargain and sell unto THOMAS L. JOHNSTON and his heirs
one full moiety of a certain tract of land with its appurtenances lying and being in the
County of Spotsylvania adjoining the Town of Freds:burg and which is particularly
described in a Deed of Indenture from BENJAMIN DAY and others, Trustees of the
CHARITY SCHOOL of Fredericksburg to said RICHARD JOHNSTON bearing date the 27th
day of August in year of our Lord one thousand eight hundred and one; and is made part
hereof, which tract of land so sold and conveyed by said BENJAMIN DAY and others,
Trustees of the CHARITY SCHOOL contains as appears by the Deed of Indenture the Quan-
tity of Ten and one half acres of land be the same more or less; To have and to hold the
one half of the aforesaid ten and one half acres of land together with one half of all its
rights members and premises unto THOMAS L. JOHNSTON his heirs and RICHARD JOHN-
STON and ANN his Wife and their heirs against all claims will warrant and forever de-
fend by these presents; In Testimony whereof RICHARD JOHNSTON & ANN his Wife do
hereunto set their hands and affix their seal the day & year first above written
Signed sealed and Delivered in the presence of
   ANTHY: BUCK, WALKER JOHNSTON,   RICHD. JOHNSTON
   JAMES ADAM, WILLIAM PORTER,   ANN T. JOHNSTON
   JOHN ALCOCK
 The Commonwealth of Virginia to DAVID C. KER, TOAMS GOODWIN & JOHN BENSON,
Gentlemen, Greeting (The Commission for the privy Examination of ANN the Wife of RICHARD
JOHNSTON); Witness JOHN CHEW Clerk of our said Court the 27th day of February 1802 &
in the 26th year of the Commonwealth   JNO: CHEW
 In Obedience to the within Order, we have this day (the return of the execution of the privy
Examination of ANN T. JOHNSTON); Given under our hands & seals this 27th February 1802
           DAVID C. KER
           THO: GOODWIN
 At a Court of Hustings held for the Town & Corporaltion of Freds:burg February the
27th 1802 This Indenture was acknowledged by the said RICHARD JOHNSTON & toge-

ther with the Commission annexed & Certificate of Execution thereof by the said ANN T. indorsed, are ordered to be recorded

Examd. & delivered T. JOHNSTON   Teste   JNO: CHEW, C. C. H.

pp.   THIS INDENTURE of Mortgage made and entered into this 27th day of August in
366-   year of our Lord one thousand eight hundred and one Between RICHARD JOHN-
369   JOHNSTON and ANN his Wife of Town of Fredericksburg of one part and THOMAS
      L. JOHNSTON of Town aforesaid of other part; Whereas THOMAS L. JOHNSTON hath
become security to said RICHARD JOHNSTON in a Bond entered into between RICHARD
JOHNSTON to the Trustees of the CHARITY SCHOOL of the Town of Fredericksburg in the
penalty of 4560 Dollars conditioned for the payment of Two thousand twohundred &
eighty dollars with an annual Interest thereon which bond bears date the 28th of Septr.
1802, And whereof RICHARD JOHNSTON and ANN his Wife by Deed of Indenture bearing
date the 27th day of August in the year 1801 have conveyed a fee simple Estate in one
moiety of a tract of land for the payment of which the said Bond was given and for
which a Mortgage was also given by RICHARD JOHNSTON and ANN his Wife, the said
THOMAS L. JOHNSTON hath become liable to pay one half of the purchase money which
was contracted to be given for the whole tract as also one half of the Interest &c. yet
there remians one half of the money contracted to be given for the whole tract & one
half of the Interest &c. &c., to be paid by RICHARD JOHNSTON; NOW THEREFORE THIS IN-
DENTURE WITNESSETH that RICHARD JOHNSTON and ANN his Wife in consideration of the
premises and the sum of One Dollars to them in hand paid, by these presents do bargain
and sell unto THOMAS L. JOHNSTON and his heirs all the other moiety of said tract of land
(which RICHARD JOHNSTON purchased from the Trustees of the CHARITY SCHOOL) not
before conveyed to the said THOMAS L. JOHNSTON Together with all it rights members
and appurtenances; Provided that if RICHARD JOHNSTON his heirs shall keep free and
save harmless the said THOMAS L. JOHNSTON his heirs from his securityship and shall
comply with the proviso in the Mortgage above recited, made by RICHARD JOHNSTON
and ANN his Wife to the Trustees of the said CHARITY SCHOOL then this Indenture and
every thing therein contained shall be void; In Testimony whereof the said RICHARD
JOHNSTON & ANN his Wife have hereunto set their hands and seals the day & year first
above written

Sealed & Delivered in presence of
    JAMES ADAM,   WILLIAM PORTER,   RICHD. JOHNSTON
    JOHN ALCOCK, WALKER JOHNSTON   ANN T. JOHNSTON
  The Commonwealth of Virginia to THOMAS GOODWIN, DAVID C. KER and JOHN BENSON
Gentlemen, Greeting, Whereas (the Commission for the privy Examination of ANN T., Wife of
RICHARD JOHNSTON); Witness JOHN CHEW Clerk of our said Court the 27th day of February
1802 and in the 26th year of the Commonwealth   JNO: CHEW
  In Obedience to the within Order we have this day proceeded (the return of the execution
of the privy Examination of ANN T. JOHNSTON); Given under our hands and seals this 27th
day of February 1802   DAVID C. KER
                                            THO: GOODWIN

  At a Hustings Court held for the Town & Corporation of Frederickburg February the
27th 1802   This Indenture of Mortgage was acknowledged by the said RICHARD
JOHNSTON and together with the Commission annexed and Certificate of the execution
thereof by the said ANN T. indorsed are ordered to be recorded

Exd. & deld. T. JOHNSTON   Teste JNO: CHEW, C. C. H.

pp.   THIS INDENTURE made this 18th day of February Anno Domini one thousand
370-   eight hundred and Two between WILLIAM WELCH of Town of Freds:burg of one
371   part and ROBERT PATTON of the Town aforesaid of other part; Witnesseth that
         WILLIAM WELCH in consideration of the Rents and Covenants hereafter
reserved on part of ROBERT PATON to be paid and peformed, WILLIAM WELCH hath
demised granted and to farm let unto ROBERT PATTON and assigns part of the tenement
now in possession of said WILLIAM WELCH lying on the Main Street of the Town aforesaid with the appurtenances thereunto belonging; To have and to hold the said Tenement with their appurtenaces unto ROBERT PATTON and assigns during the full term of
twelve years paying the yearly rent of One hundred dollars; In Witness whereof the
said parties have hereunto set their hands and seals the day & year first above written
Signed in presence of
            DAVID WILLIAMSON,   WILL: WELCH
            THOMAS WARE, FRANCIS GAINS   ROBT. PATTON
   At a Court of Hustings held for the Town & Corporation of Fredericksburg February the
27th 1802   This Indenture of Lease was acknowledged by the said WILLIAM WELCH
and ordered to be recorded
Exd. & Deld. R. PATTON   Teste JNO: CHEW C.C.H.

p.   KNOW ALL MEN by these presents that I ROBERT WALKER in consideration of
371   the Services heretofore done and performed by Milley, do by these presents
         Emancipate and set free the said Milley and do hereby absolve and discharge the
said Milley from all rights or further service whic I may ever heretofore have been
entitled to from her. In Witness whereof I have hereunto set my hand and seal this
24th day of April 1802   ROBERT WALKER
   At a Court of Hustings held for the Town & Corporation of Freds:burg April the 24th
1802   This Letter of Emancipation was acknowledged by the said ROBERT WALKER &
ordered to be recorded
Filed with Certificate Registered   Teste   JNO: CHEW C.C.H.

p.   THIS INDENTURE made this twenty first day of April One thousand Eight hun-
372   dred and Two Between ROGER DIXON of the MISSISSIPPI TERRITORY of one part
         and WILLIAM JAMES of Town of Fredericksburg and State of Virginia of other
part; Witnesseth that ROGER DIXON, Heir at Law of the late ROGER DIXON of said Town, in
consideration of One hundred and Ten Dollars by these presents doth bargain sell and
confirm unto WILLIAM JAMES his heirs one lot of land lying in Town of Fredericksburg known by the number Two hundred and nine bounded by DUNMORE STREET and
PRINCESS AUGUSTA STREET and by the lots Two hundred and two and Two hundred & ten
and said ROGER DIXON and his heirs by these presents doth warrant and defend the said
WILLIAM JAMES his heirs against the claims of every person whatsoever; In Witness
whereof ROGER DIXON hath set his hand and seal the day & year before written
Signed Sealed & Delivered in the presence of
            ANTH: THORNTON, JOHN R. THORNTON,   ROGER DIXON
            ADAM DARBY, TIMO: GREEN,
            WM. PEARSON, HENRY WHITE
   LUCY DIXON, Widow of the late ROGER DIXON of Fredericksburg doth hereby relinquish
her claim of Dower to the within mentioned lot of ground sold by ROGER DIXON of the
MISSISSIPPI TERRITORY to WILLIAM JAMES of the Town of Fredericksburg
Testes ANTH: THORNTON,   LUCY DIXON
            ADAM DARBY
(No recording shown for this Indenture.)

pp.   THIS INDENTURE made the ninth day of April one thousand Eight hundred and
373-   two Between ROGER DIXON of the Country of NATCHEZ and RICHARD PEACOCK of
374   the Town of Fredericksburg, Merchant, Witnesseth that ROGER DIXON, Heir at
        Law of the late ROGER DIXON of the aforesaid Twon for One hundred Dollars in
hand paid hath bargained and sold unto RICHARD PEACOCK and his heirs all that part or
lot of land within Town of Fredericksburg known by the number 194 and being on the
DUNMORE and FERDINAND STREETS and bounded on the other two sides by lots numbers
192 & 201; and all the estate right claim and demand of said ROGER, heir at Law as aforesaid and his heirs in the premises containing half an acre; To have and to hold the said
Tenement herein mentioned unto RICHARD PEACOCK his heirs; In Witness whereof
ROGER DIXON hath put his hand and seal the day and year above written
Signed sealed and Delivered in the presence of
        JAMES DOGGETT, DANIEL ROSS,   ROGER DIXON
        PHILIP TERRIER, JAMES ALLEN
BE IT REMEMBERED that LUCY DIXON, Widow of the late ROGER DIXON, doth by these
presents relinquish and quit claaim to all her right of Dower to the within mentioned
lot of ground sold to RICHARD PEACOCK by her Son, ROGER DIXON, being the lot number
194. Signed this twentieth day of April 1802
In presence of ANTH: THORNTON   LUCY DIXON
  At a Court of Hustings held for the Town & Corporation of Fredericksburg April the
24th 1802   This Indenture was acknowledged by the said ROGER DIXON & ordered to
be recorded
Exd. & Deld. RICHD. PEACOCK   Teste JNO: CHEW, C. C. H.

p.   KNOW ALL MEN by these presents that I do hereby bind myself in the sum of
374   of Two hundred Dollars to RICHARD PEACOCK his heirs and assigns that I will
        procure the relinquishment of my Wife's Dower or claim to the lot number one
hundred and ninety four that I have this day sold to said PEACOCK, Given this 20th day
of April 1802
Teste ADAM DARBY,   ROGER DIXON
  At a Court of Hustigns held for the Town & Corporation of Fredericksburg April the
24th 1802   This Writng was acknowledged by the said ROGER DIXON & ordered to be
recorded

pp.   THIS INDENTURE made this 28th day of August in year of our Lord one thousand
375-   eight hundred and one Between RICHARD JOHNSTON & ANN his Wife of the Town
377   of Freds:burg of one part and BENJAMIN DAY, ROBERT PATTON, DAVID HENDER-
        SON, JOHN CHEW, WM. S. STONE, WILLIAM TAYLOR & DAVID C. KER & JOHN MER-
CER, Trustees (for the time being) of the CHARITY SCHOOL of the Town of Fredericksburg of the other part. Whereas RICHARD JOHNSTON hath purchased of said Trustess of
the CHARITY SCHOOL a fee simple estate in a certain parcel of land with its appurtenances lying in County of Spotsylvania adjoining the Town of Fredericksburg containing ten and one half acres and bounded, Beginning at A at or near a line of the
land of Colo. LEWIS WILLIS, runing thence South 34 1/2 East 40 1/2 poles to B, thence
South thirty nine West 45 1/3 poles to C, thence North 74 1/2 West 22 3/4 poles to D,
thence North 25 1/2 East 69 poles to the begining for the price of Two thousand two
hundred & Eighty Dolalrs to be paid at the end of Twenty years from the 20th day of
February last past with an annual Interest of 6 pr. ct. thereon to be paid annually; Now
Therefore this Indenture Witnesseth that RICHARD JOHNSTON & ANN his Wife in consideration of the premises and the sum of One Dollar to him in hand paid, by these pre-

sents do bargain and sell unto BENJAMIN DAY, ROBERT PATTON, DAVID HENDERSON,
JOHN CHEW, WILLIAM S. STONE, WILLIAM TAYLOR & DAVID S. KER & JOHN MERCER,
Trustees of the CHARITY SCHOOL and their Successors in Office the above described
trace of land except an Avenue of thirty feet from DUNMORE STREET in Town of
Fredericksburg with the line thereof to CHRISTYs line, thence with his line to the
ACADEMY or BATH SPRING together with forty feet square round the said SPRING,
which said Avenue of thirty feet and square of Forty feet were not sold by the said
Trustees to the said RICHARD JOHNSTON but were excepted from that Sale, as by their
Deed to him bearing date the 17th day of August in the year one thousand eight hundred and one; To have and to hold the above recited tract of land with its appurtenances
(except as before excepted) to the Trustees for the time being and their Successors in
Office; Provided Nevertheless that if RICHARD JOHNSTON and ANN his Wife their heirs
shall pay the Trustees of the CHARITY SCHOOL as aforesaid or their Successors in Office
or to their assigns the aforesaid sum on or before the end of Twenty years from the
20th day of February last past which will be the 20th day of February in the year one
thousand eight hundred and twenty one and also pay the Interest accruing thereon,
provided the payments shall not be less than $400 Dollars; In Testimony whereof the
said RICHARD JOHNSTON and ANN his Wife have hereunto set their hands & seals the day
& year first above written
Signed Sealed & Delivered in presence of
    ANTHY: BUCK,   RICHD. JOHNSTON
    THOS: DOWELL, DANL: ATTWELL   ANN T. JOHNSTON
   At a Court of Hustingsheld for the Town & Corporation of Fredericksburg April the
24th 1802   This Indenture of Mortgage was proved by the Oaths of ANTHONY BUCK,
THOMAS DOWELL & DANIEL ATTWELL three witnesses thereto and ordered to be recorded
Exd. and delivered ANTHO: BUCK
   Treasurer for the Trustees   Teste JNO: CHEW, C.C.H.

p.   THIS INDENTURE made this 29th day of October in the year of our Lord one
378   thousand Eight hundred and one Between JOHN HARDIA of Town of Fredericks-
      burg of one part and WESCOM HUDGSENS of same Town of the other; Witnesseth
that JOHN HARDIA for the sum of Two hundred & fifty pounds current money of Virginia to him in hand paid; by these presents doth bargain and sell unto WESCOM
HUDGSENS all that tract of land adjoining the Lotts which the said HARDIA now pos-
sesses and bounded; Beginning on the Main Street called CAROLINE STREET and the
Cross Street called SOPHIA STREET extending fifty six feet in front on the Main Street,
and one hundred and fifteen feet deep on the Street running down to the River; To
have and to hold said parcel of land with its appurtenances to him and his heirs and
JOHN HARDIA his heirs the parcel of land with its appurtenances to the above said
HUDGSENS his heirs from the claims of any person doth warrant and for ever defend;
In Testimony whereof JOHN HARDIA has set his hand and affixed his seal hereto this
17th day of October in the year above said
Signed sealed and delivered in the presence of
    ANDERSON McWILLIAMS,   JNO: HARDIA
    JAMES NEWBY, WALTER BOURK
   At a Court of Hustings held for the Town & Corporation of Fredericksburg the 26th day
of June 1802   This Indenture for Land was proved by the oath of ANDERSON McWIL-
LIAMS, JAMES NEWBY & WALTER BOURK three witnesses thereto and ordered to be
recorded
Exd. & deld. WM. HARDIA for Mrs. HUDGIN Admx.   Teste   JNO: CHEW, C.C.H.

pp.   THIS INDENTURE made this 27th day of April 1802 Between ROGER DIXON, late
379-   of Town of Fredericksburg of one part and PHILIP TERRIER of Town of
380   Fredericksburg of other part; Witnesseth that the said ROGER for Two hundred
and Twenty Dollars to him in hand paid by the said PHILIP, doth bargain and sell
unto said PHILIP his heirs all that parcel of land in Town of Fredericksburg being part
of the lot known by the number 248, bounded Beginning at the lower corner of MRS.
TUTMONs House on CAROLINE STREET and runing along said Street twenty six feet
toward PRUSIA STREET, being the same that was leased by said ROGER to WILLIAM
JACKSON and released by said JACKSON to ROGER, thence runing at right angles from
CAROLINE STREET the whole depth of Lot number 248, thence on the back line of the
said Lot to the said TUTMANs Lot, thence along said Lot to the begining; and all appurtenances belonging; To have and to hold all the said premises with the appurtenances
unto the said PHILIP his heirs and the said ROGER and his heirs the parcel of land
against him & his heirs to said PHILIP his heirs shall warrant and forever defend by
these presents; In Witness whereof the said ROGER hath hereunto affixed his hand and
Seal the day and year aforesaid
Signed Sealed & Delivered in presence of
    JAMES ALLEN,   ROGER DIXON
    ANDERSON McWILLIAMS, JAMES DOGGETT
 At a Court of Hustings held for the Town & Corporation of Fredericksburg the 26th day
of June 1802   This Indenture for Land was proved by the oath of JAMES ALLEN,
ANDERSON McWILLIAMS & JAMES DOGGETT, three witnesses thereto & ordered to be
recorded
Exd. & delivered DAVID CHAPMAN p Order filed   Teste JNO: CHEW, C.C.H.

pp.   THIS INDENTURE made this seventeenth day of May Anno Domini Eighteen
380-   hundred and two Between JACOB KUHN of Town of Fredericksburg of one part
382   and THOMAS GOODWIN of said Town of other part; Witnesseth that JACOB KUHN
in order to secure the payment of three thousand six hundred Dollars with interest on one third part thereof from the 14th of Jany. 1802, on another third from the
14th July 1802; and on the other third from the 14th Jany. 1803 to a certain CHRISTO-
PHER JOHNSTON of BALTIMORE in the State of MARYLAND, on the 17th of May 1803; and
in consideration of the sum of one Dollar to him in hand paid by THOMAS GOODWIN by
these presents doth bargain and sell unto THOMAS GOODWIN his heirs all the Lott number Fifty Nine lying in Town of Fredericksburg and on which said KUHN now resides;
together with all houses thereon; To have and to hold the Lot number Fifty nine with
rights members and appurtenances unto THOMAS GOODWIN his heirs Upon Trust nevertheless that is JACOB KUHN should fail to apy the said sum with interest as aforesaid to
CHRISTOPHER JOHNSTON before the 17th day of May 1803, that said THOMAS GOODWIN
shall as soon as conveniently he can after such failure (having advertised the time and
place of sale of the property beforementioned in some Newspaper published in the
Town of Fredericksburg for at least thirty day) proceed to sell the same to the highest
bidder and out of the monies arising from such sale in the first place to pay and satisfy
all reasonable charges attending the Sale, then the Debt to said CHRISTOPHER JOHNSTON
with interest as aforesaid, and the residue of the monies arising from such sale to the
use of JACOB KUHN his heirs or to such person as he by writing under his hand shall
appoint; In Witness whereof the parties to these presents have hereunto set their
hands & affixed their seals the day & year first above written
Signed Sealed and Delivered in presence of
    GEO: W. B. SPOONER, JOS: F. MARTIN,   JACOB KUHN
    BEN H. BUCKNER, WILLIAM SMITH JR.   THO: GOODWIN

At a Court of Hustings held for the Town & Corporation of Fredericksburg the 24th day of July 1802   This Indenture of Trust was proved by the Oaths of JOSEPH F. MARTIN, BENJAMIN H. BUCKNER & WILLIAM SMITH JR., three of the witnesses thereto and ordered to be recorded
Exd. & deld. THO: GOODWIN   Teste JNO: CHEW, C. C. H.

pp.   KNOW ALL MEN by these presents that I CHRISTOPHER JOHNSTON of BALTIMORE
382-   in the State of MARYLAND, Merchant, do hereby appoint THOMAS GOODWIN of
383   Fredericksburg, Merchant, my true and lawfull Attorney for me to sign over &
        transfer all my right and title in a certain lot of ground No. 59 lying in Town of
Fredericksburg purchased by me at Publick Vendue the Thirteen day of January last
under Decree of the Worshipfull Court of Spotsylvania County, Hereby ratifying all acts
which my said Attorney may lawfully do in the premises in as full and ample manner
as if personally done by myself; In Witness whereof I have hereunto set my hand and
Seal this 14th day of July one thousand eight hundred and one
Signed Sealed & Delvered in presence of
    W. S. STONE,   CHR: JOHNSTON
    ROBERT CHEW,   WM. BROOKE
At a Court of Hustings held for the Town & Corporation of Freds:burg the 24th day of
July 1802   This Power of Attorney was proved by the oaths of WILLIAM S. STONE &
WILLIAM BROOKE, two of the witnesses thereto, and ordered to be recorded

pp.   THIS INDENTURE made and entered into this twenty fourth day of July in year
383-   one thousand eight hundred and two Between JAMES ALLEN of Town of
385   Fredericksburg of one part and THOMAS GOODWIN of the same place of other
        part; Witnesseth that JAMES ALLEN in order to secure the payment of Three
hundred & Seventy eight pounds 3/11 lawfull money of Virginia due & owing by JAMES
ALLEN to DAVID HENDERSON of Fredericksburg and in consideration of the sum of One
Dollar to him in hand paid by THOMAS GOODWIN, by these presents doth bargin and sell
unto THOMAS GOODWIN one Negro man named Titus aged about 70 years, one Negro boy
named Reubin aged about 17 years, one Negro woman named Francis aged about 55
years, one Mulatto girl named Charlotte aged about 15 years & her offspring, one milch
Cow, and all the household & kitchen furniture of said JAMES ALLEN as is particularly
described in the Schedule hereunto annexed as part of this Indenture; To have and to
hold the said Negroes and the offspring of said Charlotte, the household & kitchen
furniture and milch cow herein mentioned unto THOMAS GOODWIN Upon Trust Nevertheless that THOMAS GOODWIN shall at the expiration of two years from the date of these
presents (having first advertized the time & place of sale of the property in the
Fredericksburg Newpaper) proceed to sell the same & out of the monies arising from
the sale in the first place to satisfy all reasonable charges attending such sale & then
the Debt above mentioned due to DAVID HENDERSON and the residue of the monies
arising to the use of said JAMES ALLEN or assigns; But if before the expiration of two
years JAMES ALLEN shall pay the same to DAVID HENDERSON then the Trust hereby declared shall cease & be void; In Witness whereof the parties have hereunto set their
hands & seals the day & year first above written
Signed sealed and delivered in presence of   JAMES ALLEN
    (no witnesses shown)   THO: GOODWIN
    Schedule of all & singular the Household & Kitchen furniture, the property of JAMES
ALLEN conveyed by this Indenture to THOMAS GOODWIN for purposes mentioned within
& referred to in said Indenture to wit; Three feather beds & furniture, three Bedsteads,

one set of Bed & Window Curtains; one Side Board; six Mahogany Tables, one black Walnut Table, one Mahogany Dressing Table, one do. candle stand; one wash stand; one sett
of drawers; one spice press, one knife case full of knives & forks; one Mahogany Crib,
two Dressing Glasses, Two black Walnut arm'd chairs; twenty Windsor Chairs, Four
trunks to hold Cloaths, Eight small pictures; Fifty volumes of Books, Bible Included; two
large Carpets, four flower Pots, one pair fire dogs, shovel , poker & tongs; two pair of
brass candle sticks, five Japaned Waiters, one Water Pitcher, one dozen Table Spoons,
one Soup Spoon, one Punch Ladle, one set Glass castors in a plated stande; one pair of
glass Salvers, a sallad Bowl, pair of Decanters and forty five pieces of Glass assorted
mugs tumbles & wine glasses &c., three Tureens, one bowl, 2 pitchers, twenty dishes, 12
dozen other pieces Queens Ware, 12 Pickle & Butter Potts, one Sugar Cannister & box, two
tea Cannisters, one meal Cannister & Sifter; one wheel barrow, one Coal Hob, ten tubs
piggins & pales, four pots, three Dutch ovens, one Tea Kettle, one Frying Pan, four Flat
Irons, six tin Candle Moulds, one Cullender, one spinning wheel, one Grid Iron, seven
Old casks, some empty bottles,   JAMES ALLEN
   At a Court of Hustings held for the Town & Corporation of Fredericksburg the 24th day
of July 1802   This Indenture of Trust was acknowledged by the said JAMES ALLEN &
THOMAS GOODWIN, And together with the Schedule annexed which as also acknowledged
by the said JAMES ALLEN & ordered to be recorded
Exd. & delivered JAMES ALLEN   Teste JNO: CHEW, C.C.H.

pp.   I ACKNOWLEDGE this day to have received of my Mother, MARGARET JULIAN,
385-   full satisfaction for all claims and demands whatsoever which I have or may
386   have against her as Administratrix of my Father, Doctor JOHN JULIAN, or as my
         Guardian, And I do hereby release her from all such demands; In Witness
whereof I have hereunto set my hand and seal this 23rd day of April 1802
Signed & Acknowledged in presence of
     JAMES McGILLAVRAY   CHS. JULIAN
     PEGGY JULIAN, GEORGE RICHARDSON
   At a Court of Hustings held for the Town & Corporation of Freds:burg September the
25th 1802   This Release was proved by the oaths of JAMES McGILLAVRAY and
GEORGE RICHARDSON, two of the witnesses thereto, and ordered to be recorded

p.   KNOW ALL MEN by these presents taht I BARTHOLOMEW FULLER of the Town &
386   Corporation of Fredericksburg in consideration of the natural love and af-
         fection which I bear to my Children, JAMES, JEREMIAH, FRANCIS, DANIEL,
ALICE and SARAH ANN FULLER of said Town & Corporation as well as for the consideration of One Dollar to me in hand paid by the aforementioned Children, by these presents
do give and grant unto the Children and assigns one Mulatto slave woman named Mary
about twenty years of age and her increase and her mulatto Child about eleven months
old named William, To have and to hold the said slave woman & child unto them and the
said BARTHOLOMEW FULLER against the claims of all persons will warrant and forever
defend by these presents; In Witness whereof I have hereunto set my hand and affixed
my seal the 18th day of Septr. in the year of our Lord God one thousand eight hundred
and two
Signed sealed & delivered inthe presents of
     (no witnesses shown)   BARTHOLOMEW FULLER
Exd. & deld. B. FULLER
   At a Court of Hustings held for the Town & Corporation of Fredericksburg September
the 25th 1802 This Deed of Gift for slaves was acknowledged by the said BARTHOLOMEW
FULLER and ordered to be recorded   Teste JNO: CHEW, C.C.H.

pp.
387-
390

THIS INDENTURE made the thirteenth day of July in year of our Lord one thousand eight hundred and two and of our Independence the Twenty Sixth Between GEORGE FRENCH and ANN his Wife, and WILLIAM DRUMMOND and ANN FOX his Wife of Town of Fredericksburg of one part and CHARLES LANDON CARTER of the same place of other part; Witnesseth that WILLIAM DRUMMON and ANN FOX his Wife, GEORGE FRENCH and ANN his Wife for the sum of Five Shillings current money of Virginia to them in hand paid by CHARLES L. CARTER, by these presents do bargain and sell unto CHARLES L. CARTER his heirs one certain parcel of ground lying in the Town of Fredericksburg to say Twenty feet of the lot on CHARLES STREET, Beginning on said Street at Lott number one thousand and thirty three (which was sold to CHARLES L. CARTER by WILLIAM DRUMMOND, then running with and bounding on said Street twenty feet, then by a line drawn parralel to LEWIS STREET unto the Lot numbered One hundred and thirty six, thence twenty feet along the last mentioned lott to Lott No. 134; (which last is now in the possession of JOHN MINOR purchased of McWILLIAMS's Estate) thence along Lott number one hundred thirty three to the beginning; twenty feet being part of lott numbered one hundred and thirty five purchased by GEORGE FRENCH of FRAZIER, as will appear by a Deed from the party, together with all houses gardens passages profits and appurtenances (except the priviledge of getting Water from the Well being reserved to GEORGE FRENCH and his heirs) to the parcel of land belonging; To have and to hold the parcel of ground with the tenements and all premises intended to be sold (except as before excepted) unto CHARLES LANDON CARTER his heirs and GEORGE FRENCH and ANN his Wife and WILLIAM DRUMMOND and ANN FOX his Wife and their heirs shall warrant and forever defend by these presents; In Witness whereof said WILLIAM DRUMMOND and ANN FOX his Wife and GEORGE FRENCH and ANN his Wife have hereunto set their hands and seals the day and year first above written
Signed Sealed & Delivered in presence of

THOMAS LEGG,	GEO: FRENCH
WM. ALLEN,	ANN B. FRENCH
JAMES SCOTT,	WM. DRUMMOND
SAML. OWENS	ANN FOX DRUMMOND

The Commonwealth of Virginia to BENJN. DAY, STEPHEN WINCHESTER and H. T. W. MERCER Gentlemen, Greeting, Whereas (the Commission for the privy Examination of ANN B. the Wife of GEORGE FRENCH and ANN FOX, the Wife of WILLIAM DRUMMOND): Witness JOHN CHEW Clerk of our said Court the 15th day of July 1802 and in the 27th year of the Commonwealth   JNO: CHEW
Corporation of Fredg. Sct. In Obedience to the within Commision we have received the acknowledgments of the within named ANN FRENCH and ANN FOX DRUMMOND ((the return of the Execution of the privy Examinations of ANN B. FRENCH and ANN FOX DRUMMOND); Given under our hands this 17th day of July 1802
                          S. WINCHESTER
                          H. T. W. MERCER
At a Court of Hustings held for the Town & Corporation of Freds:burg September the 25th 1802   This Indenture for Land was proved by the oaths of THOMAS LEGG, WILLIAM ALLEN & JAMES SCOTT, three of the witnesses thereto and together with the Commission annexed and Certificate of the Execution thereof by ANN FOX DRUMMOND and ANN FRENCH indorsed, are ordered to be recorded
Exd. & deld. CHS. L. CARTER   Teste JNO: CHEW, C.C.H.

pp.   THIS INDENTURE made this tenth day of May in the year Eighteen hundred and
390- two Between WILLIAM SMOCK and SARAH his Wife of Town of Fredericksburg of
392   one part and JOHN LEWIS of the said Town of other part; Witnesseth that WIL-
LIAM SMOCK and SARAH his Wife for sum of Four hundred and forty pounds
lawful money to them in hand paid by JOHN LEWIS, by these presents doth bargain and
sell unto said LEWIS his heirs all that parcel of ground lying on the Main Street in said
Town being the lower part of Lott No. 39 (which said lott or parcel of ground was formerly sold by JOHN THORNTON (now of the County of CULPEPER) and JANE his Wife to
RICHARD LEWIS and conveyed by Deed on the seventh day of April 1784 by said JOHN
THORNTON and JANE his Wife to JOHN LEWIS, Son and heir of said RICHARD LEWIS, and
other representatives of said RICHARD LEWIS which lott or parcel of ground is bounded
beginning on CAROLINE or Main Street of said Town opposite the lower side of the
STONE CHIMNEY belonging to the lower Tenement on BAGGOTTs Lott, (which is the
upper part of Lott No. 39), runing thence down and with the line of said Main Street
eighty one feet six inches to Lott No. 37, thence Westwardly with the upper line of Lott
No. 37 eight poles or onehundred and thirty two feet to the lower corner of BAGGOTTs
back lott No. 38; thence up and along the said back line of Lott No. 38 in a line parralel
with the Main or CAROLINE STREET to said BAGGOTTs Corner of his part of Lott No. 39,
thence eight poles or one hundred and thirty two feet to the beginning, together with
all houses and appurtenances to said Lott belonging; To have and to hold the Lott or
parcel of ground unto JOHN LEWIS his heirs and WILLIAM SMOCK and SARAH his Wife
their heirs will warrant and forever defend by these presents; In Witness whereof
WILLIAM SMOCK and SARAH his Wife have hereunto set their hands and seals the day
and year first above written

Signed Sealed & Delivered in presence of   WM. SMOCK
    (no witnesses shown)   SARAH SMOCK

The Commonwealth of Virginia to WILLIAM DRUMMOND, STEPHEN WINCHESTER & H.
MERCER Gentlemen Greeting, Whereas (the Commission for the privy Examination of SARAH
the Wife of WILLIAM SMOCK); Witness JOHN CHEW, Clerk of our said Court, the 24th day of
August 1802 and in the 27th year of the Commonwealth   JNO: CHEW

Corporation of Fredericksburg to wit; By Virtue of the within Writ to us directed we
caused the within named SARAH SMOCK to come before us (the return of the execution of the
privy Examination of SARAH SMOCK); Given under our hands and seals this twenty eighth
day of August one thousand eight hundred & two   S. WINCHESTER
                                   H. T. W. MERCER

At a Court of Hustings held for the Town & Corporation of Fredericksburg September
the 25th 1802 This Indenture for Land was acknowledged by the said WILLIAM SMOCK
and together with the Commission annexed & Certificate of Execution thereof by the
said SARAH indorsed, are ordered to be recorded
Examined & delivered W. W. LEWIS   Teste   JNO: CHEW, C. C. H.

pp.   The Commonwealth of Virginia to STEPHEN WINCHESTER, ROBERT LEWIS and
393- WILLIAM DRUMMOND Gentlemen Greeting; Whereas RICHARD S. HACKLEY &
394   ANN his Wife and ROBERT PATTON and ANN G. his Wife by their certain Indenture of bargain and sale bearing date the 1st day of October 1799 have sold and
conveyed unto RICHARD JOHNSTON part of a lott number 14 (the Commission for the privy
Examination of ANN G. Wife of ROBERT PATTON) Witness JOHN CHEW Clerk of our said Hustings Court the 23rd day of February 1803 & in the 27th year of the Commonwealth

Agreeable to the within Commission to us directed we waited on Mrs. ANN G. PATTON
(the return of the execution of the privy Examination of ANN G. PATTON); Given under our

hands and seals this 24th day of February 1803   S. WINCHESTER
                                                                   ROBT. LEWIS
            Truly Recorded   Teste JNO: CHEW., C. C. H.
Exd. & deld. RD. JOHNSTON together with the Deed

pp.   THIS INDENTURE made this 9th day of October in year of our Lord one thousand
394-   eight hundred and two Between JAMES WALKER of Town of Fredericksburg of
395   one part and JANE LEWIS of the same Town of other part; Witnesseth that JAMES
           WALKER in consideration of Three hundred pounds lawful money of this Com-
monwealth to him in hand paid by the said JANE LEWIS, by these presents does bargain
and sell unto JANE LEWIS her heirs a certain part of a lott in Fredericksburg lying on
CAROLINE STREET and known by No. 246, begining at the Southeast corner of the House
wherein he now lives, running Northward in front Seventy eight feet and bounded by
the back lot known by No. 237, together with all houses commodites and appurtenances
belonging; To have and to hold the said aprt of a lot with all the premises herein before
mentioned unto JANE LEWIS her heirs and JAMES WALKER or his heirs will and do warrant and forever defend by these presents; In Witness whereof JAMES WALKER has
hereunto set his hand and seal the day & year first above written
Signed sealed & Delivered in the presence of
       WM. UPSHAW,   JAMES WALKER
       JNO: TALIAFERRO, A. R. FITZHUGH,
       F. STURMAN, ROBERT WALKER JR., JOHN B. BENSON
   At a Court of Hustings held for the Town & Corporation of Freds:burg the 26th of
February 1803   This Indenture was proved by the oaths of F. STURMAN, ROBERT
WALKER JR., & JOHN B. BENSON, three of the witnesses thereto and ordered to be
recorded
Exd. & deld. JNO: BENSON, Husband of JANE LEWIS   Teste JNO: JNO: CHEW, C. C. H.

pp.   THIS INDENTURE made this 26th day of February in year one thousand eight
396-   hundred and three Between JOHN LEWIS of Town of Fredericksburg of one part
398   & ROBERT LEWIS of the Town aforesaid of other part; Witnesseth that JOHN
           LEWIS for the sum of Thirteen hundred pounds Virginia Currency to him in
hand paid by ROBERT LEWIS, by these presents doth bargain and sell unto ROBERT
LEWIS and his heirs a certain parcel of ground lying in said Town and bounded, Begining on CAROLINE STREET at the upper corner of the WOODHOUSE, now in the Occupation of ROBERT LEWIS, thence along CAROLINE STREET 30 feet to the line of the Lott
rented by JAMES BROWN, Silversmith, on which a BLACKSMITHs SHOP is now erected;
thence along the line of the last mentioned Lott to PRINCESS ANN STREET, thence
runing down PRINCESS ANN STREET to the lower end of the present WAREHOUSE which
is forty feet in length, thence by a line parallel with the Cross Street which passes between TIMOTHY GREEN & WM. HERNDON and also parallel with the line which divided
this lott from the Lott rented by JAMES BROWN as aforesaid; untill it intersects the back
line of the Lott on which the first mentioned WOODHOUSE stands, which said back line is
same of the back line of TIMOTHY GREEN & WM. PEARSON, Also one certain other parcel
of ground adjoining the above described parcel of ground and on which the Dwelling
House of ROBERT LEWIS stands; and bounded, Begining on CAROLINE STREET at the lower
end of the Dwelling House now in occupation of said ROBERT LEWIS, runing thence
along CAROLINE STREET to the line of the first above described piece of ground, thence
along that line untill it intersects the line which (in the description of the first above
mentioned peice of ground) is called the back line of this Lott and the same line with

the back line of TIMOTHY GREEN and WILLIAM PEARSON's Lotts; thence along that back
line to the line of WILLIAM PEARSON, thence along PEARSONs line to the begining; the
first mentioned lott or parcel of ground being the share of a Lott which was allotted to
said JOHN LEWIS by ROBERT PATTON, WM. DRUMMOND and WM. S. STONE, three of the
Commissioners appointed by a Decree of the Worshipful Court of Spotsylvania County in
Chancery in a suit therein commenced and prosecuted by WILLIAM MORTON JR.,
JACKSON MORTON and JEREMIAH MORTON, infants of JEREMIAH MORTON & MILDRED his
Wife, deced., by URIAH MALLORY their Guardian, against said JOHN LEWIS all which
will more fully appear by the Record; To hae and to hold both lotts above described together with all rights members and appurtenances thereunto belonging and all houses
and buildings thereupon erected unto ROBERT LEWIS his heirs and JOHN LEWIS and his
heirs the lotts with all rights members and appurtenances thereunto belonging unto
ROBERT LEWIS his heirs against the claims of every person shall warrant and forever
defend by these presents; In Testimony whereof the said JOHN LEWIS doth hereunto set
his hand and seal the day & year first above written
Signed Sealed & Delivered in the presence of
     (no witnesses shown)   JOHN LEWIS
   At a Court of Hustings held for the Town & Corporation of Freds:burg the 26th day of
February 1803   This Indenture was acknowledged by said JOHN LEWIS and
ordered to be recorded
Exd. & deld. R. LEWIS   Teste JNO: CHEW, C.C.H.

pp.   WHEREAS WILLIAM S. STONE is indebted to RICHARD S. HACKLEY & CO. of NEW
398-   YORK in the sum of Seven thousand Dollars, Now This Indenture Witnesseth that
399   the said WILLIAM to secure the payment of said Seven thousand Dollars by these
         presents doth bargain and sell unto REUBEN BURNLEY the following property;
two lotts in the Town of Fredericksburg on LEWIS's STREET which said STONE bought of
STEPHEN WINCHESTER as p. Deed recorded in the District Court of Fredericksburg; with
all buildings and every other their Interest thereunto belonging; also Negroes Emanuel
Essex, Andrew, Billy, Tom & Henry males; Sue, Lucy, Matilda, Maria, Nelly, Bett &
Sukey females and their increase; To have and to hold the said Lotts & Negroes unto
REUBEN BURNLEY his heirs, Upon Trust nevertheless that REUBEN BURNLEY shall
whenever required by RICHARD S. HACKLEY & CO., or their assigns after the 25th day of
December 1800 & four proceed to sell the said property and apply the proceeds of such
sale to the use of said HACKLEY & CO., or so much thereof as may remain unpaid of the
above mentioned Debt., and the balance if any to the use of WM. S. STONE, Provided also
that if WILLIAM S. STONE doth before the twenty fifth day of December 1800 & four pay
the said sum & interest thereon then this writing to be void and of no effect, otherwise
to remain in full force; Witness our hands & seals this Second day of August 1800 & two
Attest REUBEN THOM, GEO. B. RICHARDS,   W. S. STONE
    WM. DRUMMOND, THOMAS GREEN as to S.   REUBEN BURNLEY
   At a Court of Hustings held for the Town & Corporation of Freds:burg the 26th day of
February 1803   This Indenture of Trust was proved by the Oaths of REUBEN THOM,
GEORGE B. RICHARDS and THOMAS GREEN three of the witnesses thereto and ordered to
be recorded
Exd. & Delivered D. HENDERSON   Teste JNO: CHEW C.C.H.
MEMO: An Assignment on this Deed recorded folio 446. R.S. CHEW
The Commission for the privy Examination of Mrs. STONE returned examined; Recorded
Book E, ps. 239.

pp.   THIS INDENTURE made this Eleventh day of December in year of our Lord one
400-   thousand eight hundred & two Between GEORGE RICHARDSON of Town of
403   Fredericksburg of one part and DANIEL GRINNAN of same place of other part;
Witnesseth that GEORGE RICHARDSON in order to secure the payment of the following debts namely the sum of Five hundred Dollars due by GEORGE RICHARDSON to
WINCHESTER, HOWARD & COMPANY of Town of Fredericksburg and the sum of Five
hundred Dollars due by GEORGE RICHARDSON to STEPHEN WINCHESTER of the same place
and also all sums for which the said STEPHEN WINCHESTER has become security for on
account of said GEORGE RICHARDSON, And in consideration of One Dollar to said GEORGE
RICHARDSON paid by DANIEL GRINNAN by these presents doth bargain and sell unto
DANIEL GRINNAN all the household and kitchen furniture, worktools & materials &c.,
together with one horse cart and Gears, one Colt, one Cow, one Heifer and every other
things particularly specified and named in the Schedule herein annexed as part of this
Indenture; To have and to hold the said (items mentioned) unto DANIEL GRINNAN his heirs
Upon Trust nevertheless that DANIEL GRINNAN shall as soon as he may think proper or
deem it expedient (after having advertised the time and place of sale of the property
beforementioned in the Fredericksburg Newspaper) proceed to sell the same and out of
the monies arising from the sale in the first place to pay all charges attending such
sale and then the Debts above mentioned and thre residue of monies to the use of
GEORGE RICHARDSON; But if GEORGE RICHARDSON shall pay all the Debts due for which
he may be answerable then the Trust hereby declared shall cease and be void; In
Witness whereof the parties have hereunto set their hands and seals the day and year
first above written
Signed Sealed & acknowledged in presence of
      BENJN. PARKE,   GEORGE his mark X RICHARDSON
      R. D. THROCKMORTON   DANIEL GRINNAN
      JAMES McKILDOE
  Schedule of all the household and kitchen furniture and all other the personal
property of GEORGE RICHARDSON conveyed by him to DANIEL GRINNAN and referred to
in the annexed Indenture;
  Three feather beds with bolsters and pillows with striped Virginia cloth ticken; one
feather bed bolster & pillows with an Oznabrig ticken; one large stained wood Camp
Bedstead with sacking bottom; one black Walnut Bedstead & Cord, one stained Wood
diitto & mat; one ditto old; one new black & white Virginia Cloth Counterpane fringed;
one ditto blue and white ditto; two ditto yellow & blue ditto; two white M & O. & striped
ditto; one yellow & white & one flowered ditto; one new bed quilt and one patched ditto;
one silk caddow or Rug; fine pair of sheets, one Rug, one Quilt, one pair Rose blankets;
one Mahogany Desk and Drawers; one black Walnut Desk & Drawers; one looking glass
gilt frame, seven Windsor Chairs green bottoms, four black Walnut ditto; one armed
chair painted; two wood bottom & 2 flag bottom chairs, two Silver Watches; 3 glass
decanters, 2 small ditto, six Silver tea spoons, one pair Silver sugar tongs, 6 Queensware
dishes, 1 doz. large & 1 doz. small blue edgd. plates, 1 pewter quart, 1 sett knives and
forks, chard white mettle table spoons, & 1 soup spoon; one Walnut Dining Table, 1 Pine
table; four Japaned waiters, two large chests, one hair Trunk, 1 spinning wheel & 2 pair
cards; two pair tongs, shovel & hand irons; one small looking glass & picture; one new
Tea Kettle, one black horse about 10 yrs. old, one Tumbrel Cart and gears, one large pair
waggon wheels heavily shod & ironed; one pair Coach Wheels new and neatly painted;
one red Cow, one Heifer, one Mare Colt with blaze face and one Glass eye 3 1/2 yrs. old;
one large Dutch over and one small do; one large 10 gallon iron pott, two small ditto; one
middle sized ditto; one Griddle, 1 Grid Iron, frying pany, Cross bar Iron, pot hooks, Rack

&c., one large painted Dish, one small ditto & 4 pewter plates; one large & 2 small pewter basons; one Iron Stove, one Iron Grate, all the Quary tools used in the Masonry business

At a Court of Hustings held for the Town & Corporation of Freds.burg the 26th day of February 1803   This Indenture of Trust was proved by the oaths of BENJAMIN PARKE, R. D. THROCKMORTON and JAMES McKILDOE, three witnesses thereto and together with the Schedule annexed are ordered to be recorded
Exd. & deld. S. WINCHESTER   Teste   JNO: CHEW, C. C. H.

pp.   THIS INDENTURE made this thirteenth day of July in year of our Lord one thou-
404-   sand eight hundred and two and of our Independence the Twenty sixth Between
407   WILLIAM DRUMMOND and ANN FOX his Wife of Town of Fredericksburg of one
         part and CHARLES LANDON CARTER of the same place of other part; Witnesseth
that WILLIAM DRUMMOND and ANN FOX his Wife for sum of one thousand and sixty pounds current money of Virginia to them in hand paid by CHARLES LANDON CARTER by these presents the said WILLIAM DRUMMOND and ANN FOX his Wife do bargain and sell unto CHARLES L. CARTER his heirs one certain lott or parcel of ground lying in the aforesaid Town and known by number 133, situate on CHARLES STREET and is the same Lott purchased by WILLIAM DRUMMOND of THOMAS GOODWIN and ANN MARIA his Wife and by said GOODWIN of FONTAINE MAURY and BETSY his Wife as will appear by Deeds from the several parties which said lott contains half an acre, except as to ten feet at the back of said Lott, which was sold by JOHN LEGG and BENJAMIN WEEKS to Colonel WILLIAM McWILLIAMS and adjoins the said McWILLIAMS's lott, (now the property of Colo. JOHN MINOR); together with all houses gardens profits and appurtenances to the lott belonging (except as before excepted); To have and to hold the said Lott with the tenements and all other the premises (except as before excepted) unto CHARLES L. CARTER his heirs, And WILLIAM DRUMMOND and ANN FOX his Wife or either of them their heirs will warrant and forever defend by these presents; In Witness whereof the said WILLIAM DRUMMOND and ANN FOX his Wife have hereunto set their hands and seals the day and year first above written
Signed sealed and Delivered in presence of
       THOMAS LEGG,   WM. DRUMMOND
       WM. ALLEN, SAML. OWENS   ANN FOX DRUMMOND
The Commonwealth of Virginia to BENJN. DAY, STEPHEN WINCHESTER and H. T. W. MERCER Gentlemen, Greeting, Whereas (the Commission for the privy Examination of ANN FOX the Wife of WILLIAM DRUMMOND); Witness JOHN CHEW Clerk of our said Court the 16th day of July 1802 in the 26th year of the Commonwealth   JNO: CHEW
   Corporation of Fredg. Sct. In Obedience to the within Commission, we the Subscribers have received the acknowledgment of the within named ANN FOX DRUMMOND (the return of the execution of the privy Examination of ANN FOX DRUMMOND); Given under our hands this 17th day of July 1802   S. WINCHESTER
                                               H. T. W. MERCER
   At a Court of Hustings held for the Town & Corporation of Fredericksburg the 26th day of February 1803   This Indenture was acknowledged by the said WILLIAM DRUMMOND and together with the Commission annexed and Certificate of the execution thereof by said ANN FOX DRUMMOND indorsed, are ordered to be recorded
Examined and Delivered C. L. CARTER   Teste JNO: CHEW, C. C. CH.

pp. 407-410

THIS INDENTURE made this Thirtieth day of December in year of our Lord 1802, Between WILLIAM SMOCK of one part and EDWARD S. HACKLEY of the other; Whereas by a certain Indenture bearing date the 13th day of April 1799 & 23d. of American Independence between WILLIAM S. and EDWARD S. HACKLEY reciting that Whereas the said WM. SMOCK stands indebted to said EDWARD S. HACKLEY in the sum of L. 400 current money of Virginia due by two Bonds dated the 13th of April 1799 one for the payment of the sum of L. 200 payable on the first day of April 1800 and the other for the payment of L. 200 payable on the 1st day of April 1801; & Whereas by said Indenture it was witnesseth that WILLIAM SMOCK in consideration of the premises and sum of $1., to him in hand paid, WILLIAM SMOCK sold unto EDWARD S. HACKLEY for the purpose of more effectually securing the payment of the two bonds a certain part of two lotts of ground with the appurtenances lying in the Corporation of Fredericksburg designated by number 21 & 22, supposed to contain 65 feet in front on CAROLINE STREET extending in breadth the same number of feet; to the back Street at the bottom of the Garden, & is the same part of Lotts & appurtenances purchased by said SMOCK of said HACKLEY & ANN his Wife as by Deed bearing equal date with the last mentioned Indenture from EDWARD S. HACKLEY & Wife to said SMOCK will more fully appear; To have and to hold the part of lotts of land unto EDWARD S. HACKLEY his heirs In Trust Nevertheless (as in said Indenture is recited) for the purposes therein mentioned; And whereas the two Bonds have since been paid together with Interest by said SMOCK, which payment EDWARD S. HACKLEY doth hereby acknowledge, Now This Indenture Witnesseth that EDWARD S. HACKLEY in consideration of the premises and sum of One Dollar in hand paid, by these presents does for himself his heirs bargain sell release and confirm unto said SMOCK his heirs the aforesaid two lotts, To have and to hold unto said SMOCK his heirs; In Witness whereof the said HACKLEY has hereunto set his hand and seal (date blank)

Signed Sealed and Delivered in the presence of
JNO: TALIAFERRO,   EDWARD HACKLEY
JESSE WRIGHT, JOHN ROGERS

At a Court of Hustings held for the Town & Corporation of Fredericksburg April 23d. 1803   This Indenture was acknowledged by the said EDWARD HACKLEY & ordered to be recorded

pp. 410-411

THIS INDENTURE made this eighth day of April Anno Domini one thousand eight hundred and three Between JOHN MORTIMER of Town of Fredericksburg of one part and GEORGE T. TOD of said Town of other part; Witnesseth that JOHN MORTIMER for sum of five hundred pounds by these presents doth bargain & sell part of that lot number two hundred and forty four extending on CAROLINE STREET from lot number two hundred & forty five, one hundred & thirty one feet eight inches, thence parallel with ELIZABETH STREET to the said MORTIMERs lot number two hundred and thirty five, formerly the property of Capt. WM. LEWIS, with all houses gardens ddto said lot belonging; To have and to hold the parcel of land with the appurtenances unto GEO: T. TOD his heirs and JOHN MORTIMER doth covenant that he his heirs will forever defend the title of said Land to GEO: T. TOD his heirs against the claim of any person whatsoever; In Witness whereof JOHN MORTIMER hath hereunto set his hand and seal the day & year first above written

Signed Sealed & Delivered in the presence of
THOMAS POPE BASYE,   JOHN MORTIMER
JOHN W. TIMBERLAKE,
JNO; METCALFE,   WM. SMOCK

At a Court of Hustings held for the Town & Corporation of Freds:burg April 23d 1803
This Indenture for Land was proved by the oaths of THOMAS POPE BAYSE, JOHN MET-
CALFE & WM. SMOCK three of the witnesses thereto & ordered to be recorded
Exd. & Deld. G. T. TOD   Teste JNO: CHEW, C.C.H.

pp.   This Indenture made & entered into this twentieth day of January in year of
412-   Lord one thousand eight hundred and Two between JOHN WELCH of Town of
413   Fredericksburg and NELLY his Wife of one part and HUGH MERCER of other part,
        Witnesseth that whereas there was exposed to publick sale by virtue of a Decree
of Spotsylvania Court a lott or tract of graound situate in County of Spotsylvania and
just above the Town of Fredericksburg, late the property of Capt. WM. LEWIS deced., for
the purpose in said Decree set forth and JOHN WELCH being the highest bidder became
the purchaser and being unable to give security according to the term of the sale, JOHN
MINOR & WILLIAM LEWIS having agreed to take other security; Now This Agreement
Witnesseth that JOHN WELCH and NELLY his Wife for securing the payment of Six
hundred and Sixty two Dollars and Fifty cents being the amount of the purchase money
for the said lands, in consideration of the sum of One Dollars to him paid by HUGH MER-
CER doth bargain and sell to HUGH MERCER all that lott of ground lying in Spotsylvania
County just above the Town of Fredericksburg being the same purchased by said WELCH
under the Decree above mentioned and bounded (the description of the land does not appear;
the remainder of the page is blank) also one other tract of land lying in the County of
MASON in the State of KENTUCKY lying and being bounded by the OHIO RIVER which sd.
tract of land JOHN WELCH has heretofore conveyed to JOHN MINOR by Deed of Trust for
certain purposes therein contained; which Deed is of Record now in the State of Kentucky with its appurtenances; To have and to hold the sd. tracts of land to HUGH MERCER
his heirs Upon Trust however that if the said JOHN WELCH shall not pay unto JOHN
MINOR and WILLIAM LEWIS the above sum of Six hundred and sixty two dollars & Fifty
cents with interest then sd. HUGH MERCER shall sell the said land and pay the abovesaid
Debt; In Testimony whereof JOHN WELCH hath hereunto affixed his seal & set his hand
the date above mentioned
Signed sealed and Delivered in presence of
        STA: CRUPHFIELD,   JNO: WELCH
        WM. SMOCK, WILL: WELCH,   ELEANER WELCH
        JOHN ALCOCK, WM. HERNDON,   HUGH MERCER
        THOS: SACREE
    At a Court of Hustigns held for the Town and Corporation of Fredericksburg the 25th
day of June 1803   This Indenture was acknowledged by said JOHN WELCH & HUGH
MERCER & ordered to be recorded
Exd. & Deld. Genl. MINOR   Teste JNO: CHEW, C.C.H.

pp.   THIS INDENTURE made and entered into this ninth day of July in year of our
414-   Lord one thousand Eight hundred and three Between GEORGE FRENCH and ANN
416   BRAYNE FRENCH his Wife of Town of Fredericksburg of one part and SIMON
        SEXSMITH of same place of other part; Witnesseth that GEORGE FRENCH and ANN
B. FRENCH for sum of Three hundred and ninety nine pounds lawful money of Virginia
to them in hand paid by SIMON SEXSMITH by these presents do bargain and sell unto
SIMON SEXSMITH his heirs a certain parcel of ground lying in the Town aforesaid being
part of a lott known by number Eighteen, And is bounded beginning at the upper corner of Lott 18 and running down CAROLINE STREET fifty seven feet in front, thence
through said Lott one hundred & thirty two feet back to Lott number 17, thence along
Lott 17 fifty seven feet to lott number Twenty, thence along lott number 20 one hun-

dred and thirty two feet to the beginning; Together with all buildings improvements profits and appurtenances to said parcel of ground belonging; To have and to hold the parcel of ground unto SIMON SEXSMITH his heirs, And the said GEORGE and ANN B. FRENCH and theirs heirs from the claims of every person shall and do warrant and forever defend by these presents; In Witness wehreof said GEORGE and ANN B. FRENCH have hereunto set their hands and seals the day and year first above written
Signed sealed and acknowledged in presence of

JNO: LEGG, GEO: FRENCH
JACOB G. WACKER, BENJN. PARKE ANN B. FRENCH

The Commonwealth of Virginia to ALEXANDER DUNCAN, CHARLES CARTER & HUGH MERCER, Gentlemen Greeting; Whereas (the Commission for the privy Examination of ANN B., Wife of GEORGE FRENCH); Witness JOHN CHEW, Clerk of our said Court the 20th day of July 1803 and in the 28th year of the Commonwealth   JNO: CHEW

Corporation of Fredericksburg to wit: By Virtue of the within Commission we did personally go to the within named ANN B. FRENCH (the return of the execution of the privy examination of ANN B. FRENCH); Certified under our hands and seals this 23rd day of July 1803

CHARLES L. CARTER
ALEXD. DUNCAN

At a Court of Hustigns held for the Town & Corporation of Fredericksburg July the 23rd 1803   This Indenture was acknowledged by the said GEORGE FRENCH and together with the Commission annexed and Certificate of Execution thereof by the said ANN B. FRENCH indorsed, are ordered to be recorded
Exd. & Deld. S. SEXSMITH   Teste JNO: CHEW, C. C. H.

pp. 416-419   THIS INDENTURE made and entered into this Eleventh day of July in year of our Lord one thousand eight hundred and three Between SIMON SEXSMITH and MARY his Wife of Town of Fredericksburg of one part and DAVID HENDERSON, ROBERT WALKER and JOHN SCOTT all of the same place of other part; Witnesseth that SIMON and (blank) SEXSMITH in order to secure the payment of the sum of Three hundred and ninety nine pounds lawful money of Virginia due and owing by said SIMON SEXSMITH unto GEORGE FRENCH and in consideration of the sum of One Dollar in hand paid by DAVID HENDERSON, ROBERT WALKER and JOHN SCOTT, by these presents do bargain and sell one parcel of ground lying in Town of Fredericksburg, part of a lott known by number Eighteen and bounded. (description as in the foreging Deed); Upon Trust nevertheless that DAVID HENDERSON, ROBERT WALKER and JOHN SCOTT shall at any time after the ninth day of July one thousand eight hundred and four proceed to sell the same but if SIMON SEXSMITH his heirs pay unto GEORGE FRENCH the Debt before the ninth day of July Eighteen hundred and four, then the Trust hereby declared shall cease and be void, otherwise to remain in full force. In Witness whereof the parties have hereunto set their hands and seals the day and year first above written
Signed sealed and acknowledged in presence of us

BENJN. PARKE, SIMON SEXSMITH
JOHN BROWN, MARY SEXSMITH
WM. WHITEHEAD DAVID HENDERSON
 ROBERT WALKER
 JOHN SCOTT

The Commonwealth of Virginia to ALEXANDER DUNCAN, BENJAMIN DAY and HUGH MERCER Gentlemen, Greeting, Whereas (the Commission for the privy Examination of MARY the Wife of SIMON SEXSMITH); Witness JOHN CHEW, Clerk of our said Court, the 20th day of July 1803 and in the 28th year of the Commonwealth   JNO: CHEW

Corporation of Fredericksburg; By virtue of the within Commission we did personally go to the within named MARY SEXSMITH (the return of the execution of the privy Examination of MARY SEXSMITH); Certified under our hands and seals this 21st day of July 1803
ALEXR. DUNCAN
HUGH MERCER

At a Court of Hustings held for the Town & Corporation of Fredericksburg July the 23rd 1803   This Indenture of Trust was acknowledged by the said SIMON SEXSMITH and proved by the oaths of BENJAMIN PARKE, JOHN BROWN & W. WHITEHEAD three witnesses thereto as to the execution of the said DAVID HENDERSON, ROBERT WALKER & JOHN SCOTT, and together with the Commission annexed & Certificate of Execution thereof by the said MARY indorsed are ordered to be recorded
Exd. & Deld. GEO: FRENCH   Teste JNO: CHEW, C.C.H.

pp.   THIS INDENTURE made this Second day of March in year of our Lord one thou-
419-   sand eight hundred and three Between JOHN HARDIA and CLARA his Wife of
421   Town of Fredericksburg of one part and WESCOM HUDGIN of the same place of
          other part; Witnesseth that said JOHN and CLARA HARDIA for sum of One
hundred and six pounds & 5/ current money of Virginia to them in hand paid, by these presents do bargain and sell unto WESCOM HUDGIN his heirs a certain parcel of ground lying in Town of Fredericksburg being part of Lott No. 252; and bounded, Beginning at a point 56 feet from the lower corner of said Lott and running up CAROLINE STREET twenty one feet four inches to WILLIAM ALEXANDERs line, thence along ALEXANDERs line one hundred and sixty seven feet, thence aparallel with BURKLEY STREET one hundred and sixty seven feet to the beginning; being part of the piece of ground which said HARIA occupies at present as a Garden; together with all appurtenances unto the piece of ground belonging; To have and to hold the piece of graound with the appurtenances unto WECOM HUDGIN his heirs and JOHN & CLARA HARDIA and their heirs the said premises against all persons to WESCOM HUDGIN his heirs shall warrant and forever defend by these presents; In Witness whereof JOHN HARDIA and CLARA his Wife have hereunto set their hands and seals the day and year first above written
Signed Sealed and Acknowledged in presence of
JAMES NEWBY,   BENJN. PARKE,   JNO: HARDIA
JOHN LEWIS, HENRY M. LIPSCOMB   CLARISA HARDIA
The Commonwealth of Virginia to GEO: FRENCH, BENJN. DAY & HUGH MERCER, Gentlemen Greeting, Whereas (the Commission for the privy Examination of CLARA, the Wife of JOHN HARDIA); Witness JOHN CHEW, Clerk of our said Corporation Court the 8th day of July 1803 and in 28 year of the Commonwealth   JNO: CHEW
Agreeable to the within Commission to us directed, we did personally go to the within named CLARA HARDIA (the return of the execution of the privy Examination of CLARA HARDIA); Certified under our hands & seals this 9th day of July 1803
GEO: FRENCH
HUGH MERCER
At a Court of Hustings held for the Town & Corporation of Fredericksburg July the 23rd. 1803   This Indenture for Land was proved by the oaths of BENJAMIN PARKE, JOHN LEWIS and HENRY M. LIPSCOMB, three of the witnesses thereto, and together with the Commission annexed & Certficate of the Execution thereof by the said CLARISA indorsed are ordered to be recorded
Exd. & deld. WM. HARDIA for Mrs. HUDGIN, Admx.   Teste   JNO: CHEW, C.C.H.

pp.   THIS INDENTURE made and entered into this twenty sixth day of May in year
422-   of our Lord one thosuand eight hundred and three Between RICHARD PEACOCK
424   and HANNAH his Wife of Town of Fredericksburg of one part and HENRY
         PHILIPS of same place of other part; Witnesseth that RICHARD PEACOCK and
HANNAH his Wife for one hundred Dollars to them in hand paid by these presents do
bargain and sell unto HENRY PHILIPS his heirs a certain parcel of ground lying in
Town of Fredericksburg being one half of a Lott which said PEACOCK purchased from
ROGER DIXON by a Deed bearing date the 9th day of April 1802 and recorded in the Hustings Court of said Town and known by the number One hundred and ninety four;
which parcel of ground is bounded, beginning at the upper or Southwest corner of lott
one hundred and ninety two and running up FERDINAND STREET Sixty six feet to a line
which divides lott 194 into two equal parts, thence along said division line Eighty two
feet and a half to lott number one hundred and ninety two, thence along said lott 192
sixty six feet to lott number two hundred and one; thence along lott 201 eighty two feet
and a half to the beginning, containing one quarter of an acre together with all advantages and appurtenances belonging; To have and to hold the parcel of ground with
its appurtenances unto HENRY PHILIPS his heirs and the said RICHARD and HANNAH
PEACOCK and their heirs the parcel of ground unto HENRY PHILIPS his heirs from the
claims of every person shall and do warrant and forever defend by these presents;- In
Witness whereof the said RICHARD and HANNAH PEACOCK have hereunto set their
hands and seals the day and year first above written
Signed sealed and Delivered in presence of
         BENJAN. PARKE,   RICHARD PEACOCK
         JAMES ALLEN, MICH: LEA   HANNAH PEACOCK
   The Commonwealth of Virginia to GEO: FRENCH, BENJA: DAY and HUGH MERCER,
Gentlemen Greeting; Whereas (the Commission for the privy Examination of HANNAH, the Wife
of RICHARD PEACOCK); Witness JOHN CHEW, Clerk of our said Corporation Court the 27 day
of May 1803 and in the 28th year of the Commonwealth   JNO: CHEW
   Agreeable to the within Commission to us directed we did personally go to the within
named HANNAH PEACOCK (the return of the execution of the privy Examination of HANNAH PEA-
COCK), Certified under our hands and seals this 9th day of July 1803
                           GEO: FRENCH
                           HUGH MERCER
   At a Court of Hustings held for the Town & Corporation of Fredericksburg July the 23rd
1803   This Indenture was acknowledged by the said RICHARD PEACOCK & together with
the Commission annexed & Certificate of Execution thereof by the said HANNAH
indorsed, are ordered to be recorded
Exd. & Deld. HENRY PHILIPS   Teste JNO: CHEW, C.C.H.

pp.   THIS INDENTURE made this Sixteenth day of July in year of our Lord one thou-
425-   sand eight hundred and three Between GEORGE LEWIS of the County of KING
426   GEORGE and KATHARINE his Wife of one part and WARNER WASHINGTON LEWIS
         of Town of Fredericksburg of other part; Witnesseth that GEORGE LEWIS and
KATHARINE his Wife for sum of Five shillings to them in hand paid by WARNER
WASHINGTON LEWIS by these presents do bargain and sell unto WARNER WASHINGTON
LEWIS all that tract of land lying in County of Spotsylvania near the Town of
Fredericksburg and bounded; Beginning at a Stone on the North corner of the House
formerly own'd by JOHN LEWIS Esqr., called WHITE PLAINS, and now owned by JOHN
WELCH, thence North forty five West six poles thirteen and a half feet to the line of the
Lot formally own'd by Capt. WM. LEWIS, thence with that line North fifty East ten poles
to a Stone on the side of the FERRY ROAD leading from Fredericksburg to FALMOUTH,

thence with the ROAD South forty five East six poles thirteen and half feet to a Stone on
said Road, thence South fifty West ten poles to the beginning, containing Eight square
poles more or less as by reference to Deed from JOHN LEWIS & Wife to GEO: LEWIS made
the seventh day of April Seventeen hundred and Eighty eight and recorded in the
County Court of Spotsylvania will more fully appear; Together with all the land tenements and appurtenances thereunto belonging; To have and to hold the said tract of
land with its appurtenances unto WARNER WASHINGTON LEWIS his heirs and GEORGE
LEWIS and KATHARINE his Wife or their heirs and every other person will and do warrant and forever defend by these presents; In Witness whereof GEORGE LEWIS and
KATHARINE his Wife have hereunto set their hands and seals the day and year first
above written
Signed sealed and Delivered in the presence of us
    GEO: FRENCH,   RD. JOHNSON JR.,   G. LEWIS
    BENJN. PARKE,   CHARLES DAVIS
  At a Court of Hustings held for the Town & Corporation of Fredericksburg October the
22nd. 1803   This Indenture was proved by the Oaths of GEORGE FRENCH, RICHARD
JOHNSON JR., & CHARLES DAVIS, three of the witnesses thereto & ordered to be recorded
Exd. & Deld. WARNER W. LEWIS   Teste JNO: CHEW C.C.H.

pp.   THIS INDENTURE made this the Sixth day of September in year of our Lord one
426- thousand eight hundred and three Between JAMES SUMERVILLE of one part and
428   THOMAS GOODWIN of other /both of the Town of Fredericksburg/ Witnesseth
    that JAMES SUMERVILLE for the sum of One Dollar to him in hand paid by THO-
MAS GOODWIN by these presents doth bargain and sell unto THOMAS GOODWIN all those
two WHARVES on the RIVER RAPPAHANNOCK below my present Dwelling House commonly called SUMERVILLE's WHARVES, as also my one half of the WHARF adjoining
thereto, called JOHNSON's WHARF, with the appurtenances thereunto belonging; To
have and to hold the said premises unto THOMAS GOODWIN his heirs from the date
hereof during the full term of Ten years paying to JAMES SUMERVILLE each year the
Rent of One hundred Dollars, Fifty Dollars to be allowed by the said JAMES SUMERVILLE
to be deducted from the first years Rent to repair the two Upper Wharves and the Road
thereto, which said SUMERVILLE agrees to remove his Garden Pailing to a convenient
distance and THOMAS GOODWIN will deliver up the said Tenement unto JAMES SUMER-
VILLE in as good order and condition as they are now in natural decay; and the Effects
of Floods and Ice excepted; In Witness whereof the parties to these presents have
hereunto set their hands and seals the day and year first above written
Signed sealed and delivered in presence of
    JOHN LEWIS,   JAMES SUMERVILLE
    JOS: F. MARTIN,   THO: GOODWIN
    BEN: H: BUCKNER
  At a Court of Hustings held for the Town & Corporation of Fredericksburg October the
22nd 1803   This Indenture of Lease was acknowledged by the parties thereto &
ordered to be recorded

pp.   THIS INDENTURE made this twenty sixth day of August one thousand eight hun-
428- dred and three between DANIEL GRINNAN of Town of Fredericksburg, Attorney
429   in fact for JOHN GLASSELL of LONGNIDDRY North Britain of one part and Doctor
    GEORGE FRENCH of aforesaid Town of other part; Whereas JOHN GLASSELL by his
Letter of Attorney dated the seventh of February one thousand eight hundred & one
and recorded inthe District Court of Fredericksburg did give grant and commit full
power and commission to said GRINNAN to sell and dispose of by public or private sale

and at such prices as he should think expedient the whole lands houses & tenements belonging to JOHN GLASSELL in the State of Virginia; NOW THIS INDENTURE WITNES- SETH that DANIEL GRINNAN by virtue of the Power above recited and for the sum of Four hundred and Twenty three Dollars hath sold unto GEORGE FRENCH his heirs the right title and Interest of said GLASSELL to the following lots or slips of ground lying below the lower line of the Town of Fredericksburg and the said GLASSELL's WHARF binding on the RAPPAHANNOCK RIVER & the ROAD to GLASSELL's WHARF being a con- tinuation of CAROLINE STREET, Vizt. three lots number two, three & four by a recent plat containing about one hundred and three perches each more or less, bounded, Begin- ning on the East side of said Road at ninety two feet five inches from the lower line of the said Town, corner to lot number one sold to ADAM DONALDSON, thence down the Road ninety two feet five inches the front of each lot in all two hundred and seventy seven feet three inches to the corner of Lot No. five sold to JOHN MORTIMER, thence with his line North sixty three degrees East seventy six poles twenty one links to the River, thence up the River two hundred and seventy seven feet three inches to the corner of DONALDSON's Lott, thence South sixty three and half degrees West seventy six poles twenty one links to the beginning, Together with all profits and appurtenances to the same belonging free from the claim of said JOHN GLASSELL and all persons claiming under him will warrant and forever defend; In Witness whereof DANIEL GRINNAN as Attorney aforesaid hath hereunto set his hand and seal the day within written

Signed Sealed & Acknowledged in presence of
    CHARLES GREGORY,   DANIEL GRINNAN
    DOND: CAMPBELL, HENRY GREEN   Atty. in fact for JOHN GLASSELL
  At a Court of Hustings held for the Town and Corporation of Fredericksburg October the 22nd 1803 This Indenture was acknowledged by the said DANIEL GRINNAN, Attorny in fct for JOHN GLASSELL and ordered to be recorded
Examined and Delivered BENJN. PARKE for GEO: FRENCH
                      Teste JNO: CHEW, C. C. H.

p.   KNOW ALL MEN by these presents that I LUCY ARMISTEAD do sufficient cause
429   thereunto moving Emancipate Betty, a Mulatto slave now my property and
        hereby declare that from hence forward she shall be and is free to all intents and purposes; Given under my hands and seal this 25th day of October 1803
Teste BENJN. DAY,   L. ARMISTEAD
    MARY BAGGOTT
  At a Court of Hustings held for the Town and Corporation of Fredericksburg the 26th of November 1803   This Letter of Emancipation was proved by the oath of BENJN. DAY & MARY BAGGOTT two witnesses thereto & ordered to be recorded
Examd. & deld. Betty   Teste JNO: CHEW, C. C. H.

p.   KNOW ALL MEN by these presents that I DAVID ALMOND of the Town of
430   Fredericksburg for divers good causes me thereunto moving and for One Dollar
        to me in hand paid by my Negro woman named Jenny, at or before the sealing and delivery of these presents, the receipt whereof I do acknowledge, have emanci- pated forever set free and forever discharge from Service and by these presents do hereby emancipate forever set free and discharge from Service the said Negro woman Jenny. Witness my hand and seal this Novr. 26th 1803
                         DAVID ALMOND

At a Court of Hustings held for the Town & Corporation of Fredericksburg the 28th of
November 1803   This Letter of Emancipation was acknowledged by DAVID ALMOND
& ordered to be recorded

p.   KNOW ALL MEN by these presents that I ROBERT WALKER of the Town of
430   Fredericksburg for divers good causes me thereunto moving and for and in
          consideration of One Dollar to me in hand paid by my Negro slaves, POLLY
BACKHOUSE and MARIA BACKHOUSE at or before the sealing and delivery of these
presents the receipt whereof I do acknowledge have emancipated forever set free and
discharged from further Service the said POLLY and MARIA BACKHOUSE. Witness my
hand & seal this 28th day of November 1803   ROBERT WALKER
   At a Court of Hustings held for the Town and Corporation of Fredericksburg the 28th
day of November 1803   This Letter of Emancipation was acknowledged by ROBERT
WALKER & ordered to be recorded

pp.   THIS INDENTURE made this 24th day of October in year of our Lord one thou-
431-   sand eight hundred and three Between JAMES BLAIR, DANIEL GRINNAN JUNR.,
433   and JAMES SOMERVILL, Executors of the Last Will and Testament of JAMES
          SOMERVILL deced., and WILLIAM TAYLOR & THOMAS COCHRAN, Trustees & Exe-
cutors of the last Will and Testament of THOMAS MILLER deced., of Town of Fredericksburg of one part and ELISHA THATCHER of othe other part. Whereas JAMES BLAIR,
DANIEL GRINNAN JUNR. & JAMES SOMERVILL, Executors as aforesaid by virtue of a Deed
of Trust made and executed by JOHN MITCHEL and SUSANNA his Wife in behalf of JOHN
GRAY, ARCHIBALD RITCHIE, ROBERT GILCHRIST and JAMES SOMERVILL, the Survivor or
Survivors of them, did sell unto the highest bidder a part of a certain lot or parcel of
land with all improvements thereon lying in Town of Fredg. known by the number
thirty two and the aforesaid THOMAS MILLER deced., became the purchaser thereof, but
departed this life without having received a regular and legal conveyance from the
aforesaid JAMES BLAIR, DANIEL GRINNAN JUNR. & JAMES SOMERVILLE, Executors of
JAMES SOMERVILLE deced, who was the only Survivor of the Trustees aforenamed; And
whereas the said THOMAS MILLER deced., departed this life having first made executed
& published his last Will and Testament in Writing and appointed WILLIAM TAYLOR &
THOMAS COCHRAN his Trustees & Executors, and by his last Will and Testament among
other things ordered that his Executors should expose to public sale the premises
aforesd. and should sell the same agreeable to the terms & conditions in the said Will
contained; NOW THIS INDENTURE WITNESSETH that JAMES BLAIR, DANIEL GRINNAN
JUNR. and JAMES SOMERVILLE, Executors aforessaid in consideration of the sale aforesaid made by THOMAS MILLER deced., in his life time and the said WILLIAM TAYLOR &
THOMAS COCHRAN, Trustees & Executors as aforesaid, for the sum of Three thousand six
hundred and sixty Dollars to them in hand paid by these presents do bargain and sell
unto ELISHA THATCHER his heirs that part of lot number thirty two with the improvements thereon lying in Town of Fredericksburg and bounded Beginning at a corner on
CAROLINE STREET running down the said Street seventy one feet to a House and Lot belonging to GEORGE MURRAY, thence seventy four feet backwards towards the River,
thence with a line parallel to CAROLINE STREET and thence along the Lot at present
occupied by and belonging to WALTER ROE, to the beginning corner, and all the appurtenances belonging; To have and to hold the premises and the appurtenances unto
ELISHA THATCHER his heirs, And JAMES BLAIR, DANIEL GRINNAN JUNR. and JAMES
SOMERVILL, Executors as aforesaid and said WILLIAM TAYLOR & THOMAS COCHRAN,
Trustees and Executors as aforesaid, for them and their heirs the said parcel of land and
all improvements against them and their heirs and every other person claiming under

them to said ELISHA THATCHER his heirs will warrant and forever defend by these presents; In Witness whereof the said JAMES BLAIR, DANIEL GRINNAN JUNR. & JAMES SOMERVILL Executors of the last Will & Testament of JAMES SOMERVILL deced., & WILLIAM TAYLOR & THOMAS COCHRAN, Trustees & Executors of the last Will & Testament of THOMAS MILLER deced., have hereunto set their hands and seals the day and year first above written
Signed Sealed and Delivered in presence of

FRANCIS TERRILL,	WILLIAM TAYLOR,
HENRY GREEN,	THOS: COCHRAN
JOHN MUNDELL	JAMES BLAIR
	DANIEL GRINNAN
	JAMES SOMERVILL

At a Court of Hustings held for the Town & Corporation of Fredericksburg the 25th day of February 1804   This Indenture was proved by the oaths of FRANCIS TERRILL, HENRY GREEN and JOHN MUNDELL, three witnesses thereto & ordered to be recorded Examd. & Delivered ELISHA THATCHER   Teste JNO: CHEW, C.C.H.

pp. 434-436   THIS INDENTURE made the 25th day of October one thousand seven hundred and three Between ELISHA THATCHER and BETSEY CELIA his Wife of Town of Fredericksburg of one part and WILLIAM TAYLOR and THOMAS COCHRAN, Trustees & Executors of the last Will and Testament of THOMAS MILLER deced., of the Town aforesaid of other part. Witnesseth that ELISHA THATCHER & BETSEY CELIA his Wife for the sum of One Dollar to them in hand paid by WILLIAM TAYLOR & THOMAS COCHRAN, by these presents do bargain and sell unto WILLIAM TAYLOR & THOMAS COCHRAN, Trustees and Executors as aforesaid, all that lot or parcel of ground being part of Lot number Thirty two with the improvements thereon lyinging in Town of Fredericksburg and bounded (the bounds are as described in the foregoing Deed); Provided Always and upon condition that if ELISHA THATCHER his heirs shall truly pay or cause to be paid unto WILLIAM TAYLOR and THOMAS COCHRAN, Trustees and Executors as aforesaid, the legal Interest of Six percent on the sum of Three thousand six hundred and sixty Dollars yearly to commence the first day of September last past during the life of JOHN MILLER, Brother of said THOMAS MILLER deced., and pay the sum of one thousand eight hundred and Thirty Dollars in one year from the death of said JOHN MILLER and the sum of One thousand eight hundred and thirty Dollars in two years from the death of said JOHN MILLER, then and in such case evert clause herein contained shall cease and be utterly void; In Witness whereof the said ELISHA THATCHER and BETSEY CELIA his Wife have hereunto set theirhands and annexed their seals the day and year first abovewritten
Signed sealed and delivered in presence of

| JOHN CRUMP, | ELISHA THATCHER |
| RICHARD BIBLE, HENRY GREEN | BETSEY CELEY THATCHER |

The Commonwealth of Virginia to CHARLES L. CARTER & THOMAS GOODWIN Gentlemen, Greeting, Whereas (the Commission for the privy Examination of BETSEY CELIA, Wife of ELISHA THATCHER); Witness JOHN CHEW, Clerk of our said Hustings Court the 25th day of October 1803 and in the 28th year of the Commonwealth   JNO: CHEW
Corporation of Fredericksburg, to wit: In Obedience to the within order we have this day (the return of the execution of the privy Examination of BETSEY CELIA THATCHER); Given under our hands and seals this 7th day of November 1803
CHARLES L. CARTER
THOS: GOODWIN

At a Court of Hustings held for the Town & Corporation of Fredericksburg 25th February 1804   This Indenture of Mortgage was acknowledged by ELISHA THATCHER and together with the Commission annexed and Certificate of the Execution thereof by BETSEY CELEY his Wife indorsed, are ordered to be recorded
Exd. & Deld. WM. TAYLOR   Teste JNO; CHEW, C. C. H.

p.   KNOW ALL MEN by these presents that I JOHN TALIAFERRO of the Town of
437   Fredericksburg do hereby Emancipate set free and fully discharge from Slavery
        a certain Negro man named George, alias GEORGE ALLISON, who was purchased
by me of Mrs. ANNE GATEWOOD and by the said ANNE purchased from a certain JOHN
ALLISON of PETERSBURG, Virginia. In Witness whereof I have hereunto set my hand
and seal this Twenty fourth day of March in the year of our Lord Eighteen hundred and
four   JOHN TALIAFERRO
   At a Court of Hustings held for the Town and Corporation of Fredericksburg the 24th
March 1804   This Letter of Emancipation was acknowledged by the said JOHN TALIA-
FERRO and ordered to be recorded & the said GEORGE being above the age of Forty five
years the said JOHN TALIAFERRO became Security that the said GEORGE ALLISON should
not become chargeable to this Corporation
Exd. & deld. GEORGE ALLISON   Teste JNO: CHEW, C. C. H.

pp.   THIS INDENTURE made the Twenty eighth day of December in year of our Lord
438-   one thousand eight hundred & three Between JOHN BROWNLOW of Town of
439   Fredericksburg of one part and GEORGE FRENCH, RICHARD PEACOCK and THOMAS
        GOODWIN of the same place of other part; Witnesseth that JOHN BROWNLOW in
order to secure the payment of Three thousand Dollars due and owing by him unto
Captain PRESERVELL ALGER (which sum is to be paid in three periods, to wit, one
thousand Dollars on the 15th day of April next, one thousand Dollars on the 15th day of
October next, and one thousand Dollars on the 15th day of April 1805; which several
sums said JOHN BROWNLOW hath issued his three Bonds payable at the three period and
for the sum of One Dollar paid by GEORGE FRENCH, RICHARD PEACOCK and THOMAS
GOODWIN before the sealing & delivery of these presents, by these presents doth bargain and sell unto GEORGE FRENCH, RICHARD PEACOCK and THOMAS GOODWIN one
quarter acre or hald lott of land in Town of Fredericksburg and known by number Four
which is occupied at present by Mrs. ANNE GATEWOOD as a TAVERN, together with all
houses and appurtenances to the same belonging; To have and to hold the said lot with
every of their appurtenances unto GEORGE FRENCH, RICHARD PEACOCK and THOMAS
GOODWIN their heirs Upon Trust nevertheless that if JOHN BROWNLOW shall fail to pay
and discharge the three mentioned Bonds at the periods when they shall become due
said GEORGE FRENCH, RICHARD PEACOCK and THOMAS GOODWIN proceed to sell the same
and the monies arising to pay reasonable charges attending the sale, then the before
mentioned Debt and the residue to the use of said BROWNLOW; In Witness whereof the
parties have hereunto set their hands and seals the day and year first above written
Signed Sealed & Delivered in presence of
        DANIEL ROSS,   JNO: BROWNLOW
        JOSEPH SHANNON,   GEO: FRENCH
        BENJN: PARKE   RICHARD PEACOCK
                                            THOS:GOODWIN
   At a Court of Hustings held for the Town and Corporation of Fredericksburg May the
28th 1804   This Indenture of Trust was proved by the oaths of DANIEL ROSS, JOSEPH
SHANNON and BENJAMIN PARKE, three witnesses thereto & ordered to be recorded
Exd. & Deld. THOS: GOODWIN, p. B. H. BUCKNER   Teste JNO: CHEW, C. C. H.

pp.   THIS INDENTURE made the fourteenth day of November Anno Domini Eighteen
440-   hundred & three Between ALEXANDER S. ROE of Town of Fredericksburg of one
441   part and HENRY THOMPSON of Town of BALTIMORE & State of MARYLAND of
         other part; Witnesseth that ALEXANDER S. ROE for One Dollar to him in hand
paid by HENRY THOMPSON by these presents doth bargain and sell unto HENRY THOMP-
SON his heirs all that tenement lying in Town of Fredericksburg and devised and be-
queathed to a certain ROBERT S. CHEW by the last Will and Testament of ROBERT B. CHEW
deceased bearing date the Twenty eight day of December one thousand seven hundred &
ninety one, and by ROBERT S. CHEW sold and conveyed to said ALEXANDER S. ROE &
bounded, to wit, by CAROLINE STREET twenty three feet six inches to THOMAS MILLERs
line, thence along said MILLERs line & JOHN CHEWs line one hundred and thirty two
feet to the corner of JULIANs Lott (now CHRISTYs), thence twenty three feet six inches
to LEWIS STREET, thence along LEWIS STREET one hundred & thirty two feet to the begining on CAROLINE STREET, also a parcel of ground thereto adjoining conveyed by a
certain Deed of bargain and sale bearing date the 19th day of September one thousand
eight hundred & one by JOHN CHEW & ELIZABETH his Wife to said ROBERT S. CHEW and by
ROBERT S. CHEW conveyed to said ALEXANDER S. ROE by Deed bearing date the Twentieth
day of September one thousand eight hundred & one; all of which said Deeds are of
Record in the Office of the District Court of Fredericksburg, which the said ROE
mortgaged to ROBERT S. CHEW by his certain Deed bearing date the twenty first day of
September Eighteen hundred & one, and of Record in the said Office of the Fredericksburg District Court, together with all appurtenances & improvements thereon or thereto belonging unto HENRY THOMPSON his heirs and ALEXANDER S. ROE his heirs (except
against the mortgage aforesaid) will warrant and defend by these presents; In Witness
whereof the said ALEXANDER S. ROE hath hereunto set his hand and seal the day and
year first above written
Signed Sealed & Delivered in presence of
     JOHN HACKET, FRANCIS WIATT,   ALEX: S. ROE
     JOHN B. BENSON, FRAS: TERRILL
    At a Curt of Hustings held for the Town & Corporation of Fredericksburg May the 28th
1804   This Indenture for Land was proved by the Oaths of JOHN HACKETT, JOHN B.
BENSON & FRANCIS TERRILL three of the witnesses thereto & ordered to be recorded
Exd. & Deld A. BUCK   Teste JNO: CHEW, C. C. H.

pp.   THIS INDENTURE made this ninth day of December in the year of our Lord one
441-   thousand eight hundred and three Between DAVID HENDERSON of Town of
446   Fredericksburg, Attorney in fact for JOHN KNOX, of the City of NEW YORK, of one
         part and WILLIAM S. STONE of Town of Fredericksburg of other part; Whereas
by an Indenture of bargain and sale between WM. S. STONE of one part and REUBEN
BURNLEY of other part bearing date on the second day of August in the year one thousand eight hundred and two executed by the parties thereto & recorded in the District
Court of Fredericksburg reciting that the sd. WM. S. STONE was Indebted to RICHARD S.
HACKLEY & CO., of NEW YORK in the sum of Seven thousand dollars and it was witnessed
that WILLIAM S. STONE for the purpose of securing the payment of said sum by the said
Indenture did bargain and sell to REUBEN BURNLEY two lotts in the Town of Fredericksburg, also thirteen Negro slaves; To have and to hold the lotts and Negroes to said REU-
BEN BURNLEY his heirs Upon Trust nevertheless that REUBEN BURNLEY whenever he
should be required by the said RICHARD S. HACKLEY & CO., or their assigns after the
Twenty fifth day of December in the year one thousand eight hundred and four proceed
to sell the said property and apply to proceeds of said sale to discharge the Debt, and
whereas by memorandum indorsed on the back of said Inenture between RICHARD S.

HACKLEY &c. and the said WM. S. STONE that said STONE should be at liberty at any time before the 25th day of December 1804 to convey the property to RICHARD S. HACKLEY & CO., in discharge of the said Debt and Whereas by a Deed duly executed by WILLIAM S. STONE the tenth day of November 1802, said STONE in pursuance of the above agreement did convey to said RICHARD S. HACKLEY & CO. the thirteen slaves in the Indenture mentioned to satisfy the said HACKLEY & CO. & Whereas the said HACKLEY & CO. by an Assignment on the back of the said Deed dated the 8th day of July in the year 1803, did transfer to JOHN KNOX of the City of NEW YORK the said Deed and all right and whereas JOHN KNOX by his Letter of Attorney on 21 July 1803 appointed DAVID HENDERSON to be his Attorney giving him power to sell unto any purchaser all the Estate formerly belonging to WILLIAM S. STONE of Fredsbg. NOW THIS INDENTURE WITNESSETH that DAVID HENDERSON hath this day agreed with WILLIAM S. STONE that if he shall pay on or before the Twenty fifth day of December 1804 the sum of Three thouand dollars with interest at the rate of six percent per annum that then said WILLIAM S. STONE shall be possessed of the legal Estate in all the slaves untill the said 25 day of December 1804 without any lett of them and if WILLAM S. STONE shall not pay the aforesaid sum that then the said DAVID HENDERSON take possession and sell at public sale, In Testimony whereof the said DAVID HENDERSON on behalf of the said JOHN KNOX & the said WILLIAM S. STONE have hereunto set their names & affixed their seals the day and year first above written

Signed Sealed and Delivered in the presence of

JAMES DIXON,   DAVID HENDERSON
JAMES GORDON   Attorney in fact of JOHN KNOX
                                              W. S. STONE

At a Court of Hustings held for the Town & Corporation of Fredericksburg June 25th 1804   This Indenture was acknowledged by the parties thereto & ordered to be recorded

Exd. & Delivered Mr. DIXON for D. H.   Teste JNO: CHEW, C. C. H.

We hereby assign all our right title and interest in the within Deed of Trust to DAVID HENDERSON Esqr. for the benefit of JOHN KNOX of NEW YORK, Given under our hands and Seals this 2nd day of August 1802

Witness JAMES DIXON,   RICHARD S. HACKLEY
       D. HENDERSON JR.

Memorandum: It is agreed by R. S. HACKLEY & CO. that the said W. S. STONE may at any time before the 25th day of December 1804 give up and convey in fee simple the annexed property to them or their assigns in discharge of the written debt of $7000; and that the said W. S. STONE is authorized to sell any part thereof agreeable to the within stipulations as to payments and apply the proceeds of such sales to the payment of the said $7000; to ur or our assigns with the consent of REUBIN BURNLEY aforesaid; And in such case he the said REUBIN is authorized to join in a conveyance of the same to the purchasers thereof on payment of the amount being made to us or our assigns; August 2nd 1802   RICHARD S. HACKLEY

Reacknowledged by R. S. HACKLEY this 20th April 1807 in presence of us

BENJN. PARKE,   JOHN T. PARKE
THOMAS ALLEN   WM. WELLFORD

At a Court of Hustings contd. & held for the Town and Corpo. of Fredg., May 16th 1807 The Reacknowledgment of the within Assignment of this Deed of Trust was proved by the oaths of BENJN. PARKE, JOHN T. PARKE and THOMAS ALLEN, three of the witneses thereto & ordered to be recorded

Teste R. S. CHEW, C. C. H.

Heritage Books by Ruth and Sam Sparacio:

Abstracts of Account Books of Edward Dixon, Merchant of Port Royal, Virginia, Volume I: 1743–1747

Abstracts of Account Books of Edward Dixon, Merchant of Port Royal, Virginia, Volume II

Albemarle County, Virginia Deed and Will Book Abstracts, 1748–1752

Albemarle County, Virginia Deed Book Abstracts, 1758–1761

Albemarle County, Virginia Deed Book Abstracts, 1761–1764

Albemarle County, Virginia Deed Book Abstracts, 1764–1768

Albemarle County, Virginia Deed Book Abstracts, 1768–1770

Albemarle County, Virginia Deed Book Abstracts, 1776–1778

Albemarle County, Virginia Deed Book Abstracts, 1778–1780

Albemarle County, Virginia Deed Book Abstracts, 1780–1783

Albemarle County, Virginia Deed Book Abstracts, 1787–1790

Albemarle County, Virginia Deed Book Abstracts, 1790–1791

Albemarle County, Virginia Deed Book Abstracts, 1791–1793

Augusta County, Virginia Land Tax Books, 1782–1788

Augusta County, Virginia Land Tax Books, 1788–1790

Amherst County, Virginia Land Tax Books, 1789–1791

Caroline County, Virginia Appeals and Land Causes, 1787–1794

Caroline County, Virginia Committee of Safety and Early Surveys, 1729–1762 and 1774–1775

Caroline County, Virginia Land Tax Book Alterations, 1782–1789

Caroline County, Virginia Land Tax Book Alterations, 1792–1795

Caroline County, Virginia Land Tax Book Alterations, 1795–1798

Caroline County, Virginia Order Book Abstracts, 1765

Caroline County, Virginia Order Book Abstracts, 1767–1768

Caroline County, Virginia Order Book Abstracts, 1768–1770

Caroline County, Virginia Order Book Abstracts, 1770–1771

Caroline County, Virginia Order Book, 1764

Caroline County, Virginia Order Book, 1765–1767

Caroline County, Virginia Order Book, 1771–1772

Caroline County, Virginia Order Book, 1772–1773

Caroline County, Virginia Order Book, 1773

Caroline County, Virginia Order Book, 1773–1774

Caroline County, Virginia Order Book, 1774–1778

Caroline County, Virginia Order Book, 1778–1781

Caroline County, Virginia Order Book, 1781–1783

Caroline County, Virginia Order Book, 1783–1784

Caroline County, Virginia Order Book, 1784–1785

Caroline County, Virginia Order Book, 1785–1786

Caroline County, Virginia Order Book, 1786–1787

Caroline County, Virginia Order Book, 1787, Part 1

Caroline County, Virginia Order Book, 1787, Part 2

Caroline County, Virginia Order Book, 1787–1788

Caroline County, Virginia Order Book, 1788

Culpeper County, Virginia Deed Book Abstracts, 1795–1796

Culpeper County, Virginia Land Tax Book, 1782–1786

Culpeper County, Virginia Land Tax Book, 1787–1789

Culpeper County, Virginia Minute Book, 1763–1764

Digest of Family Relationships, 1650–1692, from Virginia County Court Records

Digest of Family Relationships, 1720–1750, from Virginia County Court Records

Digest of Family Relationships, 1750–1763, from Virginia County Court Records

Digest of Family Relationships, 1764–1775, from Virginia County Court Records

Essex County, Virginia Deed and Will Abstracts, 1695–1697

Essex County, Virginia Deed and Will Abstracts, 1697–1699

Essex County, Virginia Deed and Will Abstracts, 1699–1701

Essex County, Virginia Deed and Will Abstracts, 1701–1703

Essex County, Virginia Deed and Will Abstracts, 1745–1749

Essex County, Virginia Deed and Will Book, 1692–1693

Essex County, Virginia Deed and Will Book, 1693–1694

Essex County, Virginia Deed and Will Book, 1694–1695

Essex County, Virginia Deed and Will Book, 1701–1704

Essex County, Virginia Deed, 1753–1754 and Will Book 1750

Essex County, Virginia Deed Abstracts, 1721–1724

Essex County, Virginia Deed Book, 1724–1728

Essex County, Virginia Deed Book, 1728–1733

Essex County, Virginia Deed Book, 1733–1738

Essex County, Virginia Deed Book, 1738–1742

Essex County, Virginia Deed Book, 1742–1745

Essex County, Virginia Deed Book, 1749–1751

Essex County, Virginia Deed Book, 1751–1753

Essex County, Virginia Land Trials Abstracts, 1711–1716 and 1715–1741

Essex County, Virginia Order Book Abstracts, 1695–1699

Essex County, Virginia Order Book Abstracts, 1699–1702

Essex County, Virginia Order Book Abstracts, 1716–1723, Part 1

Essex County, Virginia Order Book Abstracts, 1716–1723, Part 2

Essex County, Virginia Order Book Abstracts, 1716–1723, Part 3

Essex County, Virginia Order Book Abstracts, 1716–1723, Part 4

Essex County, Virginia Order Book Abstracts, 1723–1725, Part 1

Essex County, Virginia Order Book Abstracts, 1723–1725, Part 2

Essex County, Virginia Order Book Abstracts, 1725–1729, Part 1

Essex County, Virginia Order Book Abstracts, 1727–1729

Essex County, Virginia Order Book, 1695–1699

Essex County, Virginia Will Abstracts, 1730–1735

Essex County, Virginia Will Abstracts, 1735–1743

Essex County, Virginia Will Abstracts, 1745–1748

Fairfax County, Virginia Deed Abstracts, 1799–1800 and 1803–1804

Fairfax County, Virginia Deed Abstracts, 1804–1805

Fairfax County, Virginia Deed Book Abstracts, 1799

Fairfax County, Virginia Deed Book, 1798–1799

Fairfax County, Virginia Land Causes, 1788–1824

www.ingramcontent.com/pod-product-compliance
Lightning Source LLC
Chambersburg PA
CBHW081157270326
41930CB00014B/3187